Acclaim for Mark Bechtel's

HE CRASHED ME SO I CRASHED HIM BACK

"*He Crashed Me So I Crashed Him Back* is the first smart, funny, comprehensive telling of the 1979 Daytona 500.... Deeply researched and with scores of interviews, it is an indispensable and entertaining reference to the first season of the NASCAR we've come to know in the decades since. If you're a fan of racing, reading, or excellence, seek it out."
— Jeff MacGregor, ESPN.com

"True confession: I was part of the legion of living-room layabouts on that February afternoon of 1979 who were mobilized into the NASCAR ranks with one spectacular television moment. Reading *He Crashed Me So I Crashed Him Back* is like finding the schoolgirl who stole your heart thirty years ago. First love, first kiss are still the best. Wonderful stuff here."
— Leigh Montville, author of
At the Altar of Speed and *Ted Williams*

"Bechtel paints an excellent portrait of these colorful racers."
— Charlotte Hays, *Washington Post*

"*He Crashed Me So I Crashed Him Back* moves as fast as the race it depicts.... This is a worthy contribution to the history of the sport and will be well received by old and new fans alike."
— Lee Scott, *Florida Times-Union*

"An illuminating, informative, and entertaining read, as the engaging and droll Bechtel is in complete control from start to finish."
— *Publishers Weekly* (starred review)

"Despite being about something that happened thirty-one years ago, it's as connected to the current state of things in stock car racing as the past.... It's a quick, fun read, with the type of passion and drive the sport's brass craves so much. Whether you've been a fan since way back when or are a new follower, there's plenty to keep you entertained."

—Marty Kirkland, *Daily Citizen*

"If you're a NASCAR fan, or simply a lover of colorful stories, check out Mark Bechtel's *He Crashed Me So I Crashed Him Back*."

—Pam Kelley, *Charlotte Observer*

"Bechtel provides page after page of real-life, wouldn't-believe-it-if-it-weren't-true drama.... An understanding of NASCAR isn't necessary to read this book, just a fascination with the diversity of humanity which is as present in racing as everywhere else...and more so."

—Judy Romanowich Smith, *Minneapolis Star Tribune*

"A great read." —Tennessean.com

"What Bechtel does best is not just to tell familiar stories, but to put meat on their bones and share more of the details of what really happened. In other words, Bechtel in his book tells 'the rest of the story.'"

— Mary Jo Buchanan, Bleacher Report.com

"Bechtel's assessments are spot on.... His easy, flowing style in his well-developed account is peppered with vignettes that readers will savor."

—*Library Journal*

"Bechtel's NASCAR book is a winner.... The best suggestion I can make is to buy it." —Mark McCarter, *Huntsville Times*

HE CRASHED ME SO I CRASHED HIM BACK

Mark Bechtel

The True Story of the Year the King, Jaws, Earnhardt,
and the Rest of NASCAR's Feudin', Fightin' Good Ol' Boys Put
Stock Car Racing on the Map

BACK BAY BOOKS
Little, Brown and Company
NEW YORK   BOSTON   LONDON

For my parents

Back Bay Books / Little, Brown and Company
Hachette Book Group
1290 Avenue of the Americas, New York, NY 10104
www.hachettebookgroup.com

Originally published in hardcover by Little, Brown and Company, February 2010
First Back Bay paperback edition, February 2011

Back Bay Books is an imprint of Little, Brown and Company. The Back Bay Books name and logo are trademarks of Hachette Book Group, Inc.

The publisher is not responsible for websites (or their content) that are not owned by the publisher.

Library of Congress Cataloging-in-Publication Data
Bechtel, Mark.
    He crashed me so I crashed him back : the true story of the year the King, Jaws, Earnhardt, and the rest of NASCAR's feudin', fightin' good ol' boys put stock car racing on the map /
Mark Bechtel. — 1st ed.
        p. cm.
    Includes bibliographical references and index.
    ISBN 978-0-316-03402-9 (hc) / 978-0-316-03403-6 (pb)
    1. NASCAR (Association) — History.   2. Stock car racing — United States — History.
3. Stock car drivers — United States.   I. Title.
    GV1029.9.S74B44 2010
    796.720973 — dc22   2009031952

Contents

Introduction

NOBODY STOOD out more than the guy in the nice loafers and the suit. In addition to his sharp threads, he was carrying an eel skin briefcase as he slogged through the muddy infield at the half-mile racetrack in Richmond, Virginia. He was from the *New York Daily News*. This wasn't the kind of place he was used to.

The small band of writers who did this every week, who covered NASCAR for a living, were all thinking the same thing: *What is everyone doing here?* There were plenty of other stories out there. Some kid named Bird was finally getting a national audience in the first round of the NCAA basketball tournament. Spring training was under way, and Pete Rose was no longer a Red. Yet the press box at the Richmond Fairgrounds Raceway was overflowing. For a stock car race.

Why?

It all started with a fight.

And it wasn't even a good one.

A few punches were thrown, but mostly it was two men — two exhausted, middle-aged men — grabbing each other. Looking back on it years later, driver Buddy Baker said, "It was more of a slow waltz. If I ever get beat up, I wanna be beat up like that." Indeed, the enduring image of the fracas is of a man in a blue and white jumpsuit grabbing the foot of a man in a white and blue jumpsuit. It looked like Evel Knievel was being mugged by an Evel Knievel impersonator.

Still, it was a fight, and who doesn't love one of those?

Because of the melee, and the last-lap wreck that triggered it, the 1979 Daytona 500 got the kind of national play normally reserved for Super Bowls and All-Star Games, even in cities, such as New York, that were remote outposts in the stock car racing universe. It helped that the people across the country were a captive audience. It snowed everywhere that day. It snowed in Cleveland, Chicago, New York, and Detroit. A lot. It snowed in Atlanta and Charlotte. Not quite as much, but hard enough to put the locals off their game. It even snowed in the Sahara.* So millions of people who normally wouldn't be watching TV on a Sunday afternoon were, save for the heartiest of sledders and snowman builders, confined to their couches. And in those pre-cable days, the choices were slim. ABC showed local programming. NBC had a college basketball game. CBS showed the race live from start to finish, something no one had ever tried before.

Ten million people watched it.

They were mesmerized by what they saw. The speed! The crashes! The fighting! The sideburns! And then at the next race it happened again. Another wreck, same drivers. No fight this time, but plenty of racers who lost cars were talking like they'd be up for one, which was why Richmond was packed. They were anticipating round three.

The writers who didn't feel like cramming into the tiny press box spilled out into the pits, where it wasn't hard to tell the racing beat

---

*For the first time in recorded history. It snowed so hard for half an hour in Algeria that traffic stopped.

regulars from the interlopers. The newbies were the ones who were wearing nice shoes, looked afraid to touch anything, and jumped every time someone revved an engine. The whole scene — the carpetbaggers coming in to gawk at the feudin' good ol' boys — left the locals amused. Bill Millsaps of the *Richmond Times-Dispatch* wrote: "The grist of the mass media, publications like the *Washington Post, Washington Star, New York Daily News* and *Time* magazine are sending staff writers down here to mix with us fried-chicken-eating rednecks to discover what all the cursing is about."

But saying that NASCAR was discovered in the spring of 1979 is like saying that America was discovered in the fall of 1492. Stock car racing and the New World were both around — and, the natives would likely argue, doing just fine — long before the outsiders showed up. But stock car racing was chiefly a southern phenomenon, born on the winding Appalachian roads where bootleggers souped up their family sedans so they could outrun the revenuers. It was the one sport southerners could call their own. Until the 1960s there were no NFL, NBA, or major league baseball teams south of Washington, DC. There was racing in the North, to be sure, but if a driver wanted to see how he measured up against the best, he would have to move down south.

For years sports pages and magazines all but ignored stock car racing. Sure, a few names were universally familiar to casual sports fans. Richard Petty was recognizable to anyone who had ever seen an STP ad. And Cale Yarborough was on the cover of *Sports Illustrated* in 1977. But it's safe to say that Benny Parsons or Buddy Baker could walk down Fifth Avenue without fear of having his shirt torn by a pack of rabid fans. When NASCAR did get some coverage, the tone tended to be patronizing to the serious fan or the story read as if the author had stumbled upon a bizarre religious ritual in some faraway country. (A *People* magazine story reported, "Not so long ago, most of the big name racers on the stock-car circuit were just redneck grease monkeys who liked courting death at high speed.") Even the greatest piece of journalism ever composed about NASCAR—Tom Wolfe's 1965 *Esquire* story "The Last American Hero Is Junior Johnson. Yes!"—loses some of its bite when stripped of the details that were scandalous revelations in the halls of the Hearst Building but were nothing new south of the Mason-Dixon Line, where almost everyone knew someone who ran a 'shine still on the side.

And then the fight happened.

Virtually every list of the greatest or most seminal moments in NASCAR history is topped by the Daytona brawl. "It's astronomical how many tickets they've sold and how much money they've made because of that fight," said Donnie Allison, whose wreck with Cale Yarborough triggered it. Thirty years later, the sport's growth is undeniable. Those 10 million people who watched the 1979 Daytona 500 on TV? That's what the average weekly race draws. The 500 now pulls in 20 million viewers. Races are held everywhere from the rolling wine country of Northern California to the hills of central New Hampshire. The drivers are rock stars. Their fiercely loyal fans sustain an economy that puts the GDP of many developed nations to shame. Souvenir trucks carry shirts, hats, and every imaginable trinket for every driver. Junior Johnson has his own brand of pork rinds. Barbecue aficionados with especially discerning palates can argue over which sauce is best: Tony Stewart's Smoke barbecue sauce or Mario Batali's NASCAR-branded sauce. Harlequin has a line of NASCAR-themed bodice rippers.

Attributing all of that growth to one moment, though, to pin it all on one fight, is a little too simple, a little too neat. Many of the writers who had descended upon the Fairgrounds Raceway in Richmond would be back to covering the NCAA tournament or spring training within the week. The heartland's infatuation with NASCAR would, like the snow that still blanketed much of the country, start to melt away. No, NASCAR's growth was an achingly slow process that, like any extended period of growth in nature, was made possible by a nurturing environment. And in 1979 the world was finally ready for NASCAR.

There was a Georgian in the White House and southern culture was suddenly intriguing to the Yankees who had forever dissed it. In other words, there were cowboy hats *everywhere*. The post-Watergate distrust of government was giving way to a new, more rally-round-the-flag vibe, one that meshed perfectly with the unabashed patriotism on display at NASCAR races. The sporting landscape was changing as well. Teams and leagues were discovering that they could build around larger-than-life personalities, and NASCAR was discovering that it had a rookie driver who fit the profile. The notion of what could sensibly be broadcast on television was being challenged by the emergence of cable stations.

It all made 1979 the most significant year in the history of stock car racing. When it was over, the sport had taken its first steps on the journey from regional curiosity to national phenomenon.

HE CRASHED ME SO I CRASHED HIM BACK

Chapter One

Something Borrowed, Something Blue

Sunday, February 4
High Point, North Carolina

THE BRIDE looked stunning, wearing an immaculate gown that Irish nuns had spent nine months crocheting. The groom looked like he was auditioning to be a *Welcome Back, Kotter* extra: a gangly teenager with a frizzy perm. If he thought his mustache made him look more grown-up than he was, he couldn't have been more wrong.

Nonetheless, the guests who packed Kepley's Barn—the biggest party venue this side of Greensboro—all seemed to agree that they made quite the handsome couple. She was Pattie Huffman, a schoolteacher from High Point. He was Kyle Petty, a recent graduate of the high school just up the road in Randleman. His status as the only son of Richard Petty, stock car racing's reigning king, made their wedding the social event of the season, which explained why all nine hundred seats were filled and there were people standing in the balcony.

The resemblance between the groom and his father, who was standing beside him as his best man, was uncanny. From the back of the barn,

the only discernible difference a squinting guest could make out between the two was that one of them—the groom—was holding a top
hat. They were both wearing identical long-tailed tuxes and had the
same curly hair, the same mustache, and the same tall, angular build—a
natural frame for a growing young man like Kyle, but one that made
a forty-two-year-old, normally hearty man like Richard appear gaunt.
And they were both wearing the same wide, aw-shucks grin. That was
something the King hadn't had much reason to do recently.

Richard Petty had been driving a race car since ten days after his
twenty-first birthday. His first race at NASCAR's highest level was
in Toronto in 1958. He was knocked out by his father, Lee—a three-
time NASCAR champion—who put him into the fence on his way to
Victory Lane. "Daddy and Cotton Owens were racing for the lead halfway through the race," Richard recalled fifty years later. "They came
up to lap me, and Daddy thought I was in the way, so he hit me."

Lee loved his son. He also loved a good payday.

The winner's share that day in Toronto was $575, which Lee Petty
and his cronies didn't consider to be too bad for a few hours of work. But
Richard was young, and he looked at things differently, more optimisti-
cally. Where the old guard saw racing the family sedan as a hobby—albeit
one they took very seriously—Richard saw it as something that could
one day allow him to make a nice living. But for that to happen, there
had to be a demand from fans. For a demand to be created, there had to
be awareness. And for that reason he had been talking about driving a
race car since about eleven days after his twenty-first birthday.

Talking came naturally to Richard Petty. He was a southern gentleman, blessed with a gift for making people feel at ease, and he peppered
his speech with enough "YouknowwhatImean?'s" and "Seehere's" to
make his interviews feel as informal as a couple of old friends discussing
a hunting dog or a tractor on the front porch. He'd hold court on the pit
wall, talking to anyone with a notebook, discussing the track, his car, or

them cats he raced against. (Everyone, it seemed, was a "cat.") He was good-looking and bright, and whatever he might lack in book smarts he more than made up for in charm and an ability to think on his feet. In 1978, a racing observer described the difference between Petty and David Pearson, his main rival of the day: "The reason David doesn't say much is that he's worried about his lack of education. He'd be mortified, for instance, if somebody asked him, 'How would you compare your driving as art next to Michelangelo's?' Richard would make a joke out of not knowing it. He'd say, 'Oh, you mean Joe Michelangelo what paints the track billboards?' And that would be that." Petty was so fond of the fourth estate that he joined it: throughout the 1970s he wrote a regular column for *Stock Car Racing* magazine.*

As giving as he was with the press, Petty was even more generous with fans, who almost universally adored him—rare in a sport in which spectators take almost as much delight in booing drivers as they do in cheering for them. (Some adored him so much that they took advantage of a magazine offer to buy one square inch of the Petty compound in Level Cross, North Carolina, for $2.) No one who asked for an autograph came away unsatisfied, unless the person violated his one rule: "I do draw the line at some things, like folks following me into the bathroom or into the shower when I'm changing out of my uniform." Petty was one of the rare individuals—the president of the United States and Santa Claus also come to mind—who was recognizable enough that he'd receive mail even if it didn't have an address, as one young

---

* If the occasional literary reference he dropped was any indication, he knew good and well who Michelangelo was. "A few hundred years ago, some cat got famous in the field of literature with something he called Pepys Diary," he wrote in October 1979. "Seems his name was Sam Pepys and the hour by hour timetable of his days brought home the way folks lived during that time in merry old England." If it broke no other journalistic ground, it was probably the first time anyone had ever referred to Samuel Pepys—or any other Restoration period Englishman, for that matter—as a "cat" in print.

autograph seeker from the West Coast found out when he glued a picture of the King and his car to an envelope in lieu of a name or address and promptly received a picture adorned with the royal signature.

And when Petty gave an autograph, he didn't just scribble his name. No, his signature was an ornate collection of loops and lines that took several seconds to compose, the product of an Oriental handwriting class he had taken at King's Business College in Charlotte. Lee Petty had insisted that Richard go to business school because he knew that he would eventually take control of Petty Enterprises, the race team Lee had started at the family farm in Level Cross in 1949. Petty Enterprises didn't start as a huge operation. Lee drove, and his two preteen sons—Richard and his older brother, Maurice, who'd come to be known as "Chief"—were his crew. But by 1979 it had grown substantially. Chief was still there, building the engines. Richard's cousin Dale Inman was the crew chief. And there were a couple of dozen mechanics, fabricators, and engineers on the payroll.

Spending two decades being everything to everyone—driver, businessman, spokesman, face of his sport—had taken its toll, which is why Richard looked so frail at his son's wedding. Two months earlier, in December, he'd had nearly half of his stomach removed because of ulcers. "He internalizes a lot, so he's always had stomach trouble," says Kyle. Richard's agita was part of the Pettys' daily routine and an occasional source of amusement for Kyle. The family lived a hundred yards from Kyle's grandparents, Lee and Elizabeth. "At night," Kyle recalled years later, "my father would eat supper, and at about eight thirty or nine o'clock he'd say, 'I need some stomach pills. Run over to your grandaddy's house and get some.' They were these little pink pills or these little white pills, like Zantac or something. And I'd say, 'All right. Here's what I'm gonna do. Time me. Let's see how quick I can run over to his house, get a pill, and run back.'"

After the first race of the 1976 season, Richard developed what he called a "bellyache." Doctors told him that he had the beginnings of an ulcer and that he should take it easy and stay away from the race shop. Petty decided that the best way to remove the temptation to work was by checking himself into the hospital. "They put me in the hospital like some folks get put in jail," he said. Unable to bear the tedium, he returned to the track without missing a race. But by the end of 1978, the problem could no longer be ignored. After he returned from a cruise with his wife, Lynda, he had a three-hour procedure to remove scar tissue left by an ulcer. He was supposed to spend two or three days in the hospital, but his recovery turned into an ordeal. Petty spent twelve days in the hospital, suffering nearly constant nausea as his stomach failed to function properly. As the start of the racing season approached, Richard insisted he was fine, and no one in the Petty clan made too much of it. "We're a strange family," says Kyle. "We don't worry about each other. I don't know how to explain that. When anything happens, as long as you're walkin' and talkin', we figure you're all right. You may be slower, you may not be moving as fast, you may not be exactly 100 percent, but you're all right and that's the main thing."

The guys in the shop—who had seen Richard survive some truly horrific crashes, including one that sent him over the wall at Daytona and into the parking lot—were the same way. "It's like the old Monty Python movie where the guy's cut into pieces and just the head is still talking," says Steve Hmiel, who was a mechanic on the team. "Richard could do that. We all thought so much of Richard—they can do whatever they want to him, he's still going to be the King."

To an outsider raised in a less macho world, it was easy to see how serious the situation at the Petty household really was. And it was made even more serious when Lynda had to have an operation of her own. Things were so dicey that Kyle's fiancée moved in to help take care of his younger sisters, Lisa and Rebecca.

Petty's doctors advised him not to race in the first event of the 1979 season, at the road course in Riverside, California, on January 14. "Richard thinks he's Superman," one of his doctors told a Florida newspaper. "And he has been a remarkable patient. But he's putting himself under great stress. That was a serious operation, and it's asking too much of the body to come back this quick." Petty predictably ignored those orders, but the team arranged for Oregon driver Hershel McGriff to be on hand and relieve Petty at some point during the 312-mile race just in case. It wasn't necessary: Petty's engine blew up after just fourteen laps. He finished thirty-second, a terrible result—but the kind that was becoming all too familiar. NASCAR's King hadn't won a race since the middle of 1977.

In his first eighteen and a half seasons—from that day in Toronto when his own father wrecked him through that last win in the summer of '77—Richard Petty won 185 races, more than twice as many as any other driver except David Pearson (who had won 103). Whether that made him the best driver in the sport is a question that is still debated. It was no secret that Petty Enterprises turned out the best cars, and Petty had the wherewithal to run every race in an era when most drivers picked and chose a limited number of events. He won everywhere, from the most hallowed tracks (he had won the Daytona 500 five times) to the most rinky-dink bullrings (his 1962 win in Huntsville, Alabama, featured only sixteen cars and was over in fifty-four minutes). His six championships were twice as many as Pearson's, although Pearson ran a full season only five times in his career.

For years Petty's stiffest competition came from two teams: Wood Brothers, a Virginia outfit whose driver through most of the 1970s was Pearson, and Junior Johnson, the old moonshine hauler whose driver, Cale Yarborough, won the NASCAR Grand National* title in 1976, '77, and '78. Like Petty Enterprises, the Woods and Johnson ran down-home operations—the Wood boys up in the Blue Ridge Mountains and

---

*At the time, the highest level of NASCAR racing, what's now known as the Sprint Cup, was called the Grand National Series. The rung beneath it on the NASCAR ladder, what's now known as the Nationwide Series, was called the Sportsman division.

Johnson from his farm in Yadkin County, about seventy miles north of Charlotte. But in the mid-1970s the sport began to see a new kind of team, backed by outsiders with deep pockets—most notably DiGard, an outfit fronted by Bill Gardner, a Connecticut real estate maven. His driver was the brash young Darrell Waltrip, who was hated by many drivers and most fans for being unbearably cocky and having fancy hair that never seemed to get messed up. During Petty's winless 1978 season, Yarborough, Pearson, and Waltrip combined to win twenty of the thirty races, and Bobby Allison took another five.

But Petty's problems ran deeper than increasingly stout competition. For years Petty had been racing Dodges, but after going twelve months without winning a race, he switched to Chevrolets in the middle of the 1978 season. It was a big deal. Even though the invention of those stickers of Calvin from *Calvin and Hobbes* pissing on a Ford or Chevy logo was still years away, stock car fans were still intensely loyal to their brands. Their opinions of the products coming out of Detroit were strongly shaped by how the cars performed on the track. "Win on Sunday; sell on Monday" had been the factories' mantra for years. So when someone of Petty's stature began entertaining notions of switching models, as he first did in 1977, it raised eyebrows. *Auto Racing Digest* devoted its September 1977 cover to the question "Should Richard Petty Have Switched to Chevy?" When he made the move, *Stock Car Racing* gave the story five pages. And in early 1980 STP released a sixty-four-page comic book, with art by *Batman* creator Bob Kane, that devoted an entire page to the switch. In one frame a sober-looking man in a fedora is reading a newspaper with the banner headline PETTY SWITCHES CARS. His son, with a tear in his eye, says, "*Sob*. Is it true, Daddy?" "I'm afraid so, son!" comes the grave reply.

Switching cars, let alone makes, was uncommon at a time when drivers stuck with rides as long as they could—partly because there was no need to fix something that wasn't broken, and partly because new cars were expensive. Waltrip won the Riverside season opener in a two-year-old Chevy he called Wanda; her stablemate was a four-year-old named Bertha. When Petty abandoned his Dodges, it meant starting from scratch with Chevrolets. Nowadays, the size and shape of virtually every part of a car is dictated by NASCAR. Thirty years ago, there were only a few templates, so while the cars were supposed to resemble actual street models, a clever crew chief could manipulate the body in scores of different ways to make it sleeker — and faster. Petty's team knew none of those tricks, at least not for a Chevy.

After the fiasco in Riverside, Petty had a month to prepare for the next race: the Daytona 500, easily the biggest event on the thirty-one-race schedule. He decided to build a Chevy Caprice and took the car to the two-and-a-half-mile superspeedway shortly after New Year's to test it. "We came down and ran like a box of rocks," says Kyle. Petty decided to scrap the Caprice and run an Oldsmobile, which was the preferred ride for the rest of the drivers in the General Motors stable. The problem was, everyone loved their Oldses so much that no one would sell Petty a body, so over the next couple of weeks Kyle, Steve Hmiel, and another mechanic, Richie Barsz, built an Oldsmobile from scratch, working fourteen-hour days all month.

The uncertainty that hung over the team also caught the attention of Petty's chief sponsor, STP. The oil and gas treatment company had come on board in 1972 and immediately became NASCAR's most high-profile sponsor. Until that time, all of the Pettys' cars had been a shade of robin-egg blue that became so iconic that it was patented as Petty Blue.* When STP first expressed an interest in sponsoring Petty, the major sticking point had been what color to paint the car — Petty Blue or STP red. "I don't give a damn what color Petty likes," said STP

---

* Richard and Maurice stumbled upon the color in 1959. They were repainting a car but didn't have enough white or blue paint to handle the entire job, so they dumped the two partial cans into one tub. Lee raved about the final robin-egg blue product, but his sons hadn't written down the formula they used, so they had to go back and tinker with the ratio until they found the right mix.

president Andy Granatelli, a short, round, pushy Chicagoan who was used to getting his way.* "I happen to like red." Negotiations lasted two days; at one point, crayons were broken out. "I offered him $50,000 finally to paint it all red," Granatelli said, "and, by God, he wouldn't." Petty finally left to go to the track for the first race of the season, leaving Chief at STP headquarters in Chicago to bicker about swatches. He and Granatelli came to a compromise: blue on top, red on the sides. It quickly became auto racing's most recognizable paint scheme.

As these were the days before extensive TV coverage, the only guaranteed exposure for a sponsor came in Victory Lane. And as Richard Petty seemed to have forgotten how to get there, STP cut back its financial commitment; instead of a large logo on the hood, there would be only a small one on the rear quarter panels. The car was almost entirely blue, a fact that wasn't lost on the crew members, who had a large chunk of their salaries paid, at least indirectly, by money from STP. Says Hmiel, "I don't think people realized how close we were to not having the funding we needed."

Even Petty's wife couldn't ignore what was happening. Lynda opened an antique store. "With Richard on a losing streak," she said, "I figured somebody should start making some money."

If all of that—the surgery, the losing streak, the loss of sponsorship money, the sight of his wife selling tchotchkes—wasn't enough to tie what was left of Richard Petty's stomach in knots, he had one other thing to deal with: his son was getting into the family business.

In one of his *Stock Car Racing* columns, Petty wrote that as he was sorting through his mail, "I could hardly believe the percentage of

---

* When Petty won the 1973 Daytona 500, Granatelli barged into Victory Lane with a guest, Jordan's King Hussein, in tow ("How'd ya like it, King?" Granatelli asked him), then proceeded to pour champagne on himself and grab the microphone from Petty so that he could deliver his own remarks.

questions from young fellas, plus an increasing number of gals. They wanted me to tell 'em how to break into the racing business. In response to all of them, one more time around, my best answer is a simple negative: 'Don't.' I can't think of a tougher road to set out on." Richard had always wanted Kyle to go to college. Lynda had a more specific vision for her son: she wanted him to be a pharmacist. "She just thought that when she was growing up, the pharmacy in Randleman was the coolest place in the world," says Kyle.

Ken Squier, who had been calling races on the radio since the early 1970s, remembers playing basketball one night at the Petty house when Kyle was eleven or twelve. After Kyle went inside, Squier asked Richard, "So, is he gonna be a racer?"

Petty said, "You know, when I grew up, my dad wouldn't let me have a car until I was twenty-one. Then I could make my decision as to what I wanted to do. That's all I've ever done was cars. You know, Kyle has got so many things he can do. He can go to college, he loves music, so I don't know if he's gonna race or not." Then he paused and added, "You know, once you make up your mind in life what you want to do, you got your whole life to do it, so there ain't no sense in hurrying."

So, just as his father had done with him, Richard did his best to keep Kyle out of the driver's seat. The only time Kyle drove a race car as a kid was when he was fourteen. Richard and Kyle were in Georgia, selling Chrysler Kit Cars—basically, a Petty Enterprises race car in a box. Richard let Kyle take a finished car out onto a half-mile track, with strict orders to keep it in low gear and with the understanding that if he wrecked it, it would be the last race car he ever crashed.

Kyle had plenty of things to keep him busy. He played guitar—and he did it very well. ("He borrowed one from somebody and spent two afternoons alone in his bedroom," his grandfather Lee boasted. "The third day he was playing the thing well enough to make you want to tap your foot.") He looked after horses on the family farm. When he got to Randleman High, he lettered in golf, basketball, and football. He was a good enough quarterback to attract the attention of a few colleges: Georgia Tech, East Carolina, and some smaller schools near home. But Kyle just didn't see the use in going to school, not when he knew that he was going to end up doing what his father and grandfather had done. He'd always hung around the race shop, at first sweeping the floor or helping clean up, and as he got older he became friendly with some of the younger crew members, including Hmiel, a twenty-five-year-old sharp-tongued Yankee from upstate New York, and Barsz, who was thirty-six but didn't always act it.

Barsz was a Chicagoan who went to work for Holman Moody, the Charlotte-based outfit that built the cars for the Ford factory teams, shortly after he got out of the army in 1964. Freed from the rigors of service life, Barsz embraced his inner hippie, which made him stand out at the track. By the time he latched on with the Pettys in 1970, he says, "I had hair longer than Jesus Christ, and I protested everything."* He used nylon rope as a makeshift headband, and when it frayed, it made his hair look twice as long. The only way NASCAR officials would let him into the garage was if Richard came out to the gate and personally walked him in.†

At first Hmiel and Barsz would help Kyle work on his minibike. "We weren't supposed to do that because we weren't supposed to fool around with any of the stuff in the machine shop, so we'd do it at lunchtime when nobody was looking," says Barsz. They were then told to teach Kyle to be a mechanic by having him build kit cars. Kyle was a typical teen — "pretty wild in the street," says Barsz — and he had a tendency to wander off in search of something more exciting than welding. Barsz joked that they should weld a piece of pipe

---

* The long hair could occasionally be problematic. "You roll over it with a creeper, and it'll make you tear up," remembers Barsz.

† For a straitlaced organization, the Pettys employed a fair number of counterculture types. In the early '70s, they painted peace signs on the headrests in their race cars. No one seemed to mind the long hair or the Fu Manchus — Richard even grew one — except Lynda, who, according to Barsz, "got mad because we hated Jesus."

around his ankle and attach a cylinder head on a chain to it. "That way," says Barsz, "when Kyle would run off, you could at least see his tracks." But eventually he became pretty handy with a wrench. He fixed up a '69 Dodge Charger and sold it to a guy, who then proceeded to lead half a dozen state troopers on a chase at 140 miles per hour. "They couldn't catch him," Kyle beamed as he recounted the story. By the time he was in high school, he'd become such a valuable member of his father's crew that a team member would be charged with the task of hanging around Friday night and waiting for Kyle's football game to end, then driving with him to whatever track his father was racing at.

In the summer of '78, right around the time he graduated from high school, Kyle did an interview with Squier in which he declared his intention to drive. It aired when the family was in Daytona for the Fourth of July Firecracker 400. Richard saw it on TV at the hotel and was more than a little surprised. He found his son at a Coke machine out by the pool. The King took Kyle to an umbrella-covered table and sat him down. He pulled out a pouch of Red Man.

"Want a chew?"

"You know I don't chew."

"Well, I thought maybe you'd changed your mind about that, too."

Over the course of their talk, during which Richard smoked a cigar on top of his chew, Kyle explained that he didn't want to take a football scholarship away from another kid when racing was what he really wanted to do. Swayed by his son's argument, Richard tapped his ashes into his spit cup, got up, and said, "Oh, boy."

"It's not that bad, is it, Daddy? I mean, being a race car driver?"

"It's not the drivin' part. I gotta go tell your mother. That's the hard part."

Later in the year, after Lynda had reluctantly been sold on the idea, the King came up with a plan for Kyle. He gave him one of the

HE CRASHED ME SO I CRASHED HIM BACK • 15

old Dodge Magnums he had ditched, the one he had driven to a fourth-place finish at the Firecracker 400 in Daytona, and made Hmiel Kyle's crew chief. Newspapermen would have a field day writing that Kyle had been born with a "silver steering wheel to grasp," which stood out in a sport in which most competitors wore their past hardships like an oil- and sweat-stained badge. *(You had to steal an engine for your first car? Hell, my first car didn't even have an engine. That's how poor I was!)* But Richard made it clear that there would be no handouts; Kyle was going to have to make a go of it on his own. Everyone's first priority — including Kyle's — would still be the King's car.

That meant any work done on Kyle's car was OT. But that wasn't a problem. "It seems like everybody has a story about how hard it was coming up," says Hmiel. "Then Kyle comes along, and he's the one kid who does have everything given to him. But nobody resented him. He was just a cool kid, a really cool guy. He was real self-deprecating, too. It was a perfect opportunity for him to be a spoiled brat, and he didn't act like one. We all wanted to help him. It wasn't, *Oh my God, the boss's kid wants to start driving a race car. Ugh. More work for us.* It was, *Man, let's stay late tonight and get Kyle's car going.*"

Kyle's first race would be a 200-miler in the ARCA Series — a series for late-model cars that was similar to the Grand National circuit, but with a lot less prestige and a lot less prize money. It was a curious choice for a debut. The race was in Daytona a week before the 500. Daytona is radically different from most other tracks — two and a half miles with incredibly steep banking, which meant that you could just about run an entire race without taking the gas off the floor. It's not the kind of place where a novice can ease his way into things. "Here's the way I'm looking at it," Richard explained. "If a man's got twenty years of experience on short tracks, makes no difference. When he gets to Daytona, he's a rookie. He's got to learn about running 180 to190 miles per hour. He's got to learn about drafting. He's got to learn about crosswinds. What he has learned on a half-mile dirt or a quarter-mile asphalt [track] is good for nothing. And the future of Grand National racing is the superspeedways. That's where the money is. That's where the television's going to be. That's where the sponsors want to be. And that's where you want to be."

The first time Kyle got behind the wheel on a track—for real, not some low-speed excursion around a short track in Atlanta—was at a test session in Daytona on January 24. Goodyear had already booked the track for a motorcycle tire test that day, so Kyle could use the track only when Motorcycle Hall of Fame rider Kenny Roberts was between runs.

Before he took his car out, Kyle rode around the track in a van with his father, who drove and pointed out the preferred line and the tricky parts—most notably the fourth turn, which, because of the D shape of the tri-oval track, wasn't as sharp as the others. The finish line was just past it, and more than one race at Daytona had been decided by a driver making a bold move, or a stupid mistake, coming off of Turn 4. After the tour was over, Richard took Kyle's car out for a few laps to make sure it was running okay. Then he turned it over to the kid and went to watch with Hmiel from on top of a truck.

Kyle turned a few cautious laps at 155 miles per hour, then pulled into the pits. Feeling a little more confident, he went back out and hit 165. Then, feeling a lot more confident, he dropped the hammer. Richard looked at his stopwatch: Kyle had run a lap at 179 miles per hour. He hightailed it off the truck, yelling, "Get that kid off the racetrack! He's running too fast for his experience!"

The next afternoon, with one day of experience under his belt, Kyle ran ten consistent laps between 185 and 186 miles per hour. His top speed for the day was 187—faster than his dad had ever driven the same Dodge at Daytona. (In the King's defense, the track had been repaved over the winter, which made it a little faster.) Then Richard took his Oldsmobile out so the two could run a few laps together and Kyle could see what it was like to drive in traffic. "I noticed he didn't get too close behind me," Richard said later.

It was a hell of a crash course — sticking a newbie behind the wheel of a ridiculously fast car on a track where nine drivers had been killed in the twenty years since it had opened. "It's more bizarre to me thirty years later than it was at the time," recalls Kyle. "At the time I just assumed it was normal. Looking back on it, I'm thinking, *My God, that was wrong.*" Coming through things unscathed would have been impressive enough, but his times had everyone excited. Just about everyone. "I had to break the news gently to Lynda," Richard told a writer. "I told her by phone that Kyle had run 154. She said that wasn't too bad, not too fast. Then I told her he had run 160…and 179…and 184…and 187. She had a fit and reminded me that I'd promised not to allow him off the apron of the track."

Lest his son think that a couple of hot laps in a test session made him a big-time driver, Richard had Kyle tow the Dodge back to Level Cross by himself, a menial task that ate up most of Thursday night. When he got up Friday morning, his hometown paper, the *High Point Enterprise,* had a story about his test session under the headline KYLE'S RUNS AT DAYTONA AMAZING. He couldn't help but be optimistic about his first race. But before he hit the track again, he had another big event to prepare for.

Even by high school BMOC standards, Kyle Petty had done pretty well for himself. Before his new bride became a teacher, she had been a model. They had met two years earlier, when he was sixteen. She was eight years older.

The wedding was a lovely ceremony. The service was performed by Colonel Doug Carty. The music, which included "The Wedding Song," the Lord's Prayer, and the Everly Brothers' "Devoted to You," was performed by the colonel's wife, Mausty.* The seven bridesmaids wore calico dresses and wide-brimmed hats, looking as if they were, in the words of the bride, "dressed like Holly Hobbie dolls."

At the reception, the guests ate barbecue and danced to music provided by some of Kyle's high school friends. When it was time for the bride and groom to run the rice gauntlet, they made their way into an almost–Petty Blue Rolls-Royce Silver Shadow II limousine — worth sixty-six grand and on loan from a local dealer — with a bouquet across its hood. They were driven to the airport, where they flew to Florida for their honeymoon. Their destination wasn't uncommon for young North Carolina newlyweds, but their itinerary was. Instead of lounging on the sand, they'd spend most of their time at the track, where the young groom would do what his grandfather and father had done before him: make a name for himself on stock car racing's biggest stage.

---

* The Cartys would have a son, Austin, who'd grow up to be a contestant on *Survivor: Panama,* bringing him a level of notoriety rarely seen by non-racing High Pointers.

Chapter Two

Birthplace of Speed

Sunday, February 4
Daytona Beach, Florida

As THE Petty nuptials were wrapping up, another star-studded event of interest to the racing community was drawing to a close, this one five hundred miles to the south: the 24 Hours of Daytona. The endurance challenge kicked off Speedweeks, a fortnight of racing at Daytona International Speedway that would culminate with the 500 on February 18. The participants were driving sports cars — Porsches, Ferraris, Corvettes, and the like — and they generally weren't as recognizable, in the States at least, as the NASCAR boys who would pull into Daytona later in the week or the drivers who competed in the Indianapolis 500. But in 1979, for the third year in a row, the field included one driver everyone knew: Paul Newman.*

---

* Newman's presence as a driver for a Porsche team with Dick Barbour and Brian Redman was big news, overshadowing the race itself. The front page of Saturday's

Newman had been bitten by the racing bug when working on the 1969 movie *Winning,* in which he played a hotshot who wins both the Indy 500 and Joanne Woodward. He started racing sports cars in 1972, and by the mid-'70s he was good enough to be taken seriously at major competitions. So it was only natural that he'd eventually wind up in Daytona Beach.

In Daytona Beach driving fast is about the most natural thing a person can do. It's almost as if God created the town specifically for that purpose. The sand on central Florida's Atlantic coast comes from the shell of the coquina clam, unique to the area, and the fine, round grains naturally pack themselves into a surface that is as hard as asphalt. The city was incorporated in 1876, and it—along with Ormond Beach, its neighbor to the south—quickly became a choice destination for wintering northerners, thanks in large part to the lavish Ormond Hotel. After its expansion in 1890, the hotel was the largest wooden structure in the United States. It featured eleven miles of corridors, four hundred bedrooms, and a dining room that seated three hundred. It sat on eighty acres covered with palm trees (owner Henry Flagler removed the indigenous pines, as they were not exotic enough), and the grounds stretched from the Halifax River all the way to the Atlantic. If guests tired of the hotel's orchestra, seawater swimming pool, archery contests, dog shows, and silent movies, they could enjoy the beach, riding their bikes up and down the sand without leaving a hint of a tire mark, or taking a ride in a carriage and trying to talk over the clatter of the horses' hooves, which was so loud it sounded as if they were trotting on bricks.

Daytona Beach Morning Journal carried a story with the headline EVERYONE KNOWS PAUL NEWMAN'S HERE BUT 24 HOURS OF DAYTONA — WHAT? Most of the local mallgoers quoted in the *Journal* story were unclear on the specifics. "I know this one is at night," one helpfully pointed out. The piece ran above a picture of a bubbly Kyle and Pattie Petty and a story noting that former Sex Pistols bassist Sid Vicious had died of a heroin overdose after likely killing his new bride.

The ultimate mode of beach transportation, though, was the auto-mobile. At the turn of the century, finding a decent place to drive one's car was a chore. Asphalt had yet to be perfected, and with dirt roads one never knew what one was getting. Daytona's beach, however, was perfectly smooth and required neither construction nor upkeep. One paper wrote, "Surely it must have been made for the automobile for regardless of weather conditions, there is no dust, no mud, tires are never heated owing to the moisture and an exploded tire is unknown. Here, too, the great dangers of road racing are eliminated, and man can never build a road so hard and smooth. Repairs are unnecessary, as twice every twenty-four hours it is entirely rebuilt by the tides."

Driving at the turn of the century, before Henry Ford began pro-ducing cars the average person could afford, was a pastime of the rich. The hoi polloi were often confounded by the horseless carriage. One newspaper account noted that a car owner in Daytona "had many queer experiences with the native crackers, who at the time were very much opposed to these 'new-fangled machines.'" The "crackers," however, warmed to them when they realized just how it cool it was to watch them roar up and down the beach.

Racing was already in vogue overseas, and like so many continental fads, it was quickly adopted by well-to-do Americans. "Automobilism is the enthusiasm of the day throughout Europe," the *Times-Democrat* of Lima, Ohio, noted in 1901. "All the world loves a race and is ready to apotheosize the winner of it." The first apotheosizing in Daytona took place in March 1903, in a hastily arranged event thrown together after the owners of the Ormond Hotel agreed to foot the bill, figuring it would help drum up winter business.* The three-day event featured a handful of races involving cars and motorcycles, mostly against

---

* There's an oft-told story about a 1902 race between auto barons Ransom Olds and Alex-ander Winton, in which they finished side by side at 57 miles per hour and, being per-fect gentlemen, called it a tie. If it sounds too good to be true, that's because it probably is. No account of the race exists in either newspapers of the day or in Olds's biography.

the clock.* Media coverage of the carnival was spotty. AUTOS FLEW AT DAYTONA was the headline of the *Atlanta Constitution*'s story, which, at about one inch, was significantly shorter than the item next to it detailing the stomach contents of a recently deceased insane asylum patient.†

On the Florida coast, though, the races were an unquestioned hit. Locals with cars would drive them onto the beach and park facing the ocean, watching as the racers rolled by. Some arrived in chauffeured tricycles with one wheel in the back and two in the front, the space between being wide enough to hold a spectator. Others walked. No matter how they got there, they contributed to the festive atmosphere, forging a bond that is as strong as ever today: the union of racing and partying. The crowd was certainly not as rough as those you'll see in the infield of a race today, as many of the attendees were well-bred guests of the hotel, with names—Astor, Vanderbilt, Ford—that brought to mind brandy, cigars, and staterooms. In other words, no one was shouting "Remove your corset" or "Show us thy bosom, my good lady." But they had a good time nonetheless.

When the second Winter Speed Carnival was held, in 1904, it was a bona fide social event. The Atlanta paper noted in its Savannah Society News section that a "Mr. and Mrs. E. E. Theus left last week for Daytona to attend the automobile races." The *New York Times* reported that in Palm Beach "after the Ormond races, large dinners will be given at which New Yorkers will be prominent. Many of the automobilists will come down from the races, and they will add speed to the Palm Beach pace, making the first week of February very lively." But the races really arrived in 1905, when the *Atlanta Constitution* sent Isma Dooly, the South's foremost society editor, to write a column

---

* Alexander Winton, an automobile manufacturer from Cleveland, came the closest to breaking the most esteemed record, the one-mile timed run. At 52⅕ seconds, he was three-fifths of a second too slow.
† Included in the six pounds of junk doctors pulled out: a four-inch metal spike, twenty-seven buttons, and more than three hundred nails.

unimaginatively titled "International Automobile Races As Viewed By A Woman." In addition to marveling at the foliage and the blue sky that "subdues one into an eloquent silence and creates a longing for the talent of the painter and the expression of the poet," Ms. Dooly described the well-to-do being ferried from their yachts onto the beach and up to the clubhouse, "the social rendezvous of automobilists and an excellent point from which to view the racing machines pass on the broad expanse of white beach one after another."

Dooly also witnessed firsthand a less seemly side of racing. Frank Croker, the son of a Tammany Hall politician, crashed into the ocean when he swerved to avoid a bicyclist. His car flipped into the surf, and he and his mechanic were killed, becoming the first—but certainly not last—men to die while in search of speed in Daytona. Dooly wrote:

> Not even the tragic death of young Frank Croker more than momen-
> tarily subdued the enthusiastic interest of the hundreds of people as-
> sembled more than ten days ago at the Daytona-Ormond track for
> the automobile races that were held there the past week. There were
> expressions of sadness on all sides, that the calamity had occurred, but
> almost at the moment the sympathy was expressed there were cries of
> "Here he comes," and groups of people stood aghast as automobile
> drivers of world-wide fame came dashing along the beach, recklessly
> unmindful of the awful warning given them in the death of their com-
> rade but a few hours before.

In subsequent years, interest in beach racing slowly began to wane. The millionaires whose deep pockets made the beach races possible had a new toy to play with: the airplane. As the number of participants declined, the event became less of a moneymaker for Daytona Beach and Ormond Beach, and the cities gradually withdrew their support. Bureaucratic haggling over who had the right to sanction the races also hastened the demise of the Winter Speed Carnival, but the coup de grâce came in 1911, when the Indianapolis Motor Speedway opened its doors, bringing about the dawn of a new kind of racing in the United States.

Daytona's first golden age was over. It would take only one man to bring about a second.

By the late 1920s, keeping up with the technology necessary to even approach the land speed record made racing even more of a rich man's game than it had been two decades earlier. And Malcolm Campbell was a rich man. All you really need to know about Campbell is that his grandfather founded a diamond business and his estate in Surrey had its own nine-hole golf course. Schooled in France and Germany, the exceedingly well-bred Campbell cut a dashing figure. He was ruggedly handsome and, like Paul Newman, possessed what the morning editor of the London *Daily Herald* called "those piercing blue eyes, characteristic of lovers of speed." He was extremely fit; when he came to Daytona for the first time in 1928 as a forty-three-year-old, he could have easily passed for thirty. He had a hint of a Scottish burr, and his genial nature—one profile asserted that he knew "as many Scotch jokes as [Scottish entertainer] Harry Lauder, and can tell them delightfully"—made it hard not to love him.

When he was a kid, Campbell had been stopped by a bobby for riding a bicycle down a hill at 27 miles per hour, "to the confusion and terror of two elderly ladies." He was hauled in front of a magistrate, who gave him a 30-shilling fine and the following admonishment: "Malcolm Campbell, you have endangered life and property on the public highway. You drove this machine of yours at a totally unnecessary speed. If you come before us again, we will take a much more serious view of the matter. We hope this will be a lesson to you not to travel so fast in the future."

But Campbell was a recidivist—a serial speeder. He dabbled in racing while he worked as an insurance underwriter. His early career was interrupted by World War I, during which he served in the Royal Automobile Club, but after the armistice his day job became a thing of the past. Campbell set the land speed record at Pendine Sands in Wales in 1924 and again in 1927 in his car *Bluebird,* which was the name he gave to all his vehicles.* The mark lasted only a month before Sir Henry Segrave broke it at Daytona, which prompted Campbell to make his next attempt in Florida. He and his fellow Briton swapped the record until Segrave retired in 1929 to focus on the water speed record. At that point, with his only human competition gone, Campbell's opponent became a number: 300 miles per hour.

Campbell was often asked why he did what he did. On one occasion, he insisted that he was trying to make the world a better place, one blazing run at a time. He said that he raced "to explore every means likely to help scientists, metallurgists and engineers to make rapid transport cheaper and safer; to uphold national prestige and to provide scientists with data which might help in spheres quite apart from motoring."† Another time, he said, "If I break my neck then I'm unlucky. It's just a great adventure." Such derring-do made Campbell the most popular sportsman in England and a bona fide celebrity on both sides of the Atlantic. His every move was documented by the press, which would make for some racy reading when he and his wife divorced in 1940. Sir Malcolm accused Lady Campbell of having several affairs, and she, according to the *New York Daily News,* "charged that she had heard him invite their [grown] son Donald to go along on a tour of the more gilded bagnios. She added that Sir Malcolm had boasted how he had seduced the waitress who had served lunch to his son at a Mayfair bunshop."‡

---

* They were named after Maurice Maeterlinck's play *The Blue Bird,* which is about a boy and a girl seeking the bluebird of happiness.

† Actually, airplane mechanics worked on the car, and the technology they perfected on the beach was used in planes during the Battle of Britain.

‡ "Bagnio" is a fancy word for a brothel. Although it sounds like a euphemism for a house of ill repute, "Mayfair bunshop" literally means a shop in the town of Mayfair where buns were sold. And the next time someone tells you that people's unhealthy obsession with the private lives of famous people is a new phenomenon, remember that this story was on the front page of a New York newspaper in 1940.

Like any good immensely loaded daredevil, Campbell indulged in some seriously cool hobbies. In fact, he was something of a real-life Indiana Jones. In December 1931, nine months after he upped the land speed record to 245.73 miles per hour, Campbell went treasure hunting on Cocos, an island four hundred miles off the coast of Colombia. Club Med it was not: a month earlier three shipwrecked Americans had been rescued there after what one paper called "six months of Crusoe-like existence." Undaunted—and with the full backing of the Colombian government, which provided locals to serve as guides—Campbell went to Cocos in search of what he called "the richest and most authentic pirate treasures in the world," booty he estimated at being worth £12 million (somewhere around $1.3 billion today). Campbell said that he had received a clue from someone associated with an old Spanish pirate that was supposed to lead to a large rock that hid the entrance of the treasure cave. Alas, he and his men couldn't contend with the scorching heat, the steep hills, the prickly underbrush, and the "millions of beastly little insects" that "stung and irritated like the deuce." Campbell came home empty-handed. Three years later, while searching for Captain Kidd's treasure in Southwestern Africa, Campbell's plane crashed, leaving him stranded alone for forty hours in an area that was home to many leopards. When one happened upon him while he slept, Sir Malcolm scared it away with his flashlight.

But that was nothing compared to what happened to him following a plane crash in the Sahara in 1930. There he was held captive for several days by the indigenous Riffs in the hills of northern Morocco. Campbell hadn't been in search of treasure. Rather, he had taken his plane up over the desert so that he could scout for a better place to race *Bluebird*. He was getting worried that he was approaching the maximum speed possible in Florida. It took him nearly six miles to get *Bluebird* up to speed and six more to slow her down; soon there just wouldn't be enough sand in Daytona. Convinced that the Sahara wasn't the answer, Campbell trained his eyes west. By 1934 he had all but settled on the Bonneville Salt Flats, the dried-up bed of a lake that in prehistoric times had covered most of what is now Utah. But before he abandoned Daytona, he wanted to give the beach one last chance, in the spring of 1935.

The quest was plagued with problems from the outset. Campbell could never get the beach quite smooth enough. At night mules would pull scrapers over the course to try to smooth and level it out, the beach being lit by torches as the animals made their way across the sand. Though still not entirely satisfied with the course, Campbell grew tired of waiting, and on the morning of March 7, the siren atop the Orange Avenue Fire Station sounded, putting the town on notice that a run was imminent. A crowd of 50,000 made its the way to the beach, packing the grandstand on the Measured Mile. Those who couldn't find seats sat on the dunes or stood along the thirteen-mile route, their cars parked at odd angles wherever they could find a spot.

Bluebird could be heard before she could be seen. Then, trailing the roar, a small dot approached. By the time the spectators were able to make her out, she had disappeared in a cloud of sand. Campbell's speed on the first pass was 330 miles per hour, but for the record to be official he had to make another pass in the opposite direction within an hour, and the average of the two runs would stand as his time. As he exited the speed trap on the return run, he bit a small bump in the sand and skidded sideways through the Measured Mile. He was able to wrestle *Bluebird* under control and bring the car to a stop, its tires torn to shreds. Leaning up against the car, he related the near catastrophe to the press as nonchalantly as he might talk about his dozen Alsatians. "When the *Bluebird* hit it she shook her head sort of like a fish after a strike and headed for the soft sand," he said. "In my heart I thought I was done for." He had beaten his existing world record but hadn't come close to the magic number of 300. Campbell dismissed the run as "a picayune world's record of 276 miles per hour." That time, combined with the near-death experience, convinced him that he'd never reach his goal in Florida. His next attempt, later that summer, would take place in Utah.

The Bonneville Salt Flats were two hundred square miles of rock-hard ground three feet thick, caked hard by the desert sun and as smooth as marble. If you tried to drive a metal stake into the ground, the stake would bend. There was minimal skidding, and the salt actually cooled the car's tires. Up to that point in time, the Flats had been used for closed-track records; there were two circular tracks, of 10 and 12½ miles. For Campbell, a special 13-mile open course was laid out from north to south (so that he wouldn't have to drive into the sun), parallel to the Western Union Pacific tracks.

As Campbell made his way to the States that summer in typical luxury — he booked a stateroom on the Cunard White Star liner *Majestic* — he was not sure what to expect. When asked by Arthur Daley of the *New York Times* whether he thought he would reach 300 miles per hour, Sir Malcolm stated, with typical English understatement, "I'm none too sanguine about it." Down in Florida, his fans followed his exploits closely and with mixed emotions. Campbell was a favorite son of Daytona, and the affection went both ways. (He would later call the city his "second home.") But the locals knew that if Utah proved to be as fast as Campbell suspected it to be, he'd relocate his efforts to the desert, and they'd likely never see him behind the wheel of *Bluebird* again. So as much as they embraced Campbell, they could be forgiven for hoping he'd come up short.

On September 3, Campbell made his run. A nine-inch-wide black line had been laid down to guide him. His "good lads," as he always called his crew, shoved off the 28½-foot *Bluebird,* and the 2,500-horsepower machine began making its way across the seemingly endless field of white. Campbell described the sensation: "I could not see the line more than 100 yards ahead. I could see the earth was round, for the black line I was straddling seemed to go up to the horizon, and I had the same impression the early mariners had. When I met the horizon that was the end of the earth, I must be flying into space." When he had completed both runs, he was given his speed: 299.875 miles per hour, agonizingly close but short. Four hours later he was informed that there had been a timing error. His speed had actually been 301.33. "The news comes somewhat flat," said Campbell, his buzz nearly killed, "but I am glad to hear it."

Sensing that their status in the racing world was slipping away, as it had twenty-five years earlier, the Daytona Beach city fathers offered $10,000 to anyone who could do what Campbell couldn't: hit 300 miles per hour on the beach. The move smacked of desperation: who was going to be motivated by a $10,000 bounty when it had cost Campbell a million dollars to get his *Bluebird* past the magic number in Utah? Henry McLemore, the Daytona Beach correspondent for United Press International (UPI), wrote in December 1935:

> There are citizens here who will tell you that Campbell never drove on the beach while it was at its best. My answer to that is, if you can't get the best beach in as many tries as Campbell made, then there isn't any beach. This isn't meant as a slur on this city's beach. Certainly, it must be the greatest in the world. But it is asking too much of nature to provide 14 miles of absolutely level land. It seems to me that Daytona Beach should be satisfied with having the finest beach for bathing and pleasure car driving in the world, and let somebody else have the speed records.

And that's what happened. Never again would a record fall on the beach. But Campbell's departure didn't end the natives' quest for speed. It just made them realize that they didn't need to rely on outsiders to provide it. They could race themselves, but they needed someone to provide a little order.

When Malcolm Campbell set that last, "picayune" record in Daytona Beach in the spring of 1935, not everyone shared in his disappointment. Among the gearheads who witnessed the historic run was a bearish service station operator who was new to town. His name was Bill France, and he was mesmerized by what he saw.

Born in Horse Pasture, Virginia, France grew up in Washington, DC. His father was a bank teller who was confounded by his son's interest in cars, which France said he developed when he was "knee-high to a hubcap." The young France would sneak out in the family's Model T and take it to a speedway in Laurel, Maryland. "My dad," he said later, "never could figure out why his tires were wearing out so quickly." He met a pretty nursing student named Anne at a dance in December 1930, and they were married by the next summer. In October 1934, in the middle of the Depression, Bill and Anne loaded their one-year-old son, Bill Jr., and all their possessions into the family car, a 1928 Hupmobile Century Six, and drove south for Miami. France had $100 to his name. As they are with many larger-than-life figures, stories about France tend to be embellished. The most oft-told version of the tale of the Frances' settling in Daytona holds that the Hupmobile serendipitously broke down in town, as if the racing gods reached down and cracked its head gasket. In reality, France just wanted to have a look at the beach he had heard so much about. The empty, placid beach was inviting, so he took his family for a swim and fell in love with the place.

France got a job as a mechanic at the Daytona Motor Company, a car dealership, but shortly after he saw Campbell's last run up and down the Measured Mile, he became motivated to devote more time to racing. He bought a service station so he could be his own boss. "Business was not too good at first," France said. "So I had plenty of time to fish and race. Not bad."

France was typical of a new kind of racer emerging in Daytona: mechanically inclined men who were not especially rich and, with Campbell and his *Bluebird* three thousand miles away, who now had to make their own fun. They raced their own cars, as France put it, "mostly for fun and a little money." But they weren't racing against the clock; they were racing against each other.

In need of a tourist attraction, the city of Daytona Beach staged a race on a makeshift oval track in 1936. Parallel one-and-a-half-mile straightaways—one on the beach, the other on Highway A1A, which ran alongside it—were connected by slightly banked turns. Twenty-seven drivers turned up, including big names such as Indy 500 champ "Wild Bill" Cummings, who was drawn by the $5,000 purse, and locals such as France. The race illustrated the difficulty in staging a race on a beach. The sand that remained pristine when one car made a couple of passes over it displayed a tendency to rut when twenty-seven cars turned lap after lap in the same groove. Tow trucks dotted the course, pulling out cars that got stuck in the sand. To make matters worse, the tide came in earlier than expected, threatening to immerse the makeshift parking lot on the beach, so officials called the race early. The city lost $22,000 on the day.

The local Elks lodge took over the race the next year. Adding clay to the sand in the turns solved the rut problem, but despite the fact that the payout was significantly smaller than the year before—bar owner Smokey Purser got $43.56 for winning—the race again lost money, and the Elks cut their ties.

But France still thought that, done right, a race on the beach could be a winning proposition. He decided to call a well-known promoter who lived in Orange City Beach, which was near Daytona but still far enough away to be a toll call. France didn't have a quarter, so he called collect. The promoter refused to accept the charges, so France decided he'd promote the race himself. With a friend, France convinced the city to let him promote two races in 1938. For the first they charged 50 cents admission and ended up making $200 after expenses. So they doubled the price for the second and still drew roughly the same size crowd. Their take was $2,000. "It taught me a lesson," France said years later. "We had undersold the product the first time out. I never forgot that lesson."

As he learned more about the racing game, France started putting on more and more races in the area. At that time it seemed that most promoters were interested primarily in figuring out how to rip off the drivers and the track owners simultaneously. Stories of slick con men absconding with promised purses were the norm. But France was a forward-thinking man; he realized there was more money to be made in the long run by doing things legitimately than by scamming people for a few bucks here and there.

Of course, France wasn't the only person who realized that it might be a good idea—and a potentially lucrative one—to centralize the process of promoting races. One advantage France had over other promoters was that he had done some racing himself, which gave him a measure of credibility with the drivers. Another advantage was that he was huge, which made pretty much everyone else listen to what he had to say. France stood about six feet four inches tall and weighed around 220 pounds. (Years later *Sports Illustrated* would call him the "Cadillac-size Billy Rose of the racetrack world.") Most of the time, he was a charming southern gentleman, winning over friends and strangers alike with reasoned speech laced with the Virginia drawl he never quite lost. If he had to, though, "Big Bill" could play the heavy. "The fact that he's not by nature a good compromiser worked to his advantage in the early days," said Humpy Wheeler, a longtime race promoter and former president of Lowe's Motor Speedway outside Charlotte. "He was tough, with a one-track mind when it counted." (In the 1960s, not long after France took on the Teamsters and won, he heard the song "My Way," and it quickly became his favorite.)

After World War II, France opened a lounge in Daytona Beach's Streamline Hotel, where racers would come in and swap stories about racing or their favorite tricks for outrunning the cops while hauling moonshine into the small hours of the morning. (Anyone who admitted to throwing a glass jar out the window was considered bush league. The true artists would do things such as inject fluid into their exhaust systems to create a smoke screen.) On December 14, 1947, France welcomed more than two dozen drivers to the lounge for a meeting, with the goal of forming a unified body to promote stock car racing. At 1:00 p.m., once the room was sufficiently smoke-filled for the wheeling and dealing that was about to take place, the meeting convened.

Over the next four days, France solidified his position as the ultimate authority in the stock car universe, and he did so by convincing everyone else that it was in their best interest to endow him with that power. It was a neat trick, one that showed how savvy a negotiator France was. But if it seems slightly underhanded, it wasn't. France was genuinely convinced that the best way to run the operation was to limit the number of voices that were heard. "We had made a study of every racing organization that had ever come along," said Bill Tuthill, France's right-hand man. "I told Bill that the democratic method, where the board voted on everything, had never worked." So France and Tuthill had the body set up as a private corporation. France had been liberal in sending out the invitations; he knew that to get his new organization to work, he was going to have to get every promoter—not just the ones he was friendly with—on board. When rival promoters started clamoring for, say, bylaws to be written, France and Tuthill shut them up by forming a bunch of committees and putting them to work. Tuthill called it "a ruse to get some of the guys out of our hair." France appointed Tuthill chairman, and Tuthill in turn nominated France as president. He was voted in after he delivered the opening remarks, and he would run the National Association for Stock Car Auto Racing (NASCAR) for a quarter of a century before ceding control to his son Bill Jr.* He set up shop in a $40-a-month, second-floor walk-up office in the Selden Bank Building in Daytona Beach.

The early days of France's reign—when the fledgling organization was most in danger of coming apart—were remarkably smooth, because France kept his constituents happy. He improved payouts and safety, and perhaps more important, he didn't skim any cash. It helped that France always remembered his place: a southern man can do few

---

*Deciding on a name had been a tedious process. NASCAR originally lost out to the National Stock Car Racing Association, or NSCRA, because it sounded too much like "Nash car." But when it was discovered that an NSCRA already existed in Georgia, the previous vote was disregarded, and NASCAR was chosen instead.

things worse, at least in racing circles, than put on airs. Bill France's home number was always listed in the Ormond Beach phone book, even as the sport began its explosion in the late 1970s and '80s. France also went to great lengths to honor the sport's history and heritage, although he was never so sentimental that his judgment was clouded: he bought Malcolm Campbell's *Bluebird* but kept it locked up out of sight in the warehouse of a Daytona moving company.

As NASCAR took hold in the Southeast, France began thinking about what he could do to improve its status in his hometown. The beach course was becoming increasingly problematic. Hotels were moving farther down the beach, gradually encroaching on the course. And although there was something appealingly rustic about holding an event al fresco, having to deal with the tides was becoming a major headache. In 1949 France started talking with the city about building something bigger and more permanent. He had his eye on a piece of land just west of the airport. The city talked about issuing bonds but dragged its feet, so France set about scrounging up the money himself. The track, designed by Charles Moneypenny, was a marvel. It was two and a half miles, the same size as Indianapolis, but whereas Indy was flat and shaped like a rectangle with rounded corners, Daytona was banked at 33 degrees in the turns and 18 degrees in the tri-oval. At that point the fastest track in the world was Monza, a bowl-shaped oval outside Milan, Italy. France had Moneypenny design Daytona with consistent banking so there would be more than one groove and side-by-side racing would be possible. In addition to the main track, Moneypenny's design included a road course on the infield and a lake that would be large enough to stage boat races. (The void for the lake was created when the dirt was taken away to construct the banked turns.) The original plan called for a football field between pit road and the start/finish line. *Sports Illustrated* marveled that Daytona International Speedway was "one of the most ambitiously conceived racing plans ever blueprinted, and one of the

fastest, with a projected average lap speed for *stock cars* of 125 mph."
(Their emphasis.)

Another Bill France story that may or may not be embellished holds
that in the mid-1950s he went to the Indy 500 and was tossed out of
the pits for not having the proper credentials. Whether or not that actually happened, there's little doubt that France — who enjoyed one-
upmanship as much as the next guy — had his eye on Indy when he
built his track. "Absolutely, unquestionably, Indy was the Genesis of
the Daytona 500," says Humpy Wheeler. "The old story about not giving credentials in Indianapolis, if that's true, that was a terrible mistake, because it ended up costing them a premier spot in the U.S. for
motorsports. He built Daytona to be faster than Indianapolis."

The track was a source of pride for the locals. "If it is not the fastest in
the world," Ken Rudeen wrote in *Sports Illustrated,* "a lot of citizens will
have to eat their hats." The first race on the track was held in February
1959, in front of 41,000 fans. Although the speeds were a touch slower
than at Indy, no one felt compelled to eat his chapeau, because the track
produced a remarkable show. Johnny Beauchamp was declared the winner of the first Daytona 500, but many observers thought that Lee Petty
had beaten him to the stripe. It took three days of looking at photos and
newsreel footage before France declared Petty the winner by two feet.

Speedweek became plural in 1964 when France added a fourteen-
hour race. In typical fashion, he one-upped Sebring, also in Florida,
which had been home to the longest endurance race in the United
States, at twelve hours. In 1966 the Daytona race became a daylong affair, the equal of Le Mans. To mark the occasion, Bill France put track
workers in Charles de Gaulle caps and had signs printed in French:
drivers were directed to *les pits*.

The transition from the beach to the track was complete. France
had given the sport a signature event and a home worthy of it — a place
where drivers could fly without being at the mercy of the tides or the
wind or the sand.

Chapter Three

The Good Ol' Boys

Thursday, February 8
Drawing for the Busch Clash

THE GRAND National drivers had been off for nearly a month since their first race, Darrell Waltrip's win on the road course at Riverside. As they descended on Daytona and took over the hotel rooms of the sports car set,* the first substantial task for many of them was something most had plenty of practice doing: grabbing an ice-cold beer. It was a made-for-media dog-and-pony show to determine the starting order for the newest Speedweeks event: the Busch Clash, an all-star race for the nine drivers who'd won pole positions the year before.

---

* After his engine blew up in the 24-hour race, Paul Newman couldn't get out of town without suffering one last indignity. ARCA car owner Sap Parker checked into the suite that Newman and Joanne Woodward had stayed in and reported to the *Daytona Beach News-Journal*, "Had to wait five hours for them to check out Monday. Talked to the maid that cleaned their room and Newman gave her a little trinket that must have cost two dollars when they checked out. Here's a poor little country girl, got two kids and he gives her that. I'd thought he'd at least give her $100. Hell, I gave her $50 today. I'm just a crazy Kentucky hillbilly, but damn proud."

The Clash was a fifty-mile sprint with unheard-of stakes. First prize was $50,000, more than every race except Daytona, and second paid $18,000—an obscene amount of money for twenty minutes of work, especially considering that in the 1978 season, ten of the thirty Grand National races paid their winners less than eighteen grand. The huge difference between the payout for first and second had most everyone convinced that all hell was going to break loose. "Nobody's going to be giving any breaks," said Buddy Baker. "For $50,000, you might see a tiny hole and try to go through it." In the garage, betting pools were set up, with action offered not only on who would win but also on how many cars would be taken out in wrecks. The starting order would be determined by drawing lots: specifically, cans of Busch beer with numbers on them.

If it sounds like something a fan would dream up, it was. Monty Roberts, the marketing director for Busch beer, got the idea in 1978 while mingling with the hoi polloi at a race in Charlotte. "I like to talk to fans—you know, find out what kind of beer they like to drink, what they are interested in—and they said we should run some sort of special race to really find out who is the best," he explained. Roberts was pushing the envelope for sponsor involvement. These were the days before most big businesses recognized the potential appeal of having a stock car racer as a spokesman—which is to say, the days before drivers' suits looked like patchwork logo quilts. Of course, there were sponsors in the sport. Companies such as STP, Gatorade, and Holly Farms paid money to get their names on cars, a few races had title sponsors, and Winston had been paying big money to sponsor the Grand National season points race since 1971. But this wasn't a case of a company latching onto a popular existing event. This was a company paying to rent a track and stage its own show, an exhibition that didn't affect the driver standings at all. The kind of people who now complain that postrace interviews sound like recitations of the automotive section of the Yellow Pages might have looked at the event with a cynical eye, but at the time it was hard to find anyone who wasn't in love with the idea. "This is completely upstaging the Daytona 500," said Benny Parsons, who had won two poles and three races in 1978. "Back home in North Carolina, this is all people can talk about."

Virtually every big-name driver was in the field. Most of the attention was focused on two: Bobby Allison, the defending Daytona 500 champ, and Cale Yarborough, who had won three straight NASCAR titles—in Allison's old ride.

Richard Petty may have been the King, but Cale Yarborough was the driver with the most regal lifestyle. He designed his 7,000-square-foot house in Sardis, South Carolina, himself, sparing no expense. Adjoining the master bedroom was a sauna and a whirlpool, and Yarborough put a tennis court and a swimming pool on the grounds. Out front was a landing strip for his two airplanes, and on the roof were three 60-foot TV antennas, all pointed in different directions so that he could pick up signals from Columbia, Florence, and Charleston. ("We're a television family," his wife, Betty Jo, explained.) The house was brown brick, very long and low to the ground. Yarborough was the first to admit that the row of columns out front made the place look kind of like a motel.

Yarborough was "the Baron of Florence County." In and around Sardis and Timmonsville, the small town seven miles up the road where he had been born thirty-nine years earlier, he owned a couple of dry cleaners, a Goodyear tire shop, a carpet-yarning factory, and a feed and fertilizer store. His 1,000-acre farm in Timmonsville contained substantial lumber reserves—not to mention its own church—and was worth upwards of $1.5 million.

Still, at the end of every day, Yarborough made sure to take the loose change from his pockets and put it in a homemade piggy bank—a ten-gallon milk jar with a slotted lid welded in place. He liked having a reminder that he hadn't always been so flush.

Yarborough's father died in a plane crash when he was eleven, leaving his mother to run the family's tobacco farm, cotton gin, and country store. "I never went hungry," he said. "But we sure weren't rich, and I can remember when we didn't have any electricity, running water, or indoor toilet." Yarborough found the time to do a little racing, first in soap box derby cars and then in hot rods. In the fall of 1957, when he was eighteen—three years younger than NASCAR's minimum age requirement—Yarborough and a couple of pals took a car to nearby Darlington, at that point the largest track on the NASCAR circuit, to race in the Southern 500. They had no idea what they were getting themselves into. By the time they got the car past the NASCAR inspectors, they had missed qualifying. But the rules were fairly lax in those days, and they were still allowed to enter at the back of the fifty-car field.

Yarborough had come armed with a fake birth certificate, but the chief steward, Johnny Bruner, wasn't fooled. He pulled Yarborough out of the car and told him to get lost. Yarborough's older friend got behind the wheel until Bruner left, at which point Yarborough got back in. The race started with Yarborough driving, but he had violated the first rule of remaining inconspicuous: he was wearing a bright red shirt. Bruner noticed it and ordered the car into the pits, where he oversaw another driver change. A few laps later, Yarborough's friend pitted, and they switched positions again. Bruner caught him again. This time Bruner put Yarborough in his own car and drove Cale outside the track. Yarborough, however, had plenty of experience sneaking into Darlington. As Bruner sat in traffic trying to get back into the infield, Yarborough slithered through the fence and into his race car. When Bruner got back inside the track, he noticed the red shirt again. This time he walked onto the middle of the front straightaway and stepped in front of the Pontiac, directing it into the pits like a traffic cop. "He wouldn't even let me drive around and come in the pits," said Yarborough. "He stands there and makes me back up against all them cars back to the pit entrance."

Perhaps realizing they were beaten, NASCAR officials soon lowered its minimum age to eighteen, allowing Yarborough to run the occasional race without resorting to identity theft. He wasn't a full-timer; he figured the real money was in poultry farming. But the turkey market crashed in '63, costing him $30,000 and plunging him into a period of his life that could have supplied the plot of a very bad country song — a time of terrible living conditions (a ten-by-fifty-foot trailer), worse luck (a turkey market crash?), and abject poverty.

In 1964 a track promoter in Savannah, Georgia, called Yarborough and told him he had found him a ride if he could be there the next day. Yarborough cashed a check for his last $10, packed his pregnant wife and some sandwiches into his car, and headed off. They were more than halfway there when Yarborough got pulled over for doing 40 in a 35 mile per hour zone. The fine was — you guessed it — $10. Now completely broke, Yarborough continued along until it dawned on him that the road he was on led to a 50-cent toll bridge. Betty Jo, pregnant and hungry (those sandwiches were long gone), started crying as Yarborough tried to figure out how they were going to get across. "Then I remembered that when you wash a car and pull the backseat out, sometimes you find money that has fallen out of people's pockets," he said. So Yarborough pulled out the seat, and he and Betty Jo scrounged up 37 cents. He explained his situation to the toll taker, promising to pay the last 13 cents on his way back to South Carolina. The toll taker — moved by Yarborough's situation, or at least recognizing the makings of a good story when he saw one — waved them through, and Yarborough made it to the track, where, of course, his engine blew before the race began. That meant no prize money, which meant Yarborough had to bum twenty bucks to get home. But he did stop to pay the toll taker his 13 cents. "He is still there," Yarborough said a few years later. "I often stop and talk with him when I cross."

Not long after — apparently figuring that he had already survived the worst that racing could throw at him — Yarborough turned his attention to driving full-time. He worked his way up from a shop hand at Holman Moody, the Charlotte outfit that built race cars for Ford, and by June 1965 he had won his first NASCAR race, in Valdosta, Georgia. He won the Daytona 500 for the first time in 1968, driving a Ford for the Wood Brothers team. But after the 1970 season, Ford pulled out of stock car racing. The turkey fiasco still fresh in his mind, Yarborough was worried that without the backing of a factory, stock cars wouldn't offer the kind of financial security he needed—especially since he had just become the proud owner of a $300,000 mortgage on the farm in Timmonsville. "Everything I had made I had invested, and I had obligations I had to meet," he said. He accepted an offer from Gene White to drive in the open-wheel USAC series.

Yarborough had already had a brief dalliance with Indy cars. It hadn't gone well. He'd made it thirty yards in the 1966 Indianapolis 500 before a wreck ended his day. The next year he got arrested after scuffling with an Indianapolis sheriff's deputy at a motel, then wrecked his race car as he drove it onto the track for the first practice session. After his crew replaced the nose cone, Yarborough finally made it safely onto the track, only to be fined $25 by the stewards for running through a yellow light to get there.

Signing the deal with White meant that Yarborough would drive the entire 1971 season on a team with Lloyd Ruby, a quiet Texan whose open-wheel experience made him the operation's focus. Yarborough struggled driving on the flatter tracks, and he didn't like playing second fiddle to Ruby. ("Cale didn't have second-rate equipment, but he did have second-rate help," his crew chief confessed.) After two lackluster seasons Yarborough was ready to return to stock cars.

Many owners were excited by that news—in particular, Junior Johnson.

While Yarborough was plotting his return in late 1972, Junior Johnson was trying to figure out how to handle an increasingly pressing personnel problem—namely, that his driver, Bobby Allison, was a pain in his ass. Johnson was an old-school racer, a moonshiner who had perfected his trade running moonshine in the woods of North Carolina. Johnson could drive a car—on a racetrack or a winding mountain road—arguably better than any man before or since.* His exploits have been documented in print (Tom Wolfe's story "The Last American Hero Is Junior Johnson. Yes!") and on celluloid (the 1973 Jeff Bridges movie *The Last American Hero*). He's credited with inventing the bootleg turn—a full-speed, 180-degree spin used to avoid the revenuers—and he took great pride in the fact that the cops never caught him hauling 'shine. He only got busted when federal agents snuck up on him one morning as he stoked the family still in Wilkes County, North Carolina. That was in 1956, the year after Johnson had won five races and been NASCAR's rookie of the year. He spent eleven months in federal prison in Chillicothe, Ohio, and returned to the track in 1958. Nine years later he quit driving at age thirty-five because, he said, winning had become too easy for him.

Looking for a new challenge, Johnson began fielding cars for other drivers. He'd done all right with Lee Roy Yarbrough, but things really got interesting for him when he hired Allison in 1972—in no small part because Allison came with a handsome dowry of $85,000, courtesy of Coca-Cola, which sponsored his car. Allison was so excited at the prospect of driving for Johnson that he kicked in fifteen grand of his own money to satisfy Johnson's request for an even $100,000.

But the relationship never had a chance. Junior Johnson liked things done his way, and as the man who signed the checks, he had no qualms about exercising his authority. And Allison had problems with authority. Big problems.

The roots of Bobby Allison's attitude toward The Man could be traced back to his first boss in the racing game, Carl Kiekhaefer. Kiekhaefer

---

* In 1998 *Sports Illustrated* named him the best driver of NASCAR's first fifty years.

had made his fortune by founding Mercury Marine, which made out-
board motors. When Allison finished high school, his uncle had, at his
mother Kitty's insistence, gotten him a job testing motors in Wisconsin,
which was a dream gig* for Allison, who had grown up toying with cars
and engines at the junkyard his father owned. Eventually, he crossed
paths with the boss. "Kiekhaefer had some sort of a deal where little
people annoyed him," says Allison. That was a problem: at the time
Allison was five feet four inches tall and weighed maybe 110 pounds.
"I was very timid in nature — a wimp," Allison says. "I didn't go for
any of that he-man stuff."

Kiekhaefer had the two things any good despot needs: power and a
burly, imposing physique with which to flaunt it. (For good measure,
he also had one of the vilest mouths in the Midwest. And the cigars he
was always chewing made nice props, too.) Kiekhaefer saw racing as a
way to promote his motor company, but he insisted that the operation
people saw was first-rate. His racing crews had pressed uniforms; his
cars had shiny paint jobs, and they were carried to the track in trucks.
That was unheard-of in the mid-1950s. So unheard-of, in fact, that no
one made trucks designed for that purpose. Kiekhaefer's boys used the
same trucks they used to haul boat motors, so the tail ends of the race
cars would always stick out.

Allison got his break when Kiekhaefer sent him on an errand to the
race shop in Charlotte and told him to wait there for a company truck
to take him back to Wisconsin. Running the shop was Ray Fox, who'd
go on to become a legendary engine builder but at that point would

---

*Except for the time he flipped a boat and nearly died of exposure. Allison was in
the lake for exactly thirty-five minutes, which he knew because his watch froze as
soon as he hit the water. He eventually got out and made his way to a nearby house.
The woman who lived there put him in some dry clothes belonging to her husband
and took him to the ER — where her husband worked. After she explained what
an eighteen-year-old kid was doing in his clothes, he fixed Allison up and sent him
on his way.

have been happy just to find some good help. Allison approached him and notified him that he was, under the boss's orders, around until his ride arrived.

"Well, okay," said Fox. "Are you a good mechanic?"

"Yeah, I'm a mechanic," said Allison. "Why?"

"A lot of these people here, Kiekhaefer went up to them and said, 'You go to my race shop in Charlotte or you're fired.' So they're here, but they don't work. I need to get a car ready for tomorrow night's race. Will you work on it for me?"

Allison jumped at the chance. Fox gave him a checklist and some tools and pointed him toward the car. Four hours later Allison returned. "What's next?" he asked.

"Are you done already?"

"Well, I did what you had on the sheet..."

"Did you do it right?"

"Well, I did it like the sheet said to do it."

"Man, I gotta keep you here. Here, come on, get on this second car."

Fox convinced Kiekhaefer to let him hang on to Allison. The living conditions in Charlotte weren't ideal: Kiekhaefer put twenty-one young employees up in a three-bedroom house with one bathroom. "You had to take a number to get in the bathroom, and if you weren't done in two minutes, you got thrown out," says Allison. But Allison didn't care. He was living the life — working on cars and going to races. "I was there June and July and went to eighteen races," he says. "I never saw a car besides the Kiekhaefer car win the race."

Then Kiekhaefer's temper reared its head. Carl Kiekhaefer loved to fire people. He loved to fire people so much that he even tried to fire people who didn't work for him. On one occasion he spotted a guy standing around the shop, not doing much of anything. Enraged that someone was loafing in his presence, Kiekhaefer asked him how much he made, gave him a week's severance, and told him to get out of the shop. Needless to say, the delivery man happily took the cash and went back to his own job.

Allison's demise came about when Kiekhaefer saw Allison and three of his pals hanging out near the time clock. He accused one of them, a kid named Willard Stubby, of milking the clock. He flew into a rage that ended with him calling Stubby every name in the book and firing all three of Allison's friends, who were more expendable than Allison. Enraged, Allison quit on the spot, which made Kiekhaefer even more irate. Kiekhaefer jumped into his Chrysler Imperial, and Allison and his friends knew what was coming next: Kiekhaefer was going to lock them out of the house and hold their belongings ransom. "But I knew a shortcut," says Allison. They were just coming out of the house with their things when Kiekhaefer showed up, skidding onto the front lawn, which had just been re-sodded. As he stood on the torn-up lawn, shaking his fist at Allison and his friends, they hightailed it back to Wisconsin. Without a job to keep him there, Allison decided to go home to Miami.

The irony of Allison's exile in Wisconsin was that the whole reason his mother had sent him away in the first place was that she was concerned he was spending too much time racing. She had no idea that sending him to Kiekhaefer would be like sending a chocoholic to live with an uncle in Hershey, Pennsylvania.

Allison had first started racing when he was fourteen, because it was one of the few sports a one-hundred-pound kid could compete in and not be at a disadvantage. When some friends discovered a paved quarter-mile track at an old deserted amusement park just off the Tamiami Trail, they'd sneak onto it at night and race their jalopies, using only their headlights to illuminate the course. The thrill of beating his friends gradually subsided, and Allison started looking for better venues and better wheels. As the manager of the Archbishop Curley High School football team, Allison befriended Fran Curci, the best player on the team and owner of the coolest car, a decked-out '38 Chevy coupe that he had painted blue and yellow.* Allison liked the looks of it and the way it ran, so he sold his Harley and gave Curci the proceeds, $40, in exchange for the car. (He didn't miss the Harley much, since he had to have someone else ride it with him as ballast.) He took his new car to Hialeah Speedway and won his third race—and $8, less 50 cents for the pit pass.

Not long after, Kitty shipped her boy off to Wisconsin. Says Allison, "She called Aunt Patty and Uncle Jimmy and said, 'We gotta get Bobby away from this racetrack.'" When Allison returned following his blowup with Kiekhaefer, Kitty, realizing that subterfuge wasn't going to work, chose a more direct approach in her efforts to derail her son's career. She simply forbade it, telling him that he couldn't live in her house if he was racing. Allison was sharing his dismay with the boyfriend of one of his sisters when the two hatched a plan: the boyfriend, Bob Sundman, would give Allison his ID, allowing him to race under an alias. To make the ruse a little tougher to spot, a sympathetic pit steward changed the name to Sunderman on the entry forms. It worked for a little while: Allison had nine brothers and sisters, so it was tough for Pop and Kitty to keep an eye on them at all times. But Pop eventually caught on when he realized that the exploits of this Sunderman character he was reading so much about in the newspaper tended to coincide with periods of time when his son was out of the house. When Kitty and Pop saw the lengths their son was willing to go to drive, they relented, and when he informed them in 1959 that he was going to go racing in Alabama, where the purses were richer, they even suggested that he take his brother Donnie with him.

The Allisons' Alabama odyssey was, like so many other great journeys, undertaken because a guy was chasing a girl. The guy was Gil

---

*Curci went on to become the first All-American quarterback at the University of Miami. He also coached the Hurricanes and led Kentucky to its only two SEC championships, in 1976 and '77.

Hearne, a pal of Bobby's from Florida. He and another friend had taken their car up to Georgia and Tennessee, ostensibly to go racing, but in reality they were trying to find a girl Hearne was interested in whose family had supposedly moved to Tennessee. They made a trip back to Florida and told Allison that he should come with them to Alabama because there was a lot more money to be made at the tracks up north. They were right. "The first place we went was Montgomery," remembers Allison. "We saw this beautiful half-mile paved track, and a man comes walking out and says, 'We race here to-morrow night. Tonight we race at Dixie Speedway in Midfield. That way, one hundred miles.' So we get to Dixie, and I run fifth in the heat race, fifth in the semi, and fifth in the feature. I go to the pay window, and I tell Donnie, 'I'll get our couple bucks, and we'll go get a ham-burger and sleep in the truck on the way back to Montgomery.' I go to the pay window, and the guy gives me $135! The stack of money looked *that* high. I went down the steps from the pay shack and said to Donnie, 'We've died and gone to heaven. Look at all this money!' So we went and had a $1.99 special steak at Miss Mary's Drive-in, and we slept in a $2 hotel room."

Hearne, by the way, found the girl. Her family was living in a little place on a peach orchard outside Chattanooga. That came in handy when there was racing nearby. "They let us camp out in their peach orchard," says Allison. "That's where I worked on my car."

The Allison boys—they eventually were joined by their wives and brother Eddie—set up shop in Hueytown, a small town a few miles west of Birmingham. Bobby and Donnie won enough races at local tracks in the Southeast to support the Alabama Gang, as they came to be known. Bobby won the national modified-special championship in 1962 and '63 and the modified title in 1964 and '65. He made the deci-sion to move up from the minors to Grand National racing, securing a ride with Betty Lilly, the invalid wife of a Georgia realtor. In the end, it would only give Allison more reason to be skeptical of working for someone else. Despite Mrs. Lilly's assurances that Allison would be given whatever he needed, she decided the stock car game was too rich for her blood and pulled out after just eleven races—and four blown engines.

Allison decided to stay in Grand National as his own boss. He bought a '64 Chevelle and spent sixteen days with Donnie, Eddie, and a friend named Chuck Looney getting the car into shape. His fourth race in the Chevelle was on July 10, 1966, in Bridgehampton, New York. Allison's engine blew up eleven laps into the race, leaving him with nothing under his hood for a race two days later at Oxford Plains Speedway in Maine. So he drove to Maine, found a Chevy dealer, and asked if the dealer had any cheap engines lying around. The dealer told him he had one that had come out of a car a customer had returned—because the engine didn't work. Unable to afford anything else, Allison bought the busted engine, convinced the dealer to let him use one of the dealership's bays, and spent the whole night rebuilding it, with help from Looney and a NASCAR PR man.

The next day Allison put the car on the pole and lapped the field, winning his first Grand National race. He won again four days later in Islip, New York, but again only after getting a little help from his friends. Two days after the win in Maine, Allison was involved in a wreck at Fonda Speedway in upstate New York. Luckily, he had a cousin who owned a body shop in New Jersey, so he took the Chevelle to him and went to work. Another rookie driver, James Hylton, who was an excellent body man, lent a hand as well. Hylton's generosity ended up costing him: he finished second to Allison in Islip. Had he not spent his spare time helping Allison, he would have won his first Grand National race.

But Allison and Hylton were both independent drivers, making do without the support of the factories. There was a camaraderie, an us-against-them vibe that made the independents band together, traveling in a caravan, sharing shop space and tools, even forming one over-the-wall crew to pit all of their cars, since they couldn't afford their own full crews. It was a classic case of small-market teams versus large-market teams. They were the Royals and the Twins. The Pettys and Wood Brothers were the Yankees and the Red Sox. Allison didn't mind, at least not at first, because he was winning races—three in 1966 and six in '67—and he answered to no one. It meant a hectic schedule. While the Curtis Turners of the world (he was driving for Junior Johnson at the time) could turn their busted-up cars over to their crews between races, Allison's crew was pretty much the guy in the mirror. *Sports Illustrated* documented how frenetic his rookie season was:

> *In the space of two weeks last month—before and after the National 500 at Charlotte—Bobby was disturbed because he couldn't discover the cause of an unexpected blown engine, could not obtain vital parts for another engine he was rebuilding, had wiped out his racing budget to pay another parts bill, had been ridiculously overcharged at a Charlotte motel, had learned that [his wife] Judy was expecting Junior Allison No. 4, and had driven 650 miles to Martinsville for the privilege of tangling with Lee Roy Yarbrough.*

Allison's success on the track paled in comparison to Petty's, who won twenty-seven times in 1967, including ten in a row, two of the safest records in sports. Finishing behind the Chrysler-supported number 43 week in and week out made the chip on Allison's shoulder grow. He also wasn't crazy about the way the Pettys threw their weight around. In Peter Golenbock's book *Miracle,* Allison recounts an incident in Birmingham in 1967 when Firestone brought the wrong tires to the track. Allison had a bunch of good tires at his shop in Hueytown, so he sent someone to pick them up. Suddenly, his lap times were a second faster than anyone else's, so Petty had a Firestone rep confiscate Allison's tires for Petty's own use. Allison switched to Goodyears and won the race.

The rivalry grew more intense. In November 1967 Allison and Petty swapped the lead all afternoon at the half-mile speedway in Weaverville, North Carolina. Allison won the race with a late pass that came after he knocked Petty out of the way, which led to a near brawl between their pit crews following the race. The next summer the cars came together again in a race on Long Island. Petty wound up with a bent fender that knocked him out of contention. After the race Dale Inman and Maurice Petty went after Allison. Someone kicked him in the back (Allison thought it was Inman), and the melee grew to include Allison's cousin and aunt, whom he described as "a big woman with a big pocketbook." "I guess it was a blowoff of one of those things that happens over time," Chief explained at the time. "You might say we settled an old score."

The feud simmered for years, and it grew to include the drivers' fans. "When we were running against Allison at those short tracks, with fifty laps to go we'd have the trailer ramps down, because you knew there was going to be a fight after the race," remembers Petty crew member Richie Barsz. "You wanted to get your shit loaded. When they turned the fans loose out of the stands, you had so many people who pulled for Allison, that if you didn't fight the Allisons, you'd slap a couple of the fans. They get in your face and spit on you. That just didn't work well. I'm Polish; it don't matter to me. Someone would get up in your face and say, 'That goddamn Petty,' and that's all it took. They just got it. Most of the time you dropped something on them, like a jack or a tool or something, because if you blatantly just punched them, then NASCAR was all over you. But if you stumbled with your hands full, they wouldn't say anything." * A few years—and several

---

* Fans weren't the only ones who could be felled by equipment. "Same thing with reporters," says Barsz. "If they got in your way, the first thing you'd do is encircle their feet with the air hose, so when you had a pit stop, you'd jerk their feet out from under them."

more run-ins — after the Long Island brawl, Petty and Allison dented each other's sheet metal repeatedly late in a race in North Wilkesboro, North Carolina. It was their third dustup in a month. "He could have put me in the boondocks," said an irate Petty, who won the race. In Victory Lane, a drunken Allison fan hopped the fence and made a run at Petty, only to be stopped by Chief, who grabbed his brother's helmet and hit the intruder over the head.

The battles with the Pettys — not so much the fighting aunts or the fans getting popped with racing equipment, but the struggle of trying to compete with a team that had more backing and more pull — finally wore on Allison to the point that he decided to hook up with a factory-backed team. He drove for Holman Moody in 1971, but the team no longer had the resources to race in '72, so Allison took his Coke money and agreed to drive for Junior Johnson. It was the beginning of a not-so-beautiful relationship. Oh, they got results. That wasn't the problem. Allison won ten races and finished second twelve times in thirty-one starts in '72, finishing just behind Petty in the championship race. Their record together is all the more amazing considering they amassed it without speaking to each other for much of the year. Johnson had always set up his own cars when he was driving, which sometimes meant doing things idiosyncratically — such as attaching the track bar to the left frame, when everyone else in the world hooked it to the right. It had always worked out well for Johnson when he was behind the wheel, so he didn't see a need to alter his ways just because Allison thought it needed to be changed. It got to the point where Johnson only spoke to Allison through Herb Nab, the crew chief. The situation came to a head in August, when Allison, Johnson, and Nab were standing around the car. When Allison suggested a chassis adjustment, Johnson told Nab to tell Allison — who was standing a few feet away — that they weren't going to make it. Allison's response: "Herb, tell Junior to kiss my ass."

Allison had muscled up since his high school days.

After the season, when Johnson found out that Cale Yarborough was available, he called up Allison early one morning and said that he needed to know whether Allison wanted to return in '73 because he had a chance to "get the best driver in NASCAR right now." Allison was groggy, but he still knew when he was being insulted.

"Get him," he said, and hung up the phone.

As odd a couple as Allison and Johnson were, Yarborough and Johnson seemed made for each other. Yarborough was, like Johnson, a strong, rugged, outdoorsy type, a real man's man. Not that Allison was still a wimp. He had driven through some incredible injuries, and never backed down from a fight. But he wasn't the kind of fella who would be the subject of a magazine profile detailing his nocturnal varmint-hunting habits, as Johnson later was in the the summer of 1979, when *Stock Car Racing* ran a piece called COON HUNTIN' WITH JR. JOHNSON.*

The first sign that Yarborough and Johnson had a lot in common came in 1966, when Johnson gave Yarborough a bear as a gift and Yarborough didn't think it the least bit strange. Yarborough named her Susie. "The bear is a good conversation piece," he said, but she also played another role: occasional wrestling partner. It just seemed like the thing a man should do with his ursine pet. "Any time you raise a bear," he said, "you're probably going to wind up doing some bear wrestling."

Yarborough's menagerie also included, at one point, a lion, and in addition to grappling with Susie, he was fond of tangling with snakes and alligators. There was something very Bunyanesque about him. As a young man, he'd jump off ninety-foot cypress trees into swimming holes, and he once parachuted out of an airplane without so much as a lesson. (He missed his target by two miles and wound up on top of a

---

* "I enjoy hearing the dog run and tree," he said. "A good dog in the field is one of the finest artists in anything."

dentist's office.) That was just the way Yarborough was—impulsive, fearless, and not always as responsible as the situation might call for. Back in the mid-1960s Yarborough and Wib Weatherly pooled their money and bought a Piper J-4 airplane. When they took it out for its maiden flight, they decided that Yarborough would handle the take-off and then turn the controls over to Wib. Once they got airborne, Yarborough kept offering the stick to Weatherly, who kept declining. "Naw, Cale, you're doing just fine," he'd say. As the needle on the fuel gauge got closer to "E," Yarborough got more insistent, but Weatherly wouldn't budge. Finally Yarborough blurted out the truth: he'd never flown a plane before. Weatherly then one-upped him: not only had Wib never flown a plane, but it was only the second time he'd been in one. "Well," Yarborough recounted later, "I brought it in, bouncing all over the place and with Wib's eyes as big as saucers, and the next day I was out there and took off again and practiced landings in this field until I could do it pretty good. Never had a lesson in my life."

Of course, had the plane crashed, Yarborough likely would have walked away from it. The man seemed indestructible. He was five feet seven and 175 pounds, with a broad chest, muscular legs, and cartoon-ishly large forearms. He looked like Popeye with a comb-over. His neck—or whatever it was that his head sat on—was so thick and strong that he never used a neck strap to keep his head upright while racing, although most drivers joked that he didn't need a neck strap because he didn't have a neck. (He also refused to wear a cool suit, which kept the driver's temperature down but added fifty pounds to the car's weight.) He had the perfect build for a fullback. In fact, he had turned down a football scholarship offer from Clemson and played a little semipro ball for the Sumter Generals when it looked like he might not make it as a racer. And he boxed. Very well, in fact. In high school he had been the South Carolina Golden Gloves welterweight champion.

But Johnson didn't jump at the chance to hire Yarborough because he was tough. He jumped at the chance to hire him because Yarborough would get results—"Who's the best driver, that's who you want," Johnson says—and he'd be easy to deal with. Yarborough had plenty of things on his plate—he liked to show his face around his businesses and glad-hand the locals in Timmonsville, and he insisted on answering his own fan mail—so he wasn't going to spend all of his time at the shop looking over Johnson's shoulder. Allison was one of the best all-around mechanic/drivers the sport has ever seen, a masterful tinkerer. He'd sense a problem in the car and set about fixing it. Yarborough was just a great driver. He was happy to get out of the car, say "It was loose" or "It was tight," and leave it at that, confident that Junior and his boys could fix it.

It also helped that Yarborough and Johnson drove the same way—hard. Johnson wanted Yarborough to push the other cars from the time the green flag dropped, the idea being that nobody was going to build a sturdier car than theirs. Yarborough had finished every race in 1977 and all but two in '78. "Our racing philosophy couldn't be more identical," Yarborough said at Daytona in '79. "We both believe in putting the pedal to the floor and keeping it there. Speed is what the sport is all about. We start every race intending to lead every lap we possibly can."

"It's the crew's job to build 'em to stand up to Cale," said Johnson. "We've done okay in that regard."

Since leaving Junior Johnson, Bobby Allison had done slightly less than okay. He'd latched on with Roger Penske, but they'd had a falling out over, among other things, Penske's insistence that Allison drive one of Penske's cars in the Indy 500. So Allison went back to the one owner he truly got along with—himself—and struggled through a winless 1977, his second straight season without a trip to Victory Lane. As it did with Petty, losing literally ate at him. Stomach problems—which he attributed to fatigue, worry, disappointment, and "lack of personal care"—caused Allison to lose fifty pounds and necessitated a short stay at the Mayo Clinic. During Allison's drought, Yarborough won eighteen races and two titles. On his own again, Allison reverted to his me-against-them mode, complaining that NASCAR was turning a blind eye as Johnson and the Pettys skirted the rules. He started calling Johnson's car "the Company Car," and one of the things gnawing at him was seeing Cale Yarborough take it to Victory Lane week after week.

Being a race car driver is a peculiar way to make a living. It's sort of like being a test pilot, in that it requires a man to be able to compartmentalize his feelings and to make peace with the possibility that one day he might not make it home from work. The second he starts thinking about how dangerous his job is, or the first time he sees a bad wreck and thinks, *Shit, that could've been me,* he might as well get out. But whereas a test pilot works all alone up in the sky, pushing the envelope Tom Wolfe wrote about in *The Right Stuff,* a racer risks his neck in close proximity to forty other guys, men who, like himself, are riding on the edge—and who, if they get a little chippy, might kill him. (Not on purpose, of course.) It can make for some interesting interpersonal relationships.

Still, there were plenty of close friendships among drivers, and even when there was a fight, there was a pretty decent chance the combatants would put it behind them over a beer later that night. But in any closed circle, especially one containing so many alpha males, there are going to be personality clashes, petty jealousies, and instances of guys just not being able to stand each other. The drivers, however, couldn't let whatever animosity they might feel toward each other manifest itself on the track. That was just too dangerous. And even off the track, it was easier for them to find a way to get along than to be openly hostile, since for nine months out of the year they traveled to the same small towns, stayed at the same motels, ate at the same diners, and drank at the same bars.

One of the most entertaining examples of driver cooperation occurred in 1975, when Bobby Allison, Buddy Baker, David Pearson, Richard Petty, Darrell Waltrip, and Cale Yarborough got together and recorded the album *NASCAR Goes Country*. It's the kind of recording everybody should listen to once. (And just once.) The Jordanaires, who had backed up Elvis Presley for twenty years, were brought in to sing background vocals, allowing the drivers to more or less speak most of their parts, which is probably a good thing. The album's high point, such as it is, is probably Richard Petty's performance of Roger Miller's "King of the Road," a fitting pairing of singer and subject matter. As for the low point, the less said about Buddy Baker's rendition of "Butterbeans" the better.

The record opens with "Ninety-nine Bottles of Beer (on the Wall)." (Luckily, most of the numbers between zero and ninety-eight were skipped, and the song lasts only three and a half minutes.) Baker handles the first verse, which contains a line about what began as a social event devolving into a brawl. That was especially fitting on a record sung by stock car drivers, because so much of their time was spent with people they were just as likely to take a swing at as to pat on the back. Granted, six race car drivers spending a few days goofing off in a studio wasn't as remarkable an accomplishment as Fleetwood Mac recording *Rumours* at a time when everyone in the band was either cheating on a bandmate or breaking up with one, but there was still plenty of intrigue among the warbling drivers, the kind of lurking-beneath-the-surface tension that permeated the sport. Some of it was rooted in on-track incidents (Allison and Petty). Some of it was born of an intense rivalry (Petty and Pearson). Sometimes it was a case of general principles (no one really cared for Waltrip's mouth, which didn't bother Waltrip, because he didn't care for the old guard). And sometimes it was nothing more than two strong personalities that just seemed destined to butt heads. "Cale and Bobby had trouble," says Junior Johnson. "They were just so competitive. They hated each other."

Bobby Allison's fortunes changed in 1978. He hooked up with owner Bud Moore, a World War II veteran who had been awarded the Bronze

Star for his service during Operation Overlord. Moore didn't sweat the small stuff—landing at Normandy on D-Day will do that to you—and actually welcomed feedback from Allison. They won five races together in '78, including Allison's first Daytona 500, and finished second to Yarborough in points, making Allison—who after thirteen years in the Grand National division was still looking for that elusive season championship—one of the favorites to unseat Yarborough.* Allison didn't help his title hopes in the first race of the '79 season. He had been leading at Riverside with seventeen laps left, but his engine failed, relegating him to nineteenth place. Yarborough finished a comfortable third.

When Allison flew his plane into Daytona, he had a guest: Ken Squier of CBS, who was filming a spot with Allison for the network's coverage of the 500. Allison had been flying for years. He logged an amazing number of hours hopping from short track to short track so that he could race in between Grand National events, but he also enjoyed the serenity that came with being alone in the sky. He told Squier how when he was flying, he liked to reflect on the days when piloting his own plane wasn't an option: "I think about a lot of those times when we spent all night the night after a race getting home, all night the night before qualifying getting to the racetrack, and the times when I really would have loved to have stopped at a motel but couldn't because we didn't have the money."

It hadn't been easy, but he'd come a long way from that abandoned amusement park in Miami to the media center at Daytona, where, on the afternoon of Thursday, February 8, he was preparing to find

---

*NASCAR distributed points roughly the same way in 1979 as it does today. The race winner got 175 points, the next five spots each got five fewer than the previous position (second was 170, third 165, etc.); the five after that decreased by increments of four; and the finishers from eleventh place on decreased by increments of threes. Any driver who led at least one lap got five bonus points, and the driver who led the most laps got five more. The system was often criticized for placing too much emphasis on consistency instead of rewarding wins.

out where he'd start in the Busch Clash, which was, considering the purse and the amount of work involved, the most lucrative race in stock car history. An ice-filled tub of Busch beer was placed in front of the eight drivers, who were wearing matching Busch blazers. (The ninth, Neil Bonnett, was still in Alabama having some dental work done.) As a roomful of writers and photographers looked on, a green flag was dropped, and the drivers grabbed wildly for the cans. Allison drew number 4, while Yarborough, who cut his hand on a can, pulled number 7.

Noticeably absent from the proceedings was Richard Petty, who had failed to sit on a pole during his winless 1978 season and therefore wasn't in the Busch Clash. He wasn't even in Daytona yet. He'd be arriving on Friday, which would give him just enough time to settle in and give his son a last bit of coaching before Kyle's debut.

Chapter Four

The Prince

Sunday, February 11
Qualifying for the Daytona 500/ARCA 200/Busch Clash

THE JOB of a promoter is to drum up interest in a race and sell as many tickets as possible, and the steady stream of fans coming into the speedway seven days before the Daytona 500 served as proof that Bill France was a very good promoter. Instead of having the field for the 500 set the same way it was everywhere else — give everyone a qualifying lap or two and then order the cars from fastest to slowest — France concocted an elaborate system that increased both track time and ticket sales. Every car ran two laps the Sunday before the race, with the two fastest cars locked in to the front-row spots for the 500. The next twenty-eight spots were set by two 125-mile races held the following Thursday, with the final ten places filled based on drivers' times posted in other qualifying sessions during the week. It was far more complex than it needed to be, but it gave France the chance to sell tickets for the Thursday races, and it gave fans and writers something to pay attention to in the week leading up to the 500.

Sunday began with the qualifying laps at 11:00 a.m., followed by Kyle Petty's debut in the ARCA race, with the Busch Clash closing out the afternoon. The Clash drivers were given the opportunity to qualify first so that their crews would have time to get their cars ready for the race. Lap times had been fast all week during practice, thanks to the track, which had been completely repaved for the first time in its twenty-year history. On Saturday Cale Yarborough had broken his own nine-year-old track record* with a lap of 194.868 miles per hour, despite his insistence that his car was "not running worth a durn." He was even durn worse the next day when, near the end of his first qualifying lap, his engine blew up, sending smoke billowing from his car. Nevertheless, he made it back to the finish line with a speed of 194.321 miles per hour, the fastest up to that point. He stayed on the pole for only ten minutes, when Buddy Baker confirmed his status as the driver to beat. His lap of 196.049 miles per hour obliterated Yarborough's new track record. There were forty-three drivers left to qualify after Baker put up his time, but there was only one with a real chance of catching him: Donnie Allison.

Of all the bad deals in the long and storied history of bad deals—the Red Sox giving up Babe Ruth, the Indians giving up Manhattan—few were worse than the one Donnie Allison made Michael DiProspero and Bill Gardner, two businessmen from Connecticut who were also brothers-in-law. Over pinochle one night at DiProspero's house in the fall of 1972, the talk to turned to cars. DiProspero had a little experience in local short-track racing, and he mentioned that he was thinking of buying a Grand National car and fielding a team the following spring. Gardner had never even seen a race, but he had a sense of adventure and, thanks to his real estate holdings, the means with which

---

*Concerned that cars were traveling too fast, NASCAR mandated smaller, less-powerful engines after the 1970 season to slow them down.

to indulge it. He was on board. The brothers-in-law decided to call their operation DiGard.

DiProspero and Gardner stood out among NASCAR team owners, who were generally not the pinochle-playing types. There was also the matter of DiProspero and Gardner's provenance: they were Yankees in a southern man's sport. But where they truly broke the mold was in the way they questioned the accepted NASCAR way. The owner-driver relationship was historically a simple, informal one, binding only to the extent that a gentleman's handshake was considered such. If a driver wanted to leave, he left. If an owner got sick of his driver, he let him go. DiProspero and Gardner, however, insisted on a formal business arrangement, with written contracts. On the advice of Bobby Allison, who had built a few short-track cars for DiProspero, they hired Donnie Allison for the 1973 season. The deal they struck required Allison to sign over some equipment he had at his shop in Hueytown. In return, he was named president of DiGard as well as the team's driver.

It seemed like a good deal at the time.

Donnie Allison had had a few semi-regular gigs, but for most of his Grand National career he'd been a journeyman. DiGard provided stability. But it was an expansion team, and in its early days it had its share of '62 Mets moments—including ordering the wrong kind of car for its first race. DiGard showed up at the 1973 Daytona 500 with a short-track car, a Chevelle, which was kind of like taking a putter to the first tee at Augusta National. (Allison failed to qualify for the forty-car field.) And when Gardner was scouting territory for a race shop, he looked in Daytona, despite the fact that virtually every team was located within a two-hour drive of Charlotte. "I felt Daytona was the heart of racing," he explained. So he built a state-of-the-art, 20,000-square-foot facility within walking distance of the speedway—then found it was nearly impossible to fill it with workers. Few decent mechanics were going to uproot their families and move to Florida. The location was great for the two races at the speedway but murder for the rest of the season, which was loaded with races in the Carolinas and Virginia. Many weeks the crewmen just crashed at the shop of car builder Robert Gee outside Charlotte to save themselves the fifteen-hour round-trip drive.

The team steadily improved, thanks in no small part to the depth of Gardner's pockets. It brought the right car, a new Chevrolet, to the 1974 Daytona 500, and Allison drove it away from the rest of the field. He had a thirty-eight-second lead with eleven laps left when he ran over some debris and cut both his front tires, allowing Richard Petty to overtake him and win.* Allison came close on several other occasions, but he never took DiProspero and Gardner to Victory Lane. After a fifth-place finish in the 1975 Firecracker 400, the Fourth of July race in Daytona, Gardner summoned Allison to his hundred-foot yacht, *Captiva,* and told Allison he was being let go. "That was a tough decision because Donnie was a great person, a great family guy, and he was a hell of a driver," says Gardner. "But the guys weren't that happy at the time with his performance."

Getting fired is bad. Getting fired by a guy who has called you down to his yacht is worse. But getting fired by a guy who has called you down to his yacht and then informed you that your severance package is going to be $250 is about as bad as it gets. To his credit, Allison talked Gardner up to $500. That was all Allison had to show for his stock and for all that equipment he had signed over. Five hundred bucks. (Allison says it was worth $200,000. Gardner says that's what the gear was valued at, per the contract. "There's always two sides to every story," says Gardner. "It was in the contract, that's what you got paid. It's a way of doing business that nobody had done at the time.")

Gardner hired Darrell Waltrip to replace Allison, who returned to Hueytown and raced a Camaro at local short tracks before latching on

---

* Allison might have had a chance to catch Petty, but the race had been shortened to 450 miles due to the energy crisis.

with Hoss Ellington. Until Ellington started racing, he ran a pipe insulation company and went by his given name, Charles. But he realized that insurance was a lot cheaper for a pipe fitter than a race car driver, so he raced as Hoss. He fit in well with the raucous drivers of the 1960s. Ellington once went on a bender with Coo Coo Marlin and his wife, Eula Faye, the designated driver, near Talladega, Alabama, that ended with Ellington and Marlin getting locked up for being drunk. (It didn't help that Eula Faye, the stone-cold sober one, couldn't figure out how to lower the power windows when they were pulled over.) Ellington woke up in the middle of the night in a pitch-black cell to a loud clanking sound: Marlin was beating a metal cup with his boot in an attempt to fashion a key. He kept at it until Ellington pointed out that maybe they were safer in their cell than outside. "Don't you hear them damn bloodhounds barking?" he said.

Allison was something of a kindred spirit. "Donnie liked to hunt and fish and carry on," says Ellington. "And there ain't nothing wrong with that." Allison never minded that Ellington, who was based in Wilmington, on North Carolina's Atlantic coast, usually ran his car only on superspeedways, which had the biggest purses. But before the start of the 1979 season, Ellington and Allison decided that they were going to run the full schedule. Donnie was excited; it was a chance for him to see how he stacked up and to show that he took racing seriously enough to commit to the grind of going to the track week in and week out. Their year started out well enough, with a fifth-place finish at Riverside. And when they got to Daytona, Allison was consistently one of the fastest cars in practice.

Since he wasn't part of the Busch Clash field, Allison was one of the last cars to make a qualifying run, which put him at a distinct disadvantage. By the time he got on the track, it had gotten significantly warmer, making the surface slicker. And the gentle morning breeze had turned into a strong wind that held the cars up as they made their way down the backstretch. Still, Allison was able to turn the second-fastest lap, guaranteeing himself a front-row starting spot alongside Baker. He had to be delighted that his speed of 194 was almost two miles per hour faster than the time Waltrip posted in his old car.

Satisfied, Donnie cleaned up and headed into the garage to find out whether Richard Petty's boy merited all the attention he was getting.

The roof of the Petty Enterprises van was *the* place to be for the ARCA 200. In addition to Donnie Allison, drivers Neil Bonnett, Buddy Arrington, and Lennie Pond had flocked to higher ground in search of a better vantage point for the race. Cale Yarborough was there, too, but only because his offer to work on Kyle Petty's over-the-wall crew had been gracefully declined. (Yarborough's explanation as to why he was willing to lug tires around during pit stops was simple: "Because I admire the boy's spunk." And he wasn't the only one. Allison also offered his services.) Lee Petty was there, calmly smoking his pipe. Richard Petty was the last to arrive. After giving his son a few last-minute words of encouragement, he hopped on a bike, pedaled through the garage, and joined the party atop the van. Darrell Waltrip, Bobby Allison, and David Pearson watched from the next truck over, and A. J. Foyt was perched on a nearby van, all anxious to see what the kid could do.

While the men congregated in the garage, which was off-limits to the fairer sex, the Petty women gathered at Turn 4 atop an RV owned by Ron Bell, whose Southern Pride Car Wash was one of Kyle's sponsors. Kyle's wife, Pattie, was there, as was his mother, Lynda, and his grandmother Elizabeth. Pattie had already spent plenty of time with Elizabeth; her room at the Hawaiian Inn on the beach — ostensibly her honeymoon suite — adjoined her husband's grandparents' room.

Pattie had entered the NASCAR world two years earlier when she became a "Winston Girl," which one writer described as "those ladies in red shirts and white hotpants who pose beside the red-and-white Winston promotion autos at racetracks while gentleman fans snap pictures and get a peck on the cheek, then mutter happily, 'Ain't she enough to make a man's wife jealous?'" If that was the effect the Winston Girls had on married men, one can only imagine the effect they had on teenage boys, which is what Kyle was when they met. Pattie hadn't taken the job to widen her social circle. (Fraternization with drivers was taboo but certainly not unheard-of.) She was in it strictly for the $88 a day, which went toward putting herself through grad school. She was so set against the idea of hanky-panky that she decided she wouldn't even give the winner a kiss on the cheek. "I will shake hands," she said, "but I will not do that."

Interesting, then, that she ended up marrying the first person she met on the job.

Pattie's introduction to Grand National racing came at Nashville Speedway in the summer of 1977. She was twenty-three and felt completely lost. She vaguely knew about Richard Petty, because she lived in High Point and it was hard to live in High Point and be totally oblivious to the King. She knew of David Pearson, her father's favorite driver. And she knew of another driver in the field that day: Marty Robbins, a country music star who occasionally moonlighted as a racer. Pattie's father had never been crazy about his daughter spending so much time around racetracks, but when he found out that she might be able to meet Marty Robbins—who sang "El Paso," his favorite song—he warmed to the idea. Pattie made it a priority to get her picture taken with Robbins, so she sauntered up to a harmless-looking, frizzy-haired kid with a cast on the leg he had broken playing high school football. Kyle told her he'd be happy to introduce her. Before she knew it, Pattie had her picture. "I was his hero from that point on," she says.

Despite the difference in their ages, Pattie found herself spending more and more time with the friendly kid. She was getting close to Kyle's younger sisters as well; they loved to make trips to Pattie's farm and ride her horses. Things were going swimmingly until Kyle overplayed his hand. "Kyle and I got to be really, really good friends," says Pattie. "Then the next thing you know he's like, I want to marry you."

Cue the freaking-out music.

Pattie's reaction was exactly what one might expect: "I was like, *Okay, I can't see you anymore. Don't come back here. Your mother will have me locked up and put in jail. You're not quite seventeen yet, and I'm twenty-four. This isn't a pretty picture.*"

After a couple of weeks, though, she started to miss him. So she called the Petty house and asked Lynda to send Kyle back down to the farm. They decided that the best course of action was for Pattie to go up to Level Cross and meet the whole Petty clan. She had already won over Kyle's sisters by giving Rebecca a horse. ("You give a four-year-old a pony, and you're set for life," she says.) To their relief, his parents didn't require any grand equine gestures. If anything, Pattie's presence in their living room confirmed what they already suspected about their son. "Believe it or not, he acted more mature then than he does now," says Pattie. "He hung out with older people. He didn't have friends his age. His friends were his dad's crew. His mother said to me one day, 'It never surprised me that he brought home someone who's the same age as the guys he hangs out with.'"

Before Kyle gave her a ring, he gave her a wedding present: a two-year-old filly named Rockell Chick. In August 1978 he told Pattie that if she checked the horse's feed, she'd find another gift. "You might want to go get it before she eats it," he said. Pattie checked as instructed and found a diamond ring. Their engagement official, Kyle took his new fiancée up to the house. "They wanted to know when we were getting married," says Pattie. "His dad said, 'You'll have to get married before racing season starts because I don't have time...'"

So here Pattie was, spending the last day of her honeymoon atop an RV, watching the start of racing season—the ARCA 200, an event that would have attracted virtually no interest had her husband not been in

the field. Kyle had run well in practice and qualified on the outside of
the front row, which had more to do with what he was driving than
how he drove it. The field had a handful of drivers capable of running
up front and a whole lot of guys without the experience or the machin-
ery to keep up. Kyle qualified at just under 190 miles per hour, 2 miles
per hour behind pole sitter John Rezek; the cars at the back of the pack
were a good 40 miles per hour slower.

Despite their lack of star power, the ARCA boys could usually
be counted on to put on a pretty good show in Daytona. In 1978
leaders Jim Sauter and Bruce Hill wrecked each other on the last
lap, with Sauter hanging on to win the race. But neither driver was
in the field in '79. They had been denied entry by ARCA president
John Marcum, who wielded the same kind of absolute authority
over his series that Bill France had over his, but without France's
admirable restraint. Marcum tooled around the Daytona garage
in a gold Lincoln Continental, and he had a reputation for going
to great — and sometimes questionable — lengths to inject excitement into his races. He would purportedly stand trackside with his
houndstooth hat in hand, and if any car got too far out in front, he'd
drop the hat — a signal to the flagman to throw the caution flag and
bunch up the field.*

Marcum's rationale for keeping Sauter and Hill out was that "they
don't normally race with us," but if being an ARCA regular was truly
a prerequisite, Kyle Petty shouldn't have been allowed anywhere near
the track. That, of course, wasn't going to happen. Hill believed that he
and Sauter were being kept out for a more sinister reason: to give Kyle
a better chance to win. "Everything was certainly set up that way," Hill

---

* Although phantom cautions are fairly common in NASCAR today, they weren't in
the late 1970s, when race officials would just let cars drive away from the pack, no
matter how boring a finish that might create. In the 1978 Grand National season,
nineteen of the thirty races ended with only one or two cars on the lead lap, and no
race finished with more than six.

complained. "The more I think about it, the more it disgusts me. But if I tried to force the issue, I would have difficulty getting past the technical inspectors at NASCAR races."

Marcum did his best to sidestep the controversy. "We got the nicest bunch of cars here this year we've ever had," he said. "All of 'em are independents. Closest thing we got to a factory car is Kyle's. I figured this is his first race and I think we can give him some driving lessons."

If the boy needed lessons, he wasn't going to get them from his father. "I ain't gonna tell you how to drive," Richard told Kyle. "Ain't gonna matter to me if you win or lose." The first part of the statement was far more believable than the second. The only advice Richard gave Kyle was to be patient and use the first couple of laps to get comfortable running in traffic.

Wearing one of his father's old racing suits — he removed the RICHARD portion of the stitching on the chest so it just said PETTY — Kyle slipped behind the wheel of his Dodge. He had painted the car Petty Blue and white, with the logo of his primary sponsor, Valvoline, on the hood and white eagles on the front quarter panels. There was a small Southern Pride Car Wash logo near the rear window. Kyle had encountered ignition problems near the end of Saturday's final practice, but Steve Hmiel and his crew had worked through the night to fix the car, and as it rolled off the starting grid, it was purring.

As the field turned a few warm-up laps behind the pace car, Kyle came to a realization about Daytona: "This is the biggest place in the world until you put multiple cars out there, then it becomes one of the smallest places in the world." Then the pace car pulled onto pit road, and the thirty-one cars bunched up and approached the start/finish line. That brief interval between the time the pace car pulls off the track and the time the green flag drops — transforming a casual Sunday drive into a knuckle whitener — are four or five of the most tension-filled seconds imaginable, so an inexperienced kid could be forgiven for being a little excitable under such conditions. When the green flag flew, Kyle threw his father's advice to take it easy out the window. He tore into the first corner, riding the high line, just like his old man liked to do. As he roared into Turn 2, he got even farther up the track, slapping the wall. "He can't go any higher than that," Richard said to the men on the van. But the contact with the wall didn't slow him down. He got around Rezek and led the pack back to the start/finish line. "If nothing else," his grandfather announced, "he's going to lead at least the first lap."

On the fifteenth lap, Kyle got his first reminder of just how serious the stakes were. Back in the pack, Bobby Fisher got sideways and was broadsided by Marvin Smith and Bobby Davis. Bobby Jacks then hit Davis, and Jacks went flipping through the air. (It wasn't a good lap for Bobbys.) It was a nasty wreck — nasty enough to make Cale Yarborough, who'd seen his share of carnage, let out a long "Wooooo!" on top of the Petty van, where the conversation turned to the effect the accident might have on Kyle's psyche. Richard, who was talking to Kyle over the radio, told him, "Come on back there, and when you get there, slow way, way down." By the time Kyle got around to the site of the wreck, Jacks had scampered from his car — which was on fire and lying on its side — and was sitting on the track with his head down, car parts strewn all over the place. Kyle had been to plenty of races and seen plenty of wrecks, some involving his father, but he'd never before witnessed one as a participant. He handled it without a problem.

The same, unfortunately, could not be said about his ensuing pit stop, the first of his career. Kyle had barely mastered the concept of speeding up; the concept of slowing down was completely foreign to him. He flew into the pits way too fast and almost took out Dale Inman, who was holding the signboard telling him which pit stall was his. (On top of the hauler, Yarborough and Donnie Allison were likely thankful that their offers to work on his crew had been turned down.) As he left the pits, Kyle stalled the engine, leaving him in a situation that called for cool and calm. Instead he screamed, "What gear do I put it in?" and dumped a cup of Gatorade in his lap.

By the time he got the engine refired and left the pits, Kyle had fallen back to tenth place. He worked his way back up near the front and stayed with the leaders despite another near stall in the pits thirty laps later. Watching the kid, the vets atop the Petty Enterprises van couldn't help but feel young again. Allison turned to Yarborough and said, "You know, I wouldn't mind starting all over again. Would you?" Yarborough said nothing, but his wide grin answered the question.

With the exception of the other thirty drivers in the field, and presumably their families, everyone at the speedway was pulling for Kyle, but no one more so than John Marcum, who had visions of front-page stories dancing in his houndstooth-covered head. Alas, as the laps ticked down, it was becoming clear that the car to beat belonged to Phil Finney, a driver from Merritt Island, Florida. Kyle and Marcum needed help from above. With nine laps left, it came.

To hear Kyle tell the story, the help literally came from above. Daytona Speedway is located about two miles inland; its proximity to the beach, along with the lure of Lake Lloyd and the prospect of foraging for food scraps left by infield tailgaters, makes the track a popular hangout for seagulls. Occasionally, there are collisions with the gulls, which is what Petty thought happened. But Finney remembers very well what hit his windshield as it plowed down the backstretch at 185 miles per hour: a small piece of metal about the size of a wallet. NASCAR windshields now are made of Lexan, the same material used in fighter jet canopies. Finney's was made of glass. It cracked, forcing him to pit and relinquish first place to Petty, who had a sizable lead on Rezek. But with seven laps to go, Ramo Stott blew a tire, bringing out the caution flag and allowing Rezek to get back on Kyle's tail for the final restart. "They'll go green for four laps," Lee said. "We'll see what he's learned. See if he's listened."

Richard decided there was nothing he could tell Kyle that would help him in the shoot-out. "It's potluck," he said. "You take what you can get."

Rezek had a strong restart, pulling alongside Kyle, but he couldn't complete the pass and had to back off as they hit the first corner. That's the way it went through the final laps: Rezek making up ground on the straightaways, but Kyle getting through the turns faster.

As Kyle took the white flag, Pattie was jumping up and down, screaming, "Go, Kyle! Go, Kyle! Think about our house payments and the vet bills!" Kyle was still in the lead, but on the last lap at Daytona that wasn't necessarily a good thing. The leader had to run with his foot on the floor at all times. The guy behind him could take advantage of the hole the first car punched through the air. Facing less resistance, he could settle in behind the leader and keep pace without running wide-open. Then, when the time was right, he could pull out, use up that little bit of throttle he had in reserve, and make the pass. It was called the slingshot, and it looked like Kyle was being set up for it. Being in the lead on the last lap at Daytona was such an undesirable position that in the 1974 Firecracker 400, David Pearson had faked a blown engine by taking his foot off the gas on the front stretch and leaving Richard Petty, who was on his bumper, no choice but to go around him. Then he had floored it, caught Petty in the fourth turn, and passed him just before they reached the finish line.

Now, as the cars sped off of Turn 4 — the same spot Richard had pointed out to Kyle on their tour of the track three weeks earlier — Kyle did something he hadn't done all day. Instead of staying in the high groove and giving Rezek a chance to get under him, he swung his car down low, near the apron, leaving Rezek only one option: to take the long way and try to pass him high. Rezek got alongside the Dodge one last time, but Kyle beat him to the checkered flag. Had the finish line been farther up the track, the racing world might have been deprived of a storybook ending.

Down at Turn 4, all the Petty women were in tears. In the garage, Richard hopped off the trailer and headed for Victory Lane as the rest of the drivers took turns slapping Lee on the back. "A lot of people are going to be shaking their heads over this day for a long, long time," said Buddy Arrington.

"Whaddya think, Grandpa?" said Donnie Allison.

"Damndest thing I've seen," Lee replied.

"I believe Ol' Richard has just found his successor," Bonnett said.

"Wrong," replied Allison. "Richard had his successor the second that kid was born. I don't want to hear anyone ever tell me again that having a knack for driving can't be traced to heredity."

Down in Victory Lane, Richard was impressed with just about everything his son had done: "He showed a good driving style, but now he's got to learn how to drive a race car. And especially, he's got to learn how to stop one."

Kyle proved to be a natural at the PR side of racing, too. When a photographer asked him to take off his hat, he refused because he wanted to make sure the Valvoline logo got in as many pictures as possible. But lest anyone forget he was new at this, he actually blushed when he was asked if he should be called Prince Kyle. "Aww, no," he said. "Tomorrow I'll be back right where I was before, carrying tires and doing other chores on Daddy's crew."

Someone asked Richard—whose time in qualifying for the 500 that morning had been just eleventh fastest—if he would have done anything differently had he been behind the wheel of the car.

"Yes," the King said. "I probably would have run second."

For all of the buildup leading up to the inaugural Busch Clash—the promise of cars bouncing off one another in a mad dash for cash—Monty Roberts's brainchild turned out to be a ho-hum affair. Granted, anything short of the winner crossing the finish line on his roof was going to suffer for having to follow the Kyle Petty Show, but it would take several cans of Busch beer to convince any fan that what he saw lived up to the billing.

With Donnie Allison out of the field* and Cale Yarborough's engines blowing up on a regular basis, the only driver who had a chance to hang with Buddy Baker was Darrell Waltrip. But for the Clash, the two favorites entered into a nonaggression pact, agreeing to work together to pull away from the field and save any hard racing for the last lap or two.

Getting to the front early was something Baker always tried to do — none of this hang back, stay out of trouble, and make a move late business that Richard Petty and David Pearson were always pulling. Baker's philosophy fit his physique. He was a bear of a man, so big and strong that he looked like he might actually be able to mash the gas a little harder than anyone else. His strategy for the Clash was simple: "I'm gonna get comfortable and put both feet on the floor and see what happens."

That occasionally led to problems — blown engines, crushed fenders, dented bodies. Baker was notoriously tough on his equipment. The joke about him had always been, "Give Buddy an anvil for breakfast, and he'll break it by lunch." Baker also was cursed with horrible luck and an affinity for finding new and interesting ways to lose that would have been funny had they not been so sad. Arguably his best effort in that regard came in 1969, when he lost the Texas 400 by crashing on a caution lap — because he was looking at a sign his crew had made him telling him he had the race sewn up. Daytona had been an especially grim venue for Baker. He had been racing at the track since it opened but had never won. He'd finished second five times in the 500 and had a couple of other tantalizingly close finishes, the most recent in 1978, when he'd blown an engine with four laps left.

But he had every reason to believe that '79 would be different. He joined the team owned by Harry Ranier, a relative newcomer to the game who had deep pockets. Ranier's most significant move was to hire engine

---

* His best qualifying effort in the 1978 season had been second.

builder Waddell Wilson away from L. G. DeWitt's team. Junior Johnson was widely regarded as the best engine man of the day, but a strong case could be made for Wilson. He'd started as a helper in the engine room at Holman Moody in 1963, at the same time Cale Yarborough was sweeping the floors. Holman Moody was a massive operation that supplied equipment to several drivers, so when the engines were built, they were all thrown into a pile and distributed randomly. After Fred Lorenzen lapped the field in the 1965 Daytona 500, he started requesting engines from the same curly-haired kid who had built that one. Before long all the big-name Ford drivers were clamoring for Wilson's handiwork.

With Holman Moody, then later with Wood Brothers and DeWitt, Wilson built the engines that won four Daytona 500s for four different drivers with distinctly different styles. His most impressive win came in 1973, when he built Benny Parsons's motor. Parsons had insisted that Wilson use some drag racing pistons he had been given in California. Wilson said that the engine would blow up in a second, and it did. As they were on a shoestring budget, the only backup engine they had with them in Daytona was one Wilson had thrown together out of pieces from the scrap heap. "I wouldn't have given you $100 for that engine," Wilson says. "I wouldn't have put it in a street car." But it held up through qualifying, practice, and the race.

"He was like the fastest gun in the West," says rival engine builder Lou LaRosa. "The one you're always gunning for. If you beat him, you did something well."

So if anyone could build a motor that was powerful enough to run up front in Daytona but durable enough to stand up to Baker's heavy foot, it was Wilson. And the car that Wilson and crew chief Herb Nab built was sleek, too. The black and gray Oldsmobile rode so low to the ground and blended into the track so well that the other drivers started calling it "the Gray Ghost," because they swore it just appeared out of nowhere on their rear bumpers. "Against the field, that was about as fast a race car as I ever worked on," says Wilson.

Baker, who had drawn the number 3 beer can on Thursday, didn't waste any time showing off the power he had under his hood. He took the lead on the first turn of the second lap, and then, as planned, he and Waltrip hooked up and left the other seven cars behind. As Baker took the white flag, Waltrip was on his bumper, with the battle for third taking place about half a lap behind them.

Baker's car was clearly the class of the field, but like Kyle Petty an hour earlier, he found himself in the unenviable position of having to hold off a slingshot move in the final turn. And also like Petty, Baker protected his position by going low. "They expect you to run up against the wall on the last lap," he said. "But I got down on the apron. That way he couldn't go under me.... When you go in low like that, you are already turned when you get into the corner. The guy behind you, he hasn't turned, and when he goes in, he gets a push in the nose so he can't pass you." For the second time that day, the conventional wisdom had been upended. Maybe taking the lead into the last lap at Daytona wasn't such a bad thing after all.

Baker's $50,000 check brought his take for the day to $56,000. He had won $5,000 for taking the pole in the 500 and an extra grand for breaking the track record. Up to that point, the biggest check he'd cashed in his career had been for $32,300. But when he said that "finally winning here means more than the $50,000," those on hand believed him. In addition to snapping a seventy-race winless streak that stretched back to May 1976, Baker had finally conquered Daytona. "I've been coming here since '59, and now at least I've won something," he said.

As Baker celebrated, the 50,000 fans made their way out of the grandstands and into the parking lots, leaving in their wake piles of empty Busch beer cans. For Kyle Petty, Buddy Baker — and, not least of all, Monty Roberts — it had been a beautiful day.

Chapter Five
The Man in the White Hat

Thursday, February 15
125-Mile Qualifying Races

ALL WEEK Darrell Waltrip had been wearing a white hat. He was hard to miss in it. If the hat couldn't literally hold ten gallons, it at least looked big enough to handle a couple of two-liter bottles of Sun-Drop. If nothing else, it was spacious enough to rest on Waltrip's head without messing up his hair. But more than just a fashion statement, the lid doubled as a metaphorical device. There's a fine line between being the guy people love to hate and being the guy people legitimately loathe, and Waltrip had long ago left that line in his rearview mirror. "When they announced him at the driver introduction, you could almost feel the — I don't know if you could call it hatred — but the vibrations from the fans all saying 'Boo' and stomping their feet," remembers Gary Nelson, one of Waltrip's crew members. It had gotten to the point that he didn't even want to go to driver intros. So he made a conscious effort to remake himself as the good guy, white hat and all. "I'm going to be a nicer fellow," Waltrip said on Wednesday, the day before the twin qualifying races that would set the field for the 500. "I want to prove to everybody that I'm trying to be cooperative."

The "everybody" he was trying to win over could be forgiven if they were skeptical. For years Waltrip had been, in the words of Nelson, "raising the bar for breaking the mold." He was kind of like the protagonist in every movie ever made about racing—the young, brash, fast kid who needed to learn to harness all that energy and respect his elders. Waltrip craved attention, and if he couldn't get it with his driving, he'd get it with his mouth. That's what he had done in Nashville, where his chief competition had come from old schoolers like Coo Coo Marlin and Flookie Buford, good ol' boys who, when talking to reporters, would say things like "Yep, well, we run purty good." With some goading from track promoters, Waltrip assumed the role of the heel, getting in front of the cameras and saying things like "Aw, Flookie Buford's just a backhoe operator." The idea was to get people to recognize him, and it worked. So when he made it to Grand National racing, he started talking about other drivers, other teams, NASCAR— anything that crossed his mind. It was partly for show, but underlying the act was some sincere resentment aimed at the establishment he felt was trying to hold him back. The first time Buddy Baker ever laid eyes on Waltrip was in the early '70s when the unknown kid took the stage at a Q&A at the Hawaiian Inn in Daytona and proclaimed, "I'm the guy that's going to retire Richard Petty." Waltrip later referred to Baker as "a big elephant in a small jungle," and he once called out Junior Johnson's team for not working hard enough.

Needless to say, the subjects of his diatribes were not amused. Johnson shot back, "The trouble with Darrell is that he has hoof in mouth disease, and until he gets a bigger hoof and a smaller mouth, he's got no business talking about us." In 1977 Cale Yarborough dubbed Waltrip "Jaws," partly because Waltrip's aggressive driving left one of Yarborough's cars looking like it had been attacked by a shark, but mostly because Waltrip's jaws always seemed to be on the move. But it was a NASCAR official who probably best summed up the sport's feelings for Waltrip with one slightly haughty sentence: "Darrell's problem is that he just doesn't know his place."

Waltrip wasn't oblivious to the heat from the fans, from his fellow drivers, and from NASCAR. "They want to put a little fear in the new guy," he said in 1977. "It's like prison: when you stop bucking the system, they ease up. Pretty soon they let you get away with candy in your cell. But it's always their ballgame. They only ease up when they want to. If you play by their rules and do everything the way they want you to, you'll never be in trouble."

At first blush, that's an odd sentiment. It's not as if the NASCAR ranks have ever been bursting with corporate types. Historically, they were bootleggers, brawlers, and partyers. There was certainly room in the sport for drivers with personality. Tim Flock raced with a monkey named Jocko Flocko in his car.* "Little Joe" Weatherly drove a rental car into a motel swimming pool. One Sunday morning Curtis Turner landed his airplane on a road so that he could borrow a bottle of whiskey from a friend's house.†

But those good ol' boys had the good sense — unlike Waltrip — not to seek out cameras or microphones before putting their large personalities on display. Not that they had much cause to worry about cameras or microphones being around. One year in Riverside, a radio host looking to fill some airtime grabbed Curtis Turner and asked him

---

* Jocko's career ended after he got out of his seat belt during a race in Raleigh and climbed on Flock, necessitating a pit stop so that Flock's crew could literally get the monkey off his back.

† When Turner realized that he had landed adjacent to two churches whose congregations were just getting out, he decided to hightail it out of there. As he taxied down the road and began to lift off, he noticed a traffic light hanging from heavy wires. Knowing he couldn't get in the air fast enough to get over it, he did the next best thing, a maneuver not recommended by most reputable flight instructors. "I had to raise my wheels so's I could fly low enough to get under it," he said.

what he thought of drag racing, since the winter nationals were being held in the area a few weeks later. Turner responded, "Well, I always considered that drag racing was a little like masturbation. It's a little bit of fun, but it ain't much to look at." Not many reporters went looking for quotes from Turner after that, but it didn't bother him at all.

"So many drivers then were smarter than hell, but they lacked education," says Ken Squier. "Curtis was a disaster, and Weatherly, too. Bobby Isaac was the national champion, and I doubt that he could read. He had better answers than anybody, but he wouldn't talk to anyone from the North. He was not about to show his ass to anyone who would embarrass him. He had that pride and respect for himself."

So the press descended on Waltrip, the anti–Bobby Isaac: comfortable in front of the camera, unafraid to throw out a five-syllable word now and again (even if he wasn't always using it properly), and emanating a sense of sophistication rarely seen in the sport, with his Florsheim shoes and Brooks Brothers shirts. "He had a $25 haircut in the days when everybody had $3 haircuts," says Nelson. "Drove the biggest Lincoln he could find. Probably the first driver I know of that bought an airplane but didn't learn how to fly it."

Perhaps the most annoying thing about Waltrip, though, was that he had started winning. When he started driving in the Grand National Series as a twenty-five-year-old in 1972, he was running his own operation and, predictably, struggling. Then he took over Donnie Allison's DiGard ride in the summer of 1975 and won in his eighth start. He'd since won thirteen more races, including six each in 1977 and '78, which just meant more big talk. "He was like Muhammad Ali," remembers Nelson. "He talked big, but then he backed it up on the track. But in the garage area it didn't sit well to have this kid come along and talk about how he was going to kick everyone's ass on Sunday. That made it tough for us in the garage. We were basically living with these other race teams from track to track as we went through the season. You get relationships with these folks. And all of a sudden, they changed when Darrell would piss them off."

Waltrip didn't stop at pissing off other crews. He felt that he was the one putting his neck on the line, and he wasn't about to let some grease monkey ruin his effort. "People point the accusing finger at the driver," Waltrip said. "He's the one who's supposed to have it together. You hate it when your efforts are tarnished because someone lets you down. You hate being handicapped by other people." So he'd see his crew working and would walk by and say, "You're not going to screw up my pit stops again, are you?"

Says Nelson, "His motivational skills weren't quite honed yet."

Waltrip wanted his car running right, and he wanted it—like his uniform, which he insisted be pressed—to look good. The extent of his feedback was often to say, "That's just not gonna work. You gotta repaint that thing." When the car was slow, there were some serious blowups. "He's got a light temper, all right," his former crew chief Jake Elder once said. "He wants to run in the front bad, but Darrell don't quite always understand the circumstances why he's not running in the front. That's when he flies off the handle and throws those temper tantrums." This from a man who once went after one of his crewmen with a jack handle.

For years there had been a revolving door at DiGard. First Waltrip publicly ripped Mario Rossi and then had him fired as his crew chief. After Rossi he went through David Ifft and Darel Dieringer before Buddy Parrott was hired in 1977. Parrott was a card. Like Donnie Allison, he had been a diver when he was younger (he was the North Carolina state champion in high school; Allison was the Florida champ), and like Allison, he enjoyed a good time. Parrott looked forward to trips to Daytona because the hotel he stayed in had a pool that allowed him and Allison to hold impromptu diving competitions. "You've heard of a half gainer?" says Parrott. "My best dive was probably the half goner. I'd be half-gone when I did it."

If Parrott had managed a baseball team, he'd have been what they call a players' manager. "The guys loved him," says Waltrip. "He was a good leader of the team. But working on a car, setting a car up, that didn't interest him. What interested him was running the pits, calling the race on Sunday. And when the cameras were on, Buddy was on. I'll never forget, one of the guys said to me, 'Buddy Parrott, did you know he can't even weld?' It didn't surprise me. He was a Sunday guy." Still, Parrott and Waltrip got along well enough. "We had a lot of fun together," says Waltrip. It helped that Parrott had a very capable supporting cast. As a crew chief, Nelson would win twenty-five races and earn a reputation as one of NASCAR's most creative rule benders, while engine builder Robert Yates won the 1999 championship as an owner.*

The "Waltrip Effect" wasn't lost on other owners. In 1978 Kentucky businessman Harry Ranier began fielding a full-time team, with winless journeyman Lennie Pond behind the wheel. When Ranier saw how Waltrip had elevated a fledgling team to a championship contender, he decided to make a run at him. Waltrip was amenable to the idea. Driving for DiGard was starting to wear on him, and the money Ranier was offering was good. Poaching drivers wasn't uncommon, but Waltrip had signed a deal with Bill Gardner that ran through 1982, and Gardner (who was now running the team with his brother Jim) wasn't about to let him out of it. Waltrip figured that with the Gardners up in Connecticut, his would be the only voice anyone heard, so he started doing what he did best: making outlandish statements, such as calling the Gardners "slave dealers."

Bill Gardner, however, didn't stand by and take it. First, he sent Ranier a cease-and-desist telegram. Then he called a press conference

---

* Nelson, whose roots were in West Coast racing, had been considered for the job as Waltrip's crew chief in 1977, but the driver had nixed the idea. "I didn't like Gary," remembers Waltrip. "He was from California, and when he showed up at DiGard riding a Harley, he had long hair, like a hippie. They wanted him to be my crew chief. I said, 'He ain't working on my car.'"

the morning of the Southern 500 in Darlington to set the record straight about Waltrip's contract status. Realizing he needed his driver at least sort of happy, Gardner sat down with Waltrip and gave him an improved deal for the 1979 season—despite the fact that the driver had yet to win the sport's biggest race or its championship.

It was time to grow a bigger hoof.

Waltrip was one of the few drivers who didn't loathe the Twin 125s. He saw them as a chance to compete: "That's what we're here for, ain't it?" Most of his cohorts—especially the good ones—hated the races, though, primarily because they were being forced to share the track for one hour with some very desperate drivers. "You get seven or eight cars fighting for three or four spots in the field and it will make a guy do things he wouldn't do normally," said Richard Childress. The chief worry was getting caught up in someone else's trouble and wrecking a good Daytona 500 car. "Anytime you get into a car and race something bad can happen," said Richard Petty. "Now how do you suppose a cat is going to feel if he messes up his car in the 125-miler and can't be ready for the 500?"

Petty and Childress were in the first race, which meant they had the unenviable task of chasing Buddy Baker. NASCAR made one concession to the drivers, hoping that something—anything—could be done to take away Baker's advantage: he was required to put bright orange tape on the front of the Gray Ghost so his opponents could at least see the car as it blew past them.

The races were fifty laps each, which meant that every driver would have to make one pit stop for gas. Baker dashed to the front of the field and stayed there comfortably until it was time to refuel, on lap 36. He just needed to top off his tank, but somehow the stop took ten seconds. By the time everyone had finished their stops, Cale Yarborough, whose crew had gassed his car in five seconds, had a lead of 3.2 seconds—a lot of ground at 190 miles per hour. Baker was at the back of a pack with Benny Parsons, Bobby Allison, and Richard Petty. It took him just seven laps to pass all three and hitch himself to Yarborough's bumper. He retook the lead with two laps to go, and Yarborough never had a chance to get it back. It was a dominating performance, with Baker making up half a second per lap in traffic, and one that scared the hell out of every driver who witnessed it.

The field was more level in the second race. Donnie Allison and Darrell Waltrip started on the front row and tried to employ the same strategy Waltrip and Baker had used in the Clash. Instead of fighting each other early, they'd team up and drive away from the pack, then decide it between themselves. But Allison had engine trouble and dropped out with twelve laps to go. Four laps later Tighe Scott cut a tire, bringing out a caution and bunching up the pack for a tight finish. Waltrip was in the lead, and A. J. Foyt, the four-time Indy 500 champ, was second. Foyt was one of the drivers Waltrip got along well with because he, like Waltrip, was an outsider, a Texan who ran only a few NASCAR races a year. As the caution flag flew, he pulled up beside his buddy and gave him a friendly wave — what Waltrip called "one of those I-promise-I-won't-pass-you looks" — suggesting that they should work together at the end. "It showed how much experience I've gotten — I didn't fall for it," Waltrip said later with a laugh. Instead, Foyt tried to get around Waltrip as they headed for Turn 3 for the final time. And just as he made his move, the Daytona crowd saw for the first time a scene that would be repeated over and over for the next two decades: a smirking, mustachioed driver making a wild charge.

Behind Foyt on the final lap was Dale Earnhardt, an unknown twenty-seven-year-old who had run nine races in four seasons. Just as Foyt made his move on Waltrip's high side, Earnhardt shot low. It was a bold move, and it almost paid off. Waltrip moved up the track to block Foyt, allowing Earnhardt to see daylight. That forced Dick Brooks, the fourth-place driver, to make a decision. In the draft at Daytona, one car driving by itself won't go nearly as fast as two or more cars working together. Brooks could either cut low and try to push Earnhardt past Waltrip, or he could go high and hitch himself to Foyt. He chose to go with the veteran, and without drafting help, Earnhardt slid back into fourth.

The move didn't have a big effect on the finish—Waltrip won, Foyt was second, and Earnhardt cost himself one place. But it was a ballsy move, a rookie trying to pass two of the best drivers on the track with one move. Earnhardt pulled into the garage, hopped out of his car, and met the media at Daytona for the first time. The opening question came from Earnhardt himself, who was smiling slyly under his bushy mustache, and it was certainly rhetorical: "How 'bout it, boys? Think I'm gonna make it?"

Richard Petty had little reason to be optimistic. After coming home seventh in the first qualifier, he immediately called a team meeting, at which he made clear that nothing about the car was working. "Richard said the car wasn't handling," said Maurice Petty, "plus it wouldn't run either." He wound up one spot behind Ricky Rudd, a rookie who had never driven on the track before.

But no one was feeling good, not after Baker's display. Waltrip sang the praises of his car, Maybelline, the lone Oldsmobile in his Chevy-heavy stable. "Maybelline is one of the easiest old girls I've seen. She's a pleasure to drive. I told her not to get any bugs on her face." But his cockiness was tempered by a heavy dose of realism; the brashest statement he was willing to make about the 500 was that he and Baker were co-favorites. "But him more than me," Waltrip said, sounding nothing at all like Muhammad Ali.

The general consensus was that it was going to take, as Benny Parsons said, "some kind of miracle" to keep Baker from winning. A few drivers grumbled that he was so fast he had to be cheating, but as he watched NASCAR tear down his car in the postrace inspection, Baker said, "I just want to see all those red faces among people who thought we might be doing something illegal, because that engine is two cubic inches smaller than it's supposed to be." (The ability to get away with cheating was something many crew chiefs and engine builders wore as a badge of honor, but Waddell Wilson swore that every engine he built was legal.) Yarborough tried to remain optimistic, positing that when Wilson put a more durable race engine in the Gray Ghost, it would bring Baker back to the pack. "Only bad thing about that," said Baker, "is Waddell tells me the one we're going to put in is better than the one we're taking out."

The hardest thing for Baker to do was not to get his hopes up. "I'm going to the golf course before I get a big head," he said. "Some pals can't wait to get me over to Indigo Country Club. They know I've got a little money now, and they're circling like vultures." But after years of heartbreak at Daytona, it was hard for him to think that trouble wouldn't somehow find him. "I don't know how many parts there are in a race car, but I do know that at any time the smallest thing can put you out of a race. I just hope I can run as good as this car's been running."

Chapter Six

On the Air

OF ALL the accents in the drawl-laden Babel that was the garage at
Daytona International Speedway, the most unique probably belonged
to David Hobbs. Born in Royal Leamington Spa, England, Hobbs hit
all of his g's and was one of the few people around whose vocabulary
didn't include "y'all." He was a popular interview subject the day
before the race, partly because of his résumé — he had experience driving in Formula One, the Indy 500, the Daytona 500, and various sports
car series — and partly because he was going to be calling the 500 with
Ken Squier. "I think we're going to see a good race," Hobbs told a
couple of newspapermen, "if Buddy Baker will take the money CBS is
offering him not to run away and keep the show competitive."

They had a laugh, but there was no doubt that CBS was hoping
someone would find a way to keep up with Baker, because if he turned
the race into a snoozer, the network had no choice but to show the
whole dreary thing. It was a novel concept, showing a stock car race

from start to finish. Saturday's Sportsman 300 would be a dry run, shot but not aired. On Sunday, though, there would be no safety net, thanks to an audacious deal that had the potential to make or break the man who had agreed to it.

Neal Pilson wanted to go home. He was a thirty-eight-year-old New Yorker in Daytona, a man out of his element, and he had spent several days in intense negotiations with Bill France Jr., which would drain the energy out of even the most vigorous person. In addition to inheriting control of NASCAR and the speedway from his father when Big Bill retired, France had also inherited his dad's prowess at the negotiating table, which Pilson was finding out the hard way as they tried to hammer out a deal to broadcast the 1979 Daytona 500 on CBS. The window in the conference room next to France's office on the second floor of NASCAR's offices at the speedway afforded him a perfect view of the airport, which allowed him to gaze longingly out the window at all the planes that were leaving Daytona without him. He'd see a Delta jet take off, then get up and change his reservation to a later flight, hoping he might make that one.

Pilson had no one to blame but himself. As vice president of business affairs for CBS Sports, he had, with some urging from Ken Squier, convinced his bosses to get into the racing game. It was his idea, and if it didn't work out, it was going to be his ass, so it was in his best interest to stick around and get the best deal he could, no matter how many flights he had to rebook. The negotiations were made especially tough by the fact that what they were talking about doing—scheduling a special program to show a 500-mile NASCAR race live, from start to finish—was unprecedented.

At that time, if you wanted to see a NASCAR race, your choices were limited. You could buy a ticket and go to the track, or you could turn on ABC's *Wide World of Sports* and wait for the car racing segment, which could usually be found somewhere between the barrel racing segment and the Mexican cliff diving segment. The only time a car race was shown from start to finish was on Memorial Day weekend, when ABC would tape the Indianapolis 500 on Sunday afternoon and air it that night. The only nod to Daytona's status as the preeminent stock car event was that the TelePrompTer company would occasionally broadcast the race in theaters on closed circuit, the same way many prizefights were shown.

The thinking behind keeping cars off the air was simple: with three networks and virtually no cable, there simply wasn't room on the airwaves for a three-hour, forty-five-minute block of anything, especially something with as narrow appeal as a stock car race. Then there was the fact that live racing was unpredictable—not always in a good way. In 1970 ABC decided to air the conclusions of a few races live, to capture what it presumed would be some gripping late-lap drama. One of the first races the network tried this on was the Nashville 420, which turned out to be a battle of attrition. By the time ABC returned to the track for that gripping late-lap drama, there were only nine cars running—and none on the same lap. As part of *Wide World of Sports,* ABC also showed one race live in its entirety, the 1971 Greenville 200. The seventy-five-minute snoozer—Bobby Isaac won by two laps—was entirely unmemorable,* and the live racing experiment was soon abandoned.

France, though, thought that his race could be different. Daytona was bigger and faster and less prone to the kind of sheet metal banging that could sideline twenty or twenty-five cars. And he could also trade on the race's status as the Super Bowl of its sport. CBS started warming to the idea primarily because the race took place in the middle of winter, when nothing else was happening. The NFL season was over, baseball's spring training was just getting started, and no one seemed

---

* The broadcast was so unmemorable that it is rarely, if ever, mentioned. Virtually every story of the past thirty years credits the 1979 Daytona 500 as being the first race shown live from flag to flag.

to care that the NBA season was in full swing. Squier had also lob-bied Pilson, arguing that there were plenty of race fans out there who had no way of satisfying their racing joneses, because most local tracks weren't open yet.*

In May 1978 CBS made its move. Pilson and Barry Frank, the head of CBS Sports, went to Daytona to meet with France. Squier had already spoken to France and had given Pilson a heads-up that NASCAR's main demand was going to be that the race be aired live. When France asked if CBS would be amenable to doing that, Pilson and Frank looked at each other and said yes. France smiled, and Frank got on a plane for New York, leaving Pilson to work out the details. "Bill said to me, 'You're not leaving here until we get a signed agreement,'" says Pilson. "I was thinking, *When am I ever going to be able to leave?*"

They negotiated in the conference room, writing out provisions that France would have typed up so that Pilson could fax them back to New York. After two days they had an agreement. Then Jim France, Bill's brother and NASCAR's vice president and secretary, came into the room and offered his take: "Wow, I'm not happy with this." So Pilson and Jim went a few rounds of their own, renegotiating the deal. After six hours they settled on an agreement they could both live with. Then Bill Sr. came by to offer his thoughts. He'd been retired for seven years, but he still cut an imposing figure, and Pilson was dreading the latest in the parade of Frances. But Big Bill simply put his hand on Pilson's shoulder and said, "Looks like we have a deal, because I'm really pleased."

It was time to celebrate, which in Daytona meant one thing: Steak n Shake. France picked up the $7 lunch tab. "I told him that was very generous of him," Pilson says. Then he finally got on a plane for home, feeling, in his words, like a "limp dishrag."

---

* Squier could be trusted to speak to the mind-set of the cold-weather race fan. He has run the Thunder Road International SpeedBowl, a quarter-mile oval, in Barre, Vermont, since 1960.

Because it was NASCAR, the contract was only twelve pages long, the closest thing to a handshake deal that Pilson's bosses would stand for. (A standard contract would have run in excess of fifty pages.) The sheer number of concessions Pilson made in those twelve pages are a testament to the Frances' powers of persuasion. Not only was CBS on the hook for the Daytona 500, but Pilson also agreed to show the Talladega 500 — which was held at another track owned by the France family — live. CBS would also air the Twin 125s on tape delay. The deal ran for five years and was worth $6 million. "It was," says Pilson, "a lot of money for an event that no one had ever covered live."

CBS sent its top NFL crew, producer Bob Fishman and director Mike Pearl, along with a separate producer for the pits, Bob Stenner. None of them had any experience broadcasting racing, though, and they had a tall order. "We were trying to find this balance between not offending the people who were racing fans, who found it every weekend wherever it was, and trying to educate the people who were not usually watching," says Stenner.

They would cover the race with nine cameras, less than a quarter of the number Fox employs now. There were two on the roof of the press box, one in each of the first three turns, three in the pits, and one handheld camera behind the wall in Turn 4. The restraining wall was only about four feet high, so the handheld gig was dangerous. Every day cameraman Joe Sokota was sent to his post with a motorcycle helmet and instructions to hit the deck if he thought a runaway car was coming his way. And every day he came back looking like he had spent the afternoon rolling around a junkyard trash heap. "His helmet would be full of dirt and grease, and he couldn't see out of his visor," Fishman recalls. "He'd have little bits of sheet metal in his hair and the back of his neck. I'd say, 'Joe this is insane.' And he'd say, 'No, no, I love it. It's completely safe.'"

Other than dodging debris, the toughest task for Sokota and the other eight cameramen was covering all the action. With more than three dozen cars running around the immense track, there was plenty of action. And not just in the lead pack.

Shortly before 1:00 p.m. the thirty-eight cars in the Sportsman 300 rolled onto the track under dark skies. The race was designed to showcase drivers who raced at short tracks around the country, but there were a few big names in the field. Darrell Waltrip was racing, as were Bobby and Donnie Allison. There was some controversy over the Grand National stars dipping down into the lower ranks, but all three of them had the requisite short-track bona fides.* And no fan who had seen the previous two races was going to complain about the presence of Waltrip and Donnie Allison. They had provided photo finishes each year, with Allison winning in '77 and Waltrip returning the favor the next year.

At the other, shallower end of the talent pool were the small-timers who met the requirements: twenty bucks for a license and a car that could pass inspection. One Sportsman regular was a reverend in the Carolinas who didn't harbor any thoughts of moving up to Grand National, because he refused to race on Sunday. Perhaps the least experienced driver in the field was Don Williams, a ball bearing salesman from Madison, Florida, who hid his racing from his parents and hid the fact that he had a college education from his racing buddies. Like everyone who gets behind the wheel of a race car, Williams was curious about how he'd fare at NASCAR's biggest track against its biggest names. "My life's ambition is to race here," he had told his sisters on a trip to Daytona. His qualifying time of 170.32 miles per hour was more than 20 miles per hour slower than pole sitter Donnie Allison's, but it was fast enough to make his dream come true.

The rain clouds hanging low over the speedway made for an ominous setting, and they would also have a profound effect on strategy. In

---

* Waltrip, for instance, had raced sixty-two times in 1978 and was well on his way to doing the same in '79.

long races, the smart play is usually to lay back and stay out of trouble before making a late move. But the drivers didn't have that luxury, because the weather forecast virtually guaranteed that rain would cut the race short. Everybody's plan was to get to the front quick and hope to be there when the skies opened up.

Donnie Allison led the field to the green flag, and he and Waltrip duked it out for the first couple of laps.

Then all hell broke loose.

One thing scares a driver. Not hitting the wall. Not flipping a car.

Fire.

Crashes are an occupational hazard. They happen so frequently that every driver becomes inured to them. If he doesn't, he is never going to make it. The thing about a wreck is, you hit something — be it a car or a wall — and it's over.

Fire, though, is a different story. When a car goes up in flames, it's just the beginning of the ordeal. And since protecting against injuries in a crash requires a driver to strap himself into his seat very securely, getting out of the car is an elaborate process that involves unhooking several belts, lowering a window net, and climbing out of a very small opening while wearing a bulky suit and a helmet.

Joe Frasson, a journeyman from South Carolina, took more precautions than most. He wore a fire suit and fireproof underwear, and — unlike most drivers of the era, who steered with their bare hands — Frasson wore double-layered Nomex gloves. He entered the Sportsman 300 in a Pontiac, and it was fairly stout.* He had it running in the middle of the pack on the fourth lap, when Freddy Smith's car suddenly swerved up

---

*A few Sportsman drivers used Pontiacs, but the make had been absent from Grand National racing for years. Frasson had tried to bring it back in Charlotte in 1975. When he failed to qualify for the race, he called a press conference, produced a tire iron, and began beating the crap out of the car. "I would like to announce that Pontiac is retiring from racing," he proclaimed.

the track and pinched Frasson into the wall. Smith later said that all he knew was that "something" knocked out his windshield. (Most likely it was debris from an engine that blew in front of him.) After that, Smith swore, he couldn't remember a thing.

What he missed was one of the most spectacular wrecks Daytona had ever seen. The initial contact with Frasson's car caused a small oil fire to start in the Pontiac. Frasson was driving blind—his hood popped up after the collision—so he hit the brakes and did his best to guide the car down to the inside of the track. Just as he was coming to a stop, Del Cowart rear-ended him at about 150 miles per hour, driving Frasson's twenty-two-gallon fuel tank, which was still full, out of the trunk and up into the oil fire. The explosion sent flames dancing fifty feet into the air.

Certain situations in life call for one to keep one's composure and remain cool. This, to Joe Frasson, was not one of those situations. He wanted to get out of the oven he was in as fast as he could. He could barely tell what he was doing—it can be tough to see when your goggles are melting to your face—but he somehow unhooked his safety belts and climbed out of the window, then ran away from the car, trusting that his fellow drivers would be able to avoid him. (They did.)

As Frasson was playing Frogger, the cars behind him were swerving to miss the fireball. Dodging a wreck on a superspeedway is an art form, something that has to be learned. It's a delicate operation. One's first instinct is to stand on the brakes, but with that comes the risk of getting hit from behind. The main idea is to put the trouble in your rearview mirror as quickly as possible. Don Williams had no experience dodging superspeedway wrecks. In fact, he had no experience on pavement or on anything bigger than a half-mile track. What happened when he approached Frasson's roasting Pontiac is unclear, as none of the nine CBS cameras picked it up. Some reports said that Williams hit his brakes and was hit from behind. Others insisted that he selflessly turned his car toward the wall to avoid another car.

However it happened, Williams went into the wall. Hard. The next day the papers would report that a piece of metal had been driven under the visor of his helmet and into his forehead. He was bleeding from both ears and had multiple fractures, including one at the base of his skull. The worst fears of his mother were realized. The day before the race, a friend of Don's had let slip that he was racing. His mother, Robbie, got up at the crack of dawn to get a Jacksonville paper so that she could check the starting lineup. When she saw her son's name, she called his hotel room at 6:00 a.m. to plead with him not to race. The phone just rang and rang. He was already on his way to the track.

As rescue workers pulled Williams from his car, officials put out the red flag, which stopped the race while the mess was cleaned up.*

When the race restarted half an hour later, Bobby and Donnie Allison swapped the lead, but the brothers went out of the race when their engines expired within seven laps of each other. That left Waltrip—who was driving Wanda, the same Chevy that had won the season-opening Grand National race at Riverside—and Dale Earnhardt—who was forcing his way into the spotlight for the second time in three days—as the cars to beat.

Earnhardt took the lead on lap 60—the midpoint of the race, at which point it became official—and stayed there until he had to pit with a flat tire on lap 66. Within minutes a gentle rain began to fall, but it was hard enough to bring the race to a halt and deprive Earnhardt of the chance to catch Waltrip.

After the race Frasson met with reporters, his face covered with burn lotion and most of his bushy beard gone. "I had all my fireproof underwear on, thank goodness," he said. "Everything on my helmet was burned off."

---

* Williams lived for ten years in a near-vegetative state before passing away in May 1989.

* * *

The rain continued throughout the afternoon, and drivers were getting word from back home that the weather in North Carolina was even worse. Cale Yarborough, who had honed his piloting skills significantly since that first flight with Wib Weatherly, had flown to Daytona and came to the realization that he wasn't going to be able to fly back home if the snow that was forecast actually fell. He asked a buddy, Hoss Ellington, for a ride back after the race on Sunday. Ellington said sure. So what if Hoss owned the car Donnie Allison was driving? Cale needed a lift, and Cale was a friend. It didn't make any difference that Yarborough was the opposition.

Back at his hotel on the beach, Allison watched the raindrops pound his window. It had been a bad day all around. First Williams had crashed, then Allison's engine had blown, and then the rain had spoiled what had been shaping up to be a pretty good race. Unlike Bobby, Donnie had a well-earned reputation for having a good time, but the night before an important race he was always serious. And Daytona was as important as it got, the one race big enough to validate a driver's career, to maybe even nudge him out of his brother's shadow. As he took in the storm outside and contemplated what lay ahead of him the next day, he repeated the same four words to himself over and over: "This is not good. This is not good."

Chapter Seven

So Fair and Foul a Day

Sunday, February 18
Race Day

RICHARD PETTY awoke to troubling news. During the night someone
had broken into the Petty Enterprises van parked outside his hotel and
stolen the CB radio. They had also boosted the fuzz buster, but that
wasn't a terrible loss. Given the weather in Daytona on race day, nobody was going to be driving the van very fast.

The rain had continued all through the night, and the gray morning
sky didn't bode well. It didn't take much rain to stop the race, and even
if the weather miraculously cleared up, there was still the matter of getting the track dried. Not that there was reason to be optimistic that the
weather would cooperate. All over the country it seemed as if Mother
Nature was hell-bent on showing off her nasty side.

One of the first things a transplanted northerner learns during his first
southern winter is that the natives are so ill equipped to function in
snow that they descend into a state of near panic at the prospect, let

alone the presence, of it. And in most of the South on Sunday morning, there was plenty of snow present. Nine inches blanketed Charlotte, covering roads and race shops, closing businesses, and generally confounding the populace. Edison Searles, who had moved his family to the Queen City from Detroit three months earlier, lamented to the *Charlotte Observer,* "I can deal with the snow, but I can't deal with the city's inability to handle it or the people's inability to drive in it."

In defense of the locals, the storm had arrived with little warning. Two days earlier, temperatures in Charlotte had been up around 70 degrees. The sudden appearance of snow was followed almost immediately by a predictable, comprehensive run on provisions. The manager of one A&P reported, "They're buying out the whole store. I guess they think we're gonna be snowed in for a couple weeks." Shovels were the hottest sellers, though the quantity of booze being stockpiled suggested that a sizable chunk of the city was content to leave the snow clearing to someone else and wait out the blizzard as comfortably as possible. The A&P manager said that he was moving "a lot more beer and wine than milk and bread."

Shoppers aside, most people found the streets of Charlotte almost impossible to navigate. The staff of Town & Country Ford assembled a fleet of half a dozen four-wheel-drive pickup trucks and took to the streets, picking up doctors and hospital staffers and dropping them off at Presbyterian Hospital. A panicking bride-to-be named Debbie Holder called the police and tearfully explained that she had no way of getting to the Carmel Presbyterian Church, where she was supposed to marry Atef Sohl that afternoon. (With the law as her chauffeur, she made it on time, although the flight that was to take her and Sohl to their Hawaiian honeymoon was canceled. The newlyweds were last seen walking hand in hand down a snowy street.)

Atlanta was hit hard, too. The airport was completely shut down for the first time in its history, but the streets were still semi-drivable, which was good news for the enterprising man who put on his snow

98 • MARK BECHTEL

skis and was photographed being towed down Peachtree Street. Other citizens did their best to enjoy and preserve the novelty of a winter wonderland. Aaron's, a photofinishing store in town, would see a 5,000 percent increase in the number of rolls of film it developed in the week following the storm.

But the farther north one progressed, the more bone-chilling the stories one heard. Washington, DC, saw its heaviest snowfall in fifty years: twenty-three inches, with gusting winds creating drifts as high as five feet. The National Guard was ordered in to clear the streets, fight fires, and drive ambulances. In New York City, which had been on the verge of bankruptcy only two years earlier, Mayor Ed Koch authorized $500,000 in emergency overtime pay for a thousand sanitation workers to drive salt trucks and snowplows to help clear the six inches of snow that fell overnight. Visibility was close to zero, as was the temperature. It was the coldest the city had been in eighty-three years, but it was downright balmy compared to conditions upstate, where the village of Old Forge, in the Adirondacks, had seen an overnight low of 52 below.

In the heartland, temperatures were so low and snowfall levels so high that even the grizzled midwesterner Edison Searles would likely have had trouble dealing with the elements. Four of the five Great Lakes were completely frozen over for the first time in recorded history.* The *Chicago Tribune* couldn't help but take a defeatist tone, suggesting "that perhaps this winter will never end," and so many residents of the Windy City simply abandoned their cars on the snow-covered roads that the city's impound lots couldn't handle them. Overflow vehicles were taken to Comiskey Park, where their owners could pick them up after paying a $45 towing fee.

All over the country, the pressing question on people's minds became: *How am I going to kill a Sunday afternoon if I can't leave the house?*

---

*Lake Ontario, the deepest and fastest moving of the five, was only about 40 percent frozen.

The *Charlotte Observer* ran an article with several ideas for fighting cabin fever, including a recipe for homemade Play-Doh and a suggestion that parents let kids finger-paint using chocolate pudding and a cookie sheet: "They can eat their masterpiece. Also, they can use liquid starch and food coloring, but shouldn't try to eat that."

The paper did concede the obvious: "The old standby, of course, is TV." That was very good news for Neal Pilson and Bill France Jr.

Actually, it was good news for Pilson and France only if they could give their captive audience something to watch. The race was a sellout, which meant that the provisional blackout for the southern states France had insisted upon in his talks with Pilson was lifted. But the weather meant that there were plenty of spare tickets to be had. Outside the track a lanky fifteen-year-old who had driven down from Owensboro, Kentucky, with his family tried unsuccessfully to off-load a pair of primo grandstand tickets he had inherited from some less hearty friends. They had skipped town at the sight of the storm and told the kid he could keep whatever cash he got for the tickets. Alas, Michael Waltrip's quest for "some running-around money" would go unfulfilled. "I never did sell them," remembers Darrell's younger brother.*

In his suite above the track, Neal Pilson was protected from the rain, but he was feeling anything but secure. He had dragged two of his CBS bosses to the event. Gene Jankowski, the head of the CBS Broadcast Group, called Pilson over and said, "Neal, we don't have to pay for this if it rains, right?" Pilson told him that not only would they still have to pay, but they'd have to show the race when it was run — most likely the following afternoon, which would mean paying to keep the production crew in Daytona for another day and preempting the network's popular daytime lineup of *The Young and the Restless, Guiding Light,* and *As*

---

* Don't feel too bad for him. Twenty-two years later Daytona would finally yield that running-around money — $1,331,185 — when Michael won the 2001 Daytona 500.

the World Turns. Airing a race on a Sunday afternoon when nothing else was on was one thing; depriving America's housewives of the exploits of Julia and Katherine and the rest of the good people of Genoa City was another thing entirely. To make matters worse, Pilson didn't even have a decent backup plan if the race was postponed. Traditionally, the previous year's race would be shown, but the '78 Daytona 500 had been an ABC production. Says Pilson, "Gene kind of gave me a look like, *Well, it's your career. Call us when you get another job.*"

Bill France Jr. and his father were also sweating. They'd gone to great lengths to get the race on TV, to give Americans who wouldn't normally be paying attention their first impression of the sport. And the last thing they needed was for that impression to be of a bunch of guys—most of whom had neither the inclination nor the camera presence to give lengthy interviews—huddling under umbrellas in a garage.

The race was scheduled to start at 12:15 p.m. Shortly before noon Big Bill disappeared. Legend has it that he went onto the roof of the grandstand, held out his arms, and commanded the rain to stop. To this day, when NASCAR types speak of France's reputed supernatural powers, they tend to be dismissive without actually coming out and saying they don't believe in them, the same way that skeptical nine-year-olds hedge their declarations that they don't believe in Santa Claus on the off chance that he really does exist and just happens to be listening.

Whether he made a trip to the rooftop and conversed with the gods is debatable. What is known for certain is that France got into his Cadillac and went for a drive to check on the weather up in Ormond Beach. He gave a walkie-talkie to a NASCAR employee named Jim Bachoven and sent him in the opposite direction.

"Bachy, I've got sunshine over here," France reported.

"Well, I've got some sunshine over here, too," Bachoven responded.

"You bring your sunshine, I'll bring mine and I'll meet you at the tunnel."

NASCAR flagman Chip Warren was listening to the conversation from the flag stand. "I remember that Cadillac coming up out of that tunnel," he said years later. "It was like the sky just opened up and sun started shining. It just sent cold chills all over me. I thought, Man, this guy's got something here."

As the sky lightened, the drivers and teams prepared for the start of the race. The drivers were introduced to the crowd. As Darrell Waltrip's crew busied themselves setting up their pit box, they could tell by the thunderous boos that their driver's name had been called. As Mike Joy, then the track announcer, talked about the bad weather in the rest of the country, Waltrip's crewmen realized what the storm meant. "We knew our parents were all going to be watching back home," says Gary Nelson. "We talked about doing it for them."

Grand marshal Ben Gazzara, still a decade away from his most memorable role as Patrick Swayze's nemesis in *Road House,* gave the command for the drivers to start their engines, and the forty-one cars rolled off pit road.

On millions of couches, millions of snowbound viewers—ranging from hard-core race fans to people who simply weren't interested in watching Jimmy Swaggart or a discussion of the recently begun Islamic Revolution in Iran on *Meet the Press*—flipped on CBS's broadcast. Back in Charlotte, many a fan settled in front of the TV with a copy of the Sunday *Observer,* which featured a lengthy story in the sports section by Tom Higgins titled "A Man Called Cale." In it Yarborough told a story explaining the origin of his determined ways:

> *I was in the fourth grade. There was this big ol' boy in my class who had failed a couple grades. For some reason, he didn't like me and he whipped my fanny twice a day—once before the bell rung in the morning and again at recess. I was scared to death of him. It got so bad I'd hide behind a tree 'til classes took up and he had to go in.*
>
> *Then one day he got off the school bus and he had one arm in a cast.*

He'd fallen off a horse the evening before and broken the arm. Man, I ran out from behind that tree and jumped him.

After that, I whipped him every day for a month. When his arm got well I could still whip him. I've never backed down from any sort of challenge since then.

It wouldn't be long before Yarborough found himself challenged yet again.

Once the prerace pomp died down and the cars took the track at 12:15—right on time—television viewers were treated to fifteen of the most tedious minutes in the history of broadcasting. The track was still damp, and since jet dryers weren't yet in use, the only way to get rid of the moisture was to use the heat from the race cars. That meant starting the 500 with the caution flag out and the cars circling the track behind the pace car at a leisurely 85 miles per hour.

In addition to being boring, the caution laps—which counted toward the 200 that would make up the race—had the potential to wreak havoc. After several circuits, Darrell Waltrip started to feel Maybelline's motor skipping. He hoped the problem was something minor, or at least fixable, like a spark plug. What had actually happened was that one of the lobes on a camshaft had worn down because running so many laps at such a slow speed and on such steep banking had caused the oil to pool away from the cam. It wasn't something that could be easily diagnosed, let alone fixed. The green flag hadn't even dropped, and Waltrip, though he didn't know it, was already at a huge disadvantage: he was running on seven and a half cylinders.

As the yellow-flag laps mounted, NASCAR asked Waltrip to take a run at speed to see if the track was dry enough to race on. It was called being the rabbit, and it meant putting additional strain on the motor.*

---

* In the 1973 Daytona 500, Buddy Baker made a rabbit run. Eight laps from the finish, with Baker leading the race, his engine blew up.

Waltrip, however, was happy to do it. He thought that running a few miles wide-open might clear up whatever was clogging up Maybelline's engine. He completed a lap, then pulled into the pits to talk with a NASCAR official and Buddy Parrott. He had good news for the former, bad news for the latter. The track was fine, but Maybelline wasn't: "The thing was still missing."

Meanwhile, CBS was trying to give viewers something—anything—more interesting to watch than pavement drying. Pit reporter Brock Yates tracked down Baker's crew chief, Herb Nab, who said, "Well, this is the coolest I've ever seen Buddy in my racing career.... Maybe it's because that Spectra Oldsmobile is running so good, the engine performance is good." And in an interview Petty taped before the race aired, the King told Ned Jarrett, "Looks like for me to win I'm going to have to run wide-open every lap and just hope that I can keep up. We're not really running that good, and we're not really running that bad.... We're just going to have to run and try to keep up with the crowd and hope that we get the good breaks and somebody else gets the bad breaks."

When the real racing finally started on lap 17, Donnie Allison blew past Baker to take the lead. Since Baker was physically incapable of laying back or taking it easy, it was a sign that something was wrong with the Gray Ghost. Like Maybelline's, the Ghost's engine was skipping, and it didn't seem to want to get up to power. Earlier Sunday morning Baker's crew had found a loose strut on the back bumper, and before they'd welded it back into place, they'd unplugged the ignition box, which was standard procedure. There was a chance, Baker thought, that the ignition had been reconnected improperly. There was a backup, but changing it required someone to take a wire from the primary ignition box and plug it into the backup. Baker didn't want to make a pit stop while everyone else was racing, so he and his crew decided to ride out the problem and wait for a caution, when the entire field would pit. The Ghost labored along, well back in the pack.

Up front, Donnie and his brother Bobby were leading a seven-car breakaway pack. The brothers had done plenty of racing against each other, most of it on short tracks in and around Alabama during the 1960s. Their relationship was typical of so many sets of brothers who are nearly the same age, characterized first and foremost by a family bond that would never be broken: for years their families lived up the street from each other in Hueytown. But there was definitely a sibling rivalry.

Unlike his older brother, who had been consumed by a desire to race since he was big enough (or almost big enough) to get behind the wheel of a car, Donnie Allison just dabbled in the sport as a kid. He had other things on his mind. He loved horses so much that before he suffered a bad leg injury, his dream was to be a jockey—though given the frame he would grow into, it was probably all for the best that he didn't. He liked to fish, wrestle alligators, dive, swim, and hang out. He'd always been carefree, the mischievous Allison kid. In a big family—Donnie and Bobby had eight brothers and sisters—it's easy to pick up a tag like that but tough to lose it. It ate at Donnie. Even though he spent a lot of time practicing to be a competitive swimmer, his family thought he was just "goofing off at the pool."

Donnie's feelings about driving changed with one fateful conversation when he was eighteen. The brothers tell slightly conflicting versions of the story, but they agree on the relevant facts. One night at Miami's Medley Speedway, Bobby, who was twenty and by then a well-known driver in South Florida, won a heat race and was then coaxed into letting Donnie drive his car in another race before the main event. Fifty years later Bobby's memories of what happened next are still remarkably vivid: "Donnie comes through [turns] three and four, and he gets that thing outta shape. He overcorrects and goes into the wall right where they had had a crash. This guardrail at Medley was made out of railroad rails. This was an iron fence that you should have been able to hit with a semi, but it was beat-up enough that it was beginning to break up a little bit. He hits right at the worst place you can hit this thing, and that car digs in and turns over. I mean, it ripped that car apart. You cannot believe how bad that thing was wrecked." Donnie was okay. His helmet had a nasty dent in it, and he went to the hospital to get checked out, but he was no worse for wear. Bobby, on the other hand, was hot. His car was done for the night, which meant no prize money for the main event. In Bobby's version of the story, the wreck cost him $17.50. In Donnie's, it was $75.

Bobby took the car home to his father's shop and started working on it so that he could race it the next night. Donnie apologized and promised to come by and help with the repairs. Says Bobby, "At about five o'clock, Donnie shows up with his dancing clothes on. He was really big into roller-skating, and he did fancy dance skating. He showed up in his skating outfit. It was fairly plain in today's deal, but it was a shirt with a little extra trim on it, maybe a belt that had some kind of skating emblem on it. Anyway, it was conspicuously not something you would wear to work on a wrecked race car."

Here the brothers' stories again diverge.

Bobby recalls telling his brother, "Get the heck out of here. You will never drive one of my cars again."

Donnie remembers hearing, "You'll never make a race car driver."

Either way, in Donnie's eyes a challenge had been issued.

"At that moment," Donnie said, "my main mission in life became to prove him wrong. He got one of the toughest rivals he'd ever have to race against in his entire career."

It doesn't take much to get a car out of shape at 190 miles per hour. On the thirty-first lap Donnie had the lead in Turn 2, less than a car length ahead of his brother, who was inside him. As they came to the head of the 3,000-foot backstretch, Bobby slid up the track ever so slightly, his right front fender barely clipping Donnie's left rear quarter panel. As Donnie's Oldsmobile began to spin, the nose of Bobby's Ford dug into the driver's side door, lifting three of Donnie's wheels off the ground. For a split second the Olds hung in the air, looking like a C-130 struggling to leave the runway, before it returned to earth. Donnie and Bobby both spun into the infield. Cale Yarborough, who had been right behind Donnie, minding his own business, swerved low to avoid the wreck and also wound up in the infield, which thanks to the rain had the consistency of the Okefenokee Swamp. Today a restraining wall would stop them, but since there were no spectators on the grass, there was no wall, and the three cars started to hydroplane through the field. Bobby didn't stop until he backed into a mound on the bank of Lake Lloyd. Donnie and Yarborough finally came to rest in the marsh and immediately got bogged down.

Two workers pushed Donnie back onto the course, but Yarborough, whose car was only ten feet from the track, couldn't get out of the muck. And once he did, he couldn't get his engine to fire, so he rolled slowly down the backstretch, cars whizzing past, putting him farther and farther behind.

The caution flag the wreck brought out was a welcome sight for Baker and Waltrip, because they could pit and have their engines looked at. Baker brought the Gray Ghost to a stop in his stall, and a crew member reached in, unplugged the ignition box, and jammed the wire into the backup. Or at least he thought he did. When Baker took the Ghost back onto the track, it still wasn't pulling him like it had been all week. He took the car back into the pits, and Waddell Wilson and the crew started replacing other parts—the distributor, spark plugs, anything that might possibly be the problem. Nothing worked. Baker climbed out of the car, his day over, his Daytona drought extended to twenty-one years.

Of all the races he lost at the track, this would be the toughest to accept, especially after what Wilson learned back at the shop in Charlotte the next day. The problem had been the ignition after all. But after the crewman had unplugged the primary system, he had stuck the wire right back into the same faulty box. When Wilson made the switch and started the car, the shop was filled with the sound of a perfectly purring engine.*

* As Wilson recounted the story to me, he said, "If we don't screw that up, you don't have a book."

In Waltrip's pit stall, engine builder Robert Yates and Gary Nelson had the hood up, and they were still thinking that Maybelline's problem was a bad spark plug. They decided to change all eight of them, a laborious, time-consuming process under the best of conditions. Most of the plugs were right under the exhaust header, a piece of metal that got roasted by the engine when the car was running. Changing the plugs was Nelson's job, and he had to use his bare hands. He couldn't get at them with a wrench, and there wasn't enough room between the header and the plug for him even to wear gloves. Imagine trying to pick a paper clip off a cookie sheet in a hot oven, and you get an idea what he was up against. Nelson would change one plug, then send Waltrip back out so he wouldn't get lapped. Then they'd bring him back in and change another. Holding up his hands nearly thirty years later, Nelson said, "I really believe you could trace back some of these scars from that day."

Of the wrecked vehicles, Bobby Allison's car had the most obvious damage—a sagging left front fender that gave his Ford a hangdog look, like a seven-year-old who'd been sent to bed without dessert. Donnie had only a dent in his driver's side door, and Yarborough's Olds, which had finally been towed to the pits, had no visible damage. The undercarriage, though, was a mess. "We'd just reach under there and pull out handfuls of mud and grass," says crew member Jeff Hammond. As the crew worked on the car, CBS showed a head shot of Yarborough, grinning his big South Carolina grin. "I'll bet he's not looking like that now," said David Hobbs. "I'll bet he's absolutely fuming in there, because he had nothing to with that accident."

The caution period lasted ten laps, and by the time it was over, Neil Bonnett was in the lead, with A. J. Foyt, Richard Petty, and Waltrip right behind him.

That was about all anyone knew for sure.

Today's NASCAR fan is never starved for information. Leaders, intervals, lap times, pit times, pit windows, even how many rpm a car is turning or how much throttle a driver is using—everything is monitored electronically and disseminated in real time on TV and online. Thirty years ago scoring was far more rudimentary. The only thing anyone kept track of was the number of laps completed: a volunteer would track each car and make a mark on a pad every time it crossed the start/finish line. It invited human error. At the next-to-last race of the 1978 season, the job of scoring Donnie Allison's car for the Dixie 500 in Atlanta was given to a woman who happened to be a die-hard Richard Petty fan. At one point during the race, Allison was in the pits while Petty was making a pass in Turn 2, which excited the scorer so much that she rose to her feet and cheered wildly, oblivious to the fact that Allison had just crossed the start/finish line on pit road. That left Allison officially one lap down.

Petty took the checkered flag, but Allison drove straight to Victory Lane, insisting that his team's unofficial scoring sheets had him completing all 328 laps. At first NASCAR said the race was Petty's. Then after spending several contentious hours poring over scoring sheets and debriefing the involved parties and witnesses—including Bill France Jr.'s fifteen-year-old son, Brian, who was the one who saw the scorer on her feet cheering for Petty—Allison, who had left the track near tears, was declared the winner. *Stock Car Racing* magazine called it "NASCAR's strangest race."

Now, three races later in Daytona, another confusing situation was brewing. The problem this time wasn't the official scoring—NASCAR had credited every driver for the proper number of laps. The problem was getting the information to the TV crew, to fans, and, most important to the teams. Since there were no scoring monitors in the broadcast booth or the pits, the announcers and crews were left to collect their own information. Donnie Allison was one lap down—that much was fairly clear—and his brother was down two. But Yarborough had wallowed in the muck for so long that no one was sure how far behind he had fallen. CBS speculated one or two laps. Allison's crew got its information from a NASCAR official in the pits. Says Hoss Ellington, "He walked up to me and told me that Cale was five laps down."

But Yarborough was much closer than that. He was only three laps back.

The repaved surface at Daytona International Speedway made it possible for just about anyone to tear around the track at mind-numbing speeds. The result was a fast, tightly packed bunch of cars — some being driven by drivers who had no experience driving in a draft or going quite so fast. On lap 55 Bruce Hill got together with Gary Balough, who was making his first Grand National start, coming out of Turn 4, which led David Pearson to collide with rookie Joe Millikan. Behind them cars went skidding all over the track and into the muddy infield. The situation was perhaps summed up best by the droll Englishman David Hobbs, who commented, "Oh, crikey."

Petty's crew got him out of the ensuing round of pit stops first. He was followed by two rookies, Terry Labonte and Geoff Bodine, with another Daytona neophyte, Dale Earnhardt, in fifth. On the restart, the cars that are on the lead lap line up on the outside, while the lapped cars form a line on the inside. Donnie Allison was at the head of that queue, meaning that if he could get in front of Petty and stay there until another caution flag came out, he could then pull around to the back of the lead pack and get his lap back. Petty and the newbies proved no match for Allison. Even with his car banged up from the collision with his brother, Donnie pulled away and remained on the point for nine laps, until Neil Bonnett cut a tire, triggering yet another spectacular crash. As the cars behind Bonnett checked up coming off Turn 4, Harry Gant got nudged from the rear, sending him sliding across four lanes of traffic. He slammed into the inside wall and ricocheted back across the track. Somehow he didn't get hit. His car was crumpled, but Gant walked away from the wreckage.

With Allison back on the lead lap (albeit at the tail end), Benny

Parsons pulled to the front and stayed there for a long stretch, tow-ing Cale Yarborough—who was still three laps down, despite a CBS graphic saying he was one back—away from the rest of the field. At the midway point of the race, Parsons and Yarborough had put five seconds between themselves and the pack. But just as it looked like Parsons might turn the race into a snoozer, his gauges showed that his engine getting too hot. Yarborough got around him, and less than a minute later John Utsman's engine blew up on lap 105, bringing out another caution and allowing Yarborough to make up one of his three laps. As Parsons sat in the pits, his crew trying to diagnose the problem—a leak in the radiator or a cracked head gasket were the primary suspects—Donnie Allison, who had worked his way through traffic, assumed the lead. And Yarborough pulled up alongside him for the restart.

Yarborough tucked in behind Allison and stayed there until lap 121, when the engines of Blackie Wangerin and Dave Marcis blew up. The caution flag came out as Allison and Yarborough were in Turn 3. Thinking that Yarborough was still four laps down, Allison decided not to risk a wreck by racing him hard. He backed off, and Yarborough beat him to the stripe by half a car length. He was only one lap back.

The scene repeated itself on the next restart: Allison and Yarborough pulled away, and on lap 138 Balough's engine let go. Allison and Yarborough were again on the backstretch when the yellow flag dropped, and as they pulled into Turn 3, Yarborough again tried to pass. And again, a misinformed Allison let him go.

Unlike Allison and Ellington, CBS had finally realized that Yarborough was back on the lead lap. Said Ken Squier, "We've seen a lot of tumultuous finishes here at Daytona, but I've got a feeling we're in for one today like we've never seen before."

The hardest thing about winning a 500-mile race, especially at Daytona, is staying out of trouble for three and a half hours. The '79 event was a battle of attrition. Everyone's prerace favorite, Buddy Baker, was out of it before the green flag even dropped. Darrell Waltrip was running on a handicapped engine all day. David Pearson was caught up in someone else's wreck, his day over after fifty-three laps. A flat tire sent Neil Bonnett home early. Parsons had his engine troubles. Bobby Allison, who had caused a wreck and made contact with cars on at least two other occasions, was two laps down. Every lap was just another chance for something bad to happen. A questionable call by his crew kept Dale Earnhardt on the track during the final caution period, so he had to pit under green to refuel on lap 162—about fifteen laps before the rest of the field came in. He wasn't happy, and he said goodbye to whatever slim chance he had of becoming the first rookie to win the Daytona 500 when he showed his frustration as he pulled out of the pits. "Dale got pissed and went out of the pits really hard," says Lou LaRosa, his engine builder. "He missed a shift and over-revved the motor and broke a rocker arm and a spring." Another upstart who had been strong all day, Tighe Scott, saw his chances evaporate less than twenty-five laps from the end. Scott, a dirt tracker from Pennsylvania who had never even raced on asphalt before he went to Daytona for the first time in 1976, was nonetheless a contender because he was driving an Oldsmobile prepared by Harry Hyde, the inspiration for Robert Duvall's crusty old crew chief in the movie *Days of Thunder*. The car was in the top 5 when Scott brought it onto pit road way too fast. Scott slammed on his brakes, but he hit a giant puddle left by Parsons's crew as they'd tried to keep his engine from overheating. He hydroplaned past his stall and out of contention.

The few cars that had stayed out of trouble didn't look like they had the power to keep up with Donnie Allison and Yarborough. Petty had been lingering near the front all day, but now, twenty laps from the end, when the leaders decided it was time to put the hammer down, the Oldsmobile that Petty's crew had spent all those hours building just got smaller and smaller in the leaders' rearview mirrors.

Allison and Yarborough seemed so evenly matched that as the number of laps remaining dwindled, NASCAR officials decided it would be a good idea to test-fire the photo finish camera. They were almost a second per lap faster than everyone else. It was no coincidence that their machines had been constructed by Junior Johnson and Hoss Ellington, two of the most, shall we say, *creative* car builders of their day.

Cheating has been a part of stock car racing for about as long as there's been stock car racing. At one of the first races Bill France promoted on Daytona Beach, in 1938, Smokey Purser took the checkered flag and kept right on driving up the shore. A couple of officials figured that he must be doing something to his car — or, more likely, undoing something — so they started searching likely hiding spots. They found him at Roy Strange's garage, frantically trying to get his engine back to its intended, legal specifications. Then there was NASCAR's very first race, which produced NASCAR's very first disqualification: Glenn Dunaway was stripped of a win at Charlotte Speedway in 1949 for using an unapproved chassis.

One of the original appeals of stock car racing was that the drivers were in vehicles that might have been — and indeed sometimes were — driven straight from the showroom to the track. A race would be decided by a man, not a machine. But the desire to win often exceeds the desire to keep the playing field level, and when NASCAR gradually instituted rules allowing minor modifications, the result was, predictably, an assault on those regulations. "If you bend the rules, they might crack," says Johnson. "But if you don't go plumb to that crack, you're not gonna win."

Crew chiefs and engine builders wore their ability to approach that cracking point like a badge of honor. Ask Junior Johnson who the best rule bender of his day was, and he immediately says, "I was." Ask him who was second best, and he thinks for a while. "Well, Hoss was pretty good."

Ellington saw getting around the rules as a game. "I like to beat the other guy," he says. "That's always a lot of fun to do that." He had one advantage: he was based in Wilmington, North Carolina, so none of the other teams knew his business. "In Charlotte, everybody knows what's going on," Ellington recalled. "Crew guys would be in the same bars, and someone's going to have a loose tongue. But I was down here by my-self." Ellington's rap sheet was as long as a jack handle. In 1976 he built a car that A. J. Foyt put on the pole at Daytona. Bill Gazaway, NASCAR's top cop at the time, thought it was suspicious that Foyt was 2 miles per hour faster on his second qualifying lap than his first, so he ordered the Chevy torn down. After two hours he found what he was looking for: a steel bottle containing nitrous oxide—laughing gas—which, when injected into the intake manifold, provides a brief but potent boost in horsepower.* If anyone was disappointed in Ellington, it was because he had used such a rudimentary, unoriginal cheating device, unlike the Rube Goldberg contraptions he usually came up with.

In 1970 he built what became known as Glotzbach's Gizmo, a small apparatus that looked like a mini–moonshine still attached to Charlie Glotzbach's carburetor. A length of piano wire connected it to a lever in the cockpit. When Glotzbach hit the switch, the Gizmo would allow more air into the carburetor, and the car would take off.† Later in his career Ellington got busted running a line from the carburetor to a small box filled with dry ice, which would cool the gasoline and boost the horsepower. Of course, not all of Ellington's transgressions were his fault. He once bought an engine from another owner and then had it confiscated when it turned out to be illegal. The guy who sold it to him? His old buddy Junior Johnson. "Junior would tell on me, or he'd have Herb Nab do it," says Ellington.

---

* Gazaway also found laughing gas in the car of the second-fastest qualifier, Darrell Waltrip, and Dave Marcis, who qualified third, was caught with an unapproved radiator cover.
† When the Gizmo was discovered, Ellington was summoned to the NASCAR trailer by Gazaway, who had the device on his desk. Ellington decided to play dumb. After Gazaway demonstrated it, Ellington said, "Damn, that's slick. I wouldn't mind having one of those." To which Gazaway said, "You used to have one."

There were plenty of other ways to get around the rules. Darrell Waltrip once put a hunk of lead painted to look like a radio on his front seat as the car went through inspection. After inspection, out came the radio—which no one, presumably, would miss—and suddenly the car was fifty pounds lighter. Johnson's favorite trick was to tinker with the fuel cell. Cars were supposed to hold only twenty-two gallons, but a bigger tank meant fewer pit stops, so a clever crew chief might build an expandable cell or run extra yards of tubing from the tank to the motor. But Johnson was versatile. Listening to him tick off the areas where he bent the rules is like listening to someone read the index of an Auto Shop 101 textbook: "motor, chassis, tires, wheels, transmission, carburetor…"

Asked if they were running anything illegal in '79, Ellington and Johnson both responded with the same *What do you think?* grin.

They weren't the only ones dabbling in the dark arts. Gary Nelson, Waltrip's engineer, thought it would be nice to eavesdrop on NASCAR officials during a race. But he couldn't just buy a programmable scanner. Radios in those days had crystals that had to be set to a specific frequency. Nelson knew that NASCAR had to register its channel with the FCC, and he also knew of a Motorola shop in Charlotte that had a huge book of every licensed frequency in the country. So he went to the shop and convinced the guy behind the counter to look up NASCAR's frequency and build a radio that would allow him to listen in. It wasn't illegal, but it was devious.* And it would let him pick up the unique play-by-play call for the bizarre finish that was to come.

Finding a vantage point at Daytona International Speedway that allows you to see everything is not easy. All over the infield, fans were set

---

* Later in his career Nelson would become so adept at chicanery—he designed a system that would drop buckshot from a car's rails in mid-race to shed weight—that NASCAR, figuring it takes a thief to catch a thief, finally threw up its hands and hired him to police the garage.

up atop cars, trucks, and campers, watching the action on the slice of track in front of them. The Petty women were behind pit road in the vacated Sportsman garage, listening to the race on their car radios and eating food set out on long tables. Terry Labonte, whose clutch gave out, was watching from the back of a wrecker parked on the backstretch. Geoff Bodine, who had led for six laps in his first 500 before his engine expired, was standing on the roof of a car in the infield. And down between Turns 3 and 4, Michael Waltrip was standing with his sister, watching their brother battle Richard Petty and A. J. Foyt for third place. They all adhered to the same routine: they'd look right and see the leaders blaze into view, rotate their heads to the left, crane their necks as they followed the cars until they disappeared from sight, then wait forty seconds and do it all over again on the next lap. The PA system offered some idea of what was happening, but it wasn't always audible over the din of so many engines.

Donnie Allison passed in front of Michael Waltrip for the 199th time, with Cale Yarborough riding in his wake. Twenty seconds later Darrell came by, sandwiched between Petty and Foyt. Michael watched his brother disappear into the dogleg, then turned his attention back to Turn 3 to wait for Allison and Yarborough to make their final appearance. He waited. And waited. And waited some more, like a NASA mission control worker anxiously waiting for an Apollo capsule to return from the dark side of the moon into radio range. Then, finally, some activity. "We could see all the ruckus," says Michael. "But we couldn't see a whole lot of what was going on."

It happened right where Donnie Allison thought it would. Before the race he had taped an interview with CBS in which he'd discussed his endgame strategy: "If it comes down to a last-lap run for the checkered flag, I'm going to do it on the backstretch, because I just don't think we have enough room from the fourth turn to the finish line to beat anybody. The cars are all too equal for that. You have to do it on the backstretch." So he couldn't have been surprised when Yarborough made his move coming out of Turn 2.

Yarborough had been getting anxious. For the past few laps he had noticed Bobby Allison, three laps down, lurking a couple of hundred feet ahead. Yarborough radioed Junior Johnson, telling him he was afraid that Bobby would slow down and run interference for his brother. "You worry about Donnie," Johnson told him. "Bobby ain't nothing you need to be worried about. He ain't a factor. You won't catch him before the race is over."

When they got to the backstretch, Yarborough decided he couldn't wait any longer. He tugged the steering wheel hard to the left and mashed the gas. The Holly Farms Olds started to pick up ground on Allison, who couldn't do much to stop the slingshot except to cut Yarborough off.

No driver likes to throw a block, a defensive maneuver that just ain't racing. "When I was a driver, I would have wrecked everyone who blocked me," says Junior Johnson. "That's not racing. When they block you, they deserve to be wrecked. It's like you're in a fight. You defend yourself. That just didn't happen back in my day. If it did, you were out of there, and it didn't make no difference who you were. Lee Petty, Curtis Turner—you blocked one of them, they'd knock you plumb out of the racetrack. So would I."

But Allison didn't consider what he was doing blocking; he saw it as "protecting his position." He crowded Yarborough down the track, hoping he could hold him off over the mile or so that stood between him and glory. Yarborough, down near the apron, was running out of asphalt. They ran side by side, each waiting for the other to back down in a strange game of chicken. Neither blinked. They touched, sending Yarborough even farther down the apron. Yarborough slid up, and they hit again, harder. The first tap might have been incidental. This one wasn't. "I was going to pass him and win the race," Yarborough said years later, "but he turned left and crashed me. So, hell, I crashed him back. If I wasn't going to get back around, he wasn't either."

Down on pit road, Gary Nelson was listening to Bill Gazaway describe the action on his pirated signal: "Don't chop him off. He's cutting him off! Look out! Oh no!" Allison and Yarborough banged doors a third time, and when they did, the cars locked together and shot up into the outside wall, then slid down the banking to the infield, where they came to a stop.

In the CBS truck, Bob Fishman couldn't believe what he was seeing. The lead camera positioned just past the start/finish line had caught the wreck perfectly, giving him magnificent footage. But now Fishman had a problem. That camera was the only one that could give him a head-on shot of the winner crossing the line. It had to pick up the new leader. Only no one seemed to know where—or even who—the new leader was.

Richard Petty, Darrell Waltrip, and A. J. Foyt were so far behind Allison and Yarborough that they could no longer see them. As the leaders went crashing into the wall, the trio was all the way back between Turns 1 and 2. So when the caution lights came on, they didn't know where the accident was or whom it involved. The crew members they were talking to on the radio were in the pits and couldn't see which cars were in trouble either. The drivers' first instinct when they saw the yellow lights was to lift off the gas. Waltrip remembers: "Richard backed off; I backed off; A.J. backed off. Then we realized—it's the last lap. You race back to the flag. Better get going. So everybody takes off." They stayed in formation down the backstretch, but Foyt—who was used to open-wheel racing, in which there is no racing back to the flag under yellow, and had stayed off the gas the longest—was falling off the pace. When Petty and Waltrip approached Turn 3 and saw Allison and Yarborough in the mud, it finally hit them. They were racing for the win.

In the CBS booth Ken Squier was playing two roles: play-by-play man and spotter. He had picked up Petty as the new leader and was incorporating hints for the cameramen in his call of the race. After a few seconds a camera locked in on a car with the familiar red and blue scheme. Alas, it was Buddy Arrington, who bought much of his equipment from the Pettys and used their colors. "They're still up in Turns 3 and 4," Squier said, his rising voice conveying both his excitement at the events and his dismay at the fact that the camera was still on the wrong car. "The leaders ARE UP IN TURNS 3 AND 4."

Everywhere spectators rose to their feet—even in the press box, where a few writers had climbed onto their desks to see over the standing, screaming crowd in front of them—in anticipation of the finish. (Except for Tom Higgins of the *Charlotte Observer,* who presciently declared, "I don't care about the finish. I want to see the fight!") The lead camera finally picked up the new leaders as they passed an ecstatic Michael Waltrip. They exited Turn 4, and Darrell Waltrip sized up Petty for a slingshot. The King was known to prefer the high line, so Waltrip looked low. But Petty took a cue from an unlikely teacher—his eighteen-year-old son. Just as Kyle had done on the last lap of the ARCA race a week earlier, Richard dropped his car down the track, giving Waltrip no way around him. Unlike Donnie Allison, Petty had slammed the door shut before the guy chasing him was able to get a foot in it. It was a clean move. Waltrip had nowhere to go. The King's forty-five-race losing streak was over.

Petty took one victory lap, then pulled down pit road, where he was met by twenty mechanics in bright red pants and navy blue Petty Enterprises shirts, who turned the Oldsmobile into something resembling an oversize Independence Day parade float. Included in the mob that obstructed Petty's view was a grinning tire carrier whose frizzy hair was jammed under an STP hat.

"Where's Victory Circle?" asked Richard.

"I'll show you," replied Kyle. "I know the way."

Chapter Eight
The Fight

Sunday, February 18

It's no stretch to say that winning the Daytona 500 changes a driver's life. Wherever he goes, whatever he does, "Daytona 500 Champion" will precede his name the same way "the Godfather of Soul" always prefaces "James Brown" or "Wild" comes before "Bill Hickock." Derrike Cope won two races in his career. So did Gober Sosebee and Emanuel Zervakis. But only Cope won at Daytona, which explains why, of the three drivers, Cope's is the name fans remember. There are also more tangible benefits to winning the race: that oversize novelty check pays a lot of bills, and no sponsor in its right mind is going to distance itself from a Daytona 500 winner.

So Richard Petty drove to Victory Lane, where a cold glass of milk — a nod to his stomach problems, not the traditional Indy 500 victory celebration — and a new beginning were waiting for him. STP would be back, and all the talk that he was washed-up would be silenced. As Petty was driving toward his brighter future, Donnie Allison was getting out of his car on the grass in Turn 3. His dream of winning the race that would guarantee he would finally be taken seriously was, like his Oldsmobile, in tatters. Allison had climbed out without trying to refire the engine. Getting the car started and back around to the checkered flag had been a long shot, but given the size of the lead Allison had had on Petty, it was one Hoss Ellington maintains to this day was possible.

Cale Yarborough was pissed, too. Pissed because he thought he had been ganged up on. Pissed about the first wreck. Pissed that, in his mind, both incidents had been caused by Bobby Allison. Just then, the object of his ire came driving up.

Bobby pulled onto the grass to see if his brother needed a lift back to the garage. Donnie waved him off, saying no, he'd make his way back on his own. Yarborough, who had already had a few choice words for Donnie as he sat in his car, approached Bobby's Ford, yelling that he had caused the wreck. A bemused Bobby wondered how he could have caused a wreck he was nowhere near and punctuated his rebuttal by, in his words, "questioning Cale's ancestry." More screaming from Yarborough was met with more familial insults. "That," says Bobby, "did not calm him down any."

Fighting has always been inextricably linked with racing. "It happened all the time on the short tracks, the dirt tracks," says Humpy Wheeler. "I remember operating dirt racetracks back in the '60s and the early '70s, and it was so common for a fight to break out among drivers—on the track after a wreck, in the pits after a wreck, or after the race was over. It was just par for the course. What you would do is try to keep it from becoming a riot, which usually you were successful at. Not all the time."

"One of my earliest memories was of being at a stock car race at a dirt track," says Fox NASCAR analyst Dick Berggren. "The guy that won the race had lost a left front wheel in the process. And somebody argued that therefore he didn't have four-wheel brakes [and should be disqualified]. An argument broke out, and the next thing you knew there were fifty people, all fighting, slinging fists. For me, having been through fight after fight after fight at local short tracks, a fight was never a surprise whatsoever."

One of the best fighters ever to drive a car was Tiny Lund. His nickname was ironic—there was nothing little about him. In 1959 at Lakewood Speedway, a one-mile dirt track south of Atlanta, he tangled with Curtis Turner, who had put Lund into the fence when he couldn't get around his car. Lund was livid. After he pulled his fenders out as best he could, he went back on the track and slowed to a crawl on the front stretch, waiting for Turner. But Curtis was no fool; he refused to go fast enough to let Lund wreck him.

Still thirsty for vengeance, Lund went looking for Turner after the race. He found him washing up at the lake in the track's infield. "I just made a damned run like a bull and grabbed him under one arm, and when I stopped running, we was standing in water up to my chest," Lund remembered years later. "But it was about over his head. Turner was praying. He was scared of water anyway."

"Now, Pops," said Turner, who called everyone Pops.* "What are you getting mad at me for? You know I wouldn't wreck you purposely. You got in my way."

"I didn't get in the way," Lund said. "Goddamn you. You think you can run over everybody."

"You know I wouldn't run over you," Turner said. "We're buddies. We party together. We race together."

"Yeah, but you don't have to fix your goddamned race car. You don't depend on it for a living. That old raggedy race car is all I got. You got that sonofabitch tore up, and now I'm fixing to drown your ass."

---

*Pops was also Turner's nickname, one he acquired for his propensity for popping other drivers on the track.

Turner offered Lund anything he wanted—first-place money, anything. Lund emerged from his red mist long enough to look up and see the people on the shore: "I seen all the people on the bank hollerin' and yellin'—part of 'em to drown him and part of 'em to save him. Shit." Lund loosened his grip on Turner.

A few years later Lund got into it with Lee Petty in Greensboro. Lund's car blew a head gasket, but he was trying to finish as many laps as he could so he could win enough money to get home. Petty, who even then had the best equipment around, had bolts sticking out of his door from where it was bolted shut. Every time Petty would lap Lund's car, he'd give him a good get-out-of-my-way bang. "He had four of those goddamn things," Lund said. "And when he hit a car, it'd be like a can opener."

Back then, drivers were paid on the spot after the race. Most of them put the money to use on the trip home. "So we're in line at the payoff getting our money, and ol' Lee was standing right behind me," said Lund. "We're on a platform, oh, a good fifteen feet in the air. So Lee says, 'Don't you know where to go when you're getting lapped?'"

Lund wasn't in the mood for a lecture. "Goddamn, you don't have to run over me just because you've got enough goddamn sheet metal and parts down there at your place to build more race cars than what there is on the racetrack. You like to tear everyone's car up, but you ain't gonna tear mine up no goddamn more."

Petty, no small man himself, took a swing at Lund. After he got his money—first things first—Lund took off after Petty, who was at the edge of the platform. "I kicked him in the ass, and I mean he took off of there like a big damned bird," said Lund.

From the ground, Petty looked up at Lund. "Is that the way you fight?"

"Hell no," Lund said. "Stay there. I'm coming down." He jumped off and, he recalled later, "commenced to knocking the shit out of him." Soon the Petty boys, Richard and Maurice, showed up along with their cousin Dale Inman, brandishing screwdrivers and pop bottles. Lund had some support—sort of: "Ol' Speedy Thompson, he jumped in there and was gonna help me, but he'd been frog hunting and shot a hole through his toe, and he was on a cane. One of them hit him in the goddamned toe, and he went hobbling off, holding his foot."

Another driver, Jack Smith, arrived, and just when things were about to get really interesting, Lund felt something hit the back of his head. "I seen butterflies and everything," he said. "It was ol' Liz Petty—Lee's wife. She had a pocketbook. I don't know what she had in it, but she was going *Pow! Pow! Pow! Pow!* just wearing my damned head out. And this broke things up."

On another occasion Lee Petty went after Curtis Turner with a tire iron, but that was nothing compared to the time a driver named Bobby Myers brandished a billy club at Turner. Pops pulled out a .32 pistol. "Bobby," he said, "if I was you, I'd lay that club down."

"Curtis, old man," replied Myers, "I'm just lookin' for a place to put it."

Why is brawling a natural by-product of racing? First, consider the obvious answer, courtesy of Richard Petty: "Ever driven a race car?" After three hours of defying death, a man might understandably emerge from his car a little on edge. But there's more to it than that. Formula One racing is just as dangerous, and yet its history, though occasionally colorful, isn't checkered with tales of drivers packing heat. And while A. J. Foyt did his best to bring a rollicking, ass-kicking vibe to U.S. open-wheel racing, it should be noted that the most memorable Indy car fight in recent years was a shriekfest between two female drivers that culminated with Milka Duno throwing a towel at Danica Patrick.

No, stock car racing is different from open-wheel racing because the cultures that gave birth to them are so different. Formula One and, to a slightly lesser extent, Indy car racing have aristocratic roots, bringing to mind dashing continental playboys in leather goggles and silk scarves, the kind of men who were occasionally knighted and could be invited to a dinner party without fear that the good china would be broken, stolen, or used as a spittoon. By contrast, stock car racing sprang up in a hardscrabble part of the United States where rough-and-tumble was the way of life.

James Webb, U.S. senator from Virginia, wrote a very entertaining and informative book in 2004 called *Born Fighting: How the Scots-Irish Shaped America,** which argues that the inherent feistiness found in Appalachian culture can be traced back nineteen centuries to the Roman emperor Hadrian. The Romans had been having trouble subduing the local tribes in northern Britain, and after the Ninth Legion was wiped out trying to quell a minor rebellion, Hadrian decided that it might not be such a good idea to keep fighting them. So he ordered his men to pen them in. In A.D. 122 construction began on a fifteen-foot-high wall constructed across the breadth of Great Britain from the North Sea to the Irish Sea, cutting off what is now northern England and Scotland from the rest of the island. In doing so, he made an already clannish people even more isolated.

Beginning in the early eighteenth century, the Scots-Irish began immigrating to America in droves. Being late to the colonial party, they found the good coastal land already snatched up, so they made their way inland, where the land was cheaper and more easily had. By the time the Declaration of Independence was written, a quarter of a million Scots-Irish had settled in America, primarily in the Carolinas and Virginia, where vestiges of the old country are still evident. On the drive east from NASCAR's hub in Charlotte to the Atlantic coast, you pass through Scotland County and see signs for the town of Aberdeen and for St. Andrews Presbyterian College.

---

* The cover of Webb's book features, among other images, pictures of Ronald Reagan, George Patton, Andrew Jackson, William Wallace, Robert the Bruce, and three stock cars.

Many of the pejoratives used to demean modern-day inhabitants of the area — and a lot of race fans — have their roots in Scotland and Ireland: *redneck* (the Presbyterian followers of King William and Queen Mary in the Battle of the Boyne in 1690 wore red neckerchiefs), *hillbilly* (*billy* being Scottish for friend), and *cracker* (from *craic,* a term still used in Ireland and Scotland for conversation, which begat *cracker,* a term that originally meant someone who boasted or talked too much).*

"Because Hadrian's Wall cut them off, the Scots-Irish developed different, socially, than the English did," says Humpy Wheeler. "And then they had to live off a terrible land. Even today in Scotland, there's nothing there. Sheep and rocks and whiskey. And how the Scots-Irish people — and I'm one of them, so I can talk bad about them — just love misery. They love it. They're followers of misery. The worse it is, the better they are.

"I remember Harry Gant won his first race here in '82. Harry is from Taylorsville, which is right in the semi-hills of North Carolina. In twenty minutes you'd be deep in the mountains, up near Wilkes County. This is a celebration of Harry's first victory. A celebration. I went up there for it, because Harry's a dear friend of mine. They have it at the high school in the gym. It's a dreary January, just one of those depressing days. I walk in there a little bit before it started. The place is packed full of Taylorsvillians plus people from the racing industry. Harry's up on the stage, and the country gentlemen are playing bluegrass music, singing a dour, mournful song, 'Legend of the Rebel Soldier,' which is the saddest song you could possibly sing.† It's about

---

* Of course, etymology is often an inexact science. Alternative theories hold that *redneck* comes from the sunburn patterns prevalent on farmers and that *cracker* comes from the sound made by a slave master's whip.

† He's not exaggerating. The song begins with the soldier lying in a dreary prison and ends with him dying. In between, we learn he left behind a wife and a young daughter. It's not the kind of thing you'd hear Up with People singing.

a Civil War soldier dying in prison up north. It comes from an Irish ballad about a guy dying in Brixton prison. And I'm thinking, *Is this Harry's funeral? Is there anybody in here happy?* I kept looking around, and I couldn't find anybody. It's just the way it is. It was as typical a Scots-Irish thing as I've ever seen in my life, yet it was in celebration of Harry's victory.

"All that led to people that would literally fight at the drop of a hat. Now the kind of fighting they did was primarily with their fists. So, when I was coming up in the '50s, all these mill towns in North and South Carolina, hundreds of them, were populated primarily by Scots-Irish people. In the wintertime, the sport was not basketball, as a lot of people would assume. It was boxing. Every little town had a boxing club. They had tournaments galore. These were Scots-Irish kids fighting Scots-Irish kids. That's what it was. Mean group of people."

So Cale Yarborough, the Timmonsville native, one of those kids who'd boxed competitively in high school, the man who days earlier had related the story of how he'd whipped that fourth-grade bully, approached Bobby Allison's car. With his helmet in hand, he took a swing at Allison, who was still belted into the driver's seat. "Blood was dripping in my lap," says Allison. "I said to myself, 'I gotta get out of this car and handle this right now or run from him the rest of my life.'"

Getting out of a race car is no easy feat, especially not when there's a miffed former Golden Gloves champion standing next to your car waiting to pummel you. But Allison got all his belts undone and slithered out the window in what had to be record time. As is so often the case with fights, what transpired after the punches started flying depends on whom you ask. Allison's standard line is "Cale started beating my fist with his nose. That's my story, and I'm sticking to it." Yarborough says, "I went over and knocked the hell out of Bobby." Donnie said, "Bobby kicked the shit out of him." Truth is, no one walked away much worse for wear — physically at least. At one point Yarborough tried to karate kick Bobby, which is never a good idea in a racing suit. Allison, still wearing his helmet, grabbed Yarborough's leg, and they both wound up on the ground. The Thrilla in Manila it wasn't.

The only thing that truly took a beating was Donnie's reputation, at least among people who didn't follow NASCAR closely but looked at the sports page. Donnie arrived at the melee, helmet in hand. "I have a helmet, too, if you want to fight with helmets," he yelled at Yarborough, who had just used his on Bobby's nose. Unfortunately for Donnie, that's the pose he had assumed in the most famous picture of the fight. Never mind that he never so much as threw a punch; the enduring image is of Donnie looking as if he's about to brain Yarborough with a cheap shot. "If Cale Yarborough would have raised his fist to Donnie, Cale Yarborough wouldn't be here," said the Allisons' brother Eddie, who watched the fight back home in Hueytown. "If Cale had wanted to fight Donnie, Cale would have been dead, and Donnie would be in the penitentiary."

It didn't last long, and by the time CBS cut to it, the skirmish was almost over. Viewers saw less than ten seconds of grappling before track workers pulled the two men apart. But it made for incredible theater. It wasn't so much the action that gripped fans, but the idea that this was how disagreements were dealt with in the racing universe. "For something like that to happen in stock car racing was a common, ordinary, everyday thing almost," says Wheeler. "But to happen on TV in front of the American public just brought out this hidden culture that we had, where you settle things like a man, with your fists. None of this shouting, throwing handkerchiefs at each other. Let's settle it now, like a man."

Word of the fight traveled fast. "As anxious as I was to get to Victory Lane, I was tempted to stop over there after getting the checkered flag and watch them cats go at it," Petty joked. But since no one in the garage actually saw what transpired in Turn 3, it was like a game of telephone. The smart money in the Allison-brother-most-likely-to-get-into-a-fight-on-national-TV pool had always been on Donnie, so most everyone assumed he was one of the combatants. "Donnie was the biggest fighter of them all," says Wheeler. "He was very feisty. If you had one of those 1868 pictures of gold miners in the Yukon wearing tin cloth, Donnie Allison would've been one of them." Even Kitty Allison, Donnie's own mother, was so sure he was at fault that when he showed up in the garage, she began berating him for fighting until he explained to her that it was Bobby.

Bobby was sitting on a bench with his wife, Judy. He was blasé about the fight. "Nothing happened," he said.

"Yarborough said he hit you," a reporter offered.

"He got a little excited," Allison said. "I didn't block anybody. I wasn't even close." Then two of his crew members shooed away the reporters.

Yarborough was stalking through the garage, fists clenched, calling what the Allisons had done—or what he thought they had done—"the worst thing I've ever seen in racing. I had him beat."

Donnie, meanwhile, was in his semitrailer, his face smudged with dirt and his eyes red with rage. When informed of Yarborough's assertion that he had him beat, Allison said, "I'll be damned if he did. He was just going to win the race or else. I was down as low as I could go. And Cale got off in the infield grass and came up and hit me. He wasn't going to give, and I wasn't going to. I figured if I hit that wall hard, he's going to hit it hard, too." As for his role as a bystander in the fight, Allison explained that if he had been as proficient as his brother at getting his belts off, the fight might have ended differently: "He called me those names, and I told him to wait until I was out of the car and he could call me anything he wanted. I'd have beat his brains out."

Bill France told them all to come to his office the next morning. Nobody was going anywhere anyway.

The snow and ice that focused the attention of a captive TV audience on Daytona Beach also made getting out of the city next to impossible for teams, journalists, and fans. Most flights that left from Daytona

Beach went through Atlanta or Charlotte, which meant that most flights were canceled. Dick Berggren, who was covering the 500 for *Stock Car Racing* magazine, was flying to Boston via Charlotte. He and his boss were anxious to get out of the airport, in no small part because his boss was carrying a duffel bag filled with $10,000 in small bills, the proceeds from subscriptions sold to fans during Speedweeks. "If anybody had known how much money he was carrying, he absolutely would have been knocked off," says Berggren.

Among the airline officials milling about the airport was the pilot of Berggren's flight. The writer proposed a novel idea: why not bypass Charlotte and just fly straight to Boston, where the airport was open. These being heady, pre-TSA days, the pilot said he thought it was a great idea. He hollered that anyone in the gate area who wanted to go straight to Boston should get on board.

Most travelers weren't so lucky, but not everyone was in a hurry to get out of Daytona. STP and Petty Enterprises threw a celebratory dinner at Indigo Lakes, the fanciest golf club in the area. Given all that had happened in the past year and a half, it came as no surprise that Richard Petty, who earlier in the day had issued a reminder of just how tough he was, choked up while making a speech. They laughed and celebrated into the night, aware that a long trip back to North Carolina awaited them the next day.

When they got home, they'd find that their sport would never be quite the same.

For the seventh time in as many attempts, Darrell Waltrip left the Daytona 500 without the Harley Earl Award.* But he was a happy

---

*Earl was a car designer—known as "the Father of the Corvette" and the inventor of tail fins—who served as a NASCAR commissioner in the 1950s. For years the winner had his name engraved on the Harley J. Earl Trophy and was given a smaller wooden trophy, called the Harley Earl Award. Since 1998 the winner has been given a miniature replica of the trophy.

man nonetheless. He'd finished second in a car that had no business finishing second. And it didn't even bother him that one of his many nemeses had won (though it's a pretty safe bet that whoever won would have fallen under the heading of "Waltrip nemesis"). Waltrip didn't want to ascend to the King's throne. He wanted to take it away. Two years earlier he had explained his motivation: "I want to set some records. That's why I'd like to win some more races before those guys retire. Then people won't be able to say I couldn't beat 'em." Waltrip needed a foil. And to get that, he had to hope that Daytona was, in fact, a sign that Petty was rejuvenated. He needed the sleeping giant to wake up and give him a fight.

It was a dangerous thing to wish for.

One of the few people to get back to Charlotte on race day was Humpy Wheeler.* Wheeler was an old track operator, and track operators, like farmers who took cues from the posture of their cows, tended to be avid amateur weathermen. He fancied himself a pretty good prognosticator and felt in his bones that things were going to get nasty in Daytona, so he left town Sunday morning a couple of hours before the race and headed for Charlotte, with a pit stop in St. Augustine so he could to go to Mass. Since Big Bill France's weather mojo trumped Wheeler's intuition, Humpy ended up missing all the excitement at the track, settling for the CBS feed on his car radio. As Bobby Allison and Cale Yarborough were duking it out in Turn 3, Wheeler was in lower South Carolina, dealing with what he says was "a raging snowstorm where there had never been a raging snowstorm before."

But Wheeler made it home on Sunday night and was able to keep his Monday morning appointment to speak at a meeting of the Charlotte

---

* We've talked so much about Humpy that we might as well answer the question that's probably on your mind. He's called Humpy because that was his father's nickname. His father got it for his penchant for smoking Camels.

Rotary Club, an august, archconservative club of downtown business-men. Because nothing stops the Rotary Club, Wheeler found himself playing to a full house of starched gentlemen who had braved the elements just to see him. "There's a bunch of guys who have never expressed any interest in racing whatsoever, and all they could tell me about was the finish at the Daytona 500, which I had not even seen yet," says Wheeler. "I knew that something monumental had happened because these guys were talking about it. You could have finished upside down at the World 600 [at Charlotte Motor Speedway], and they might have said, 'Well I heard you had a good finish.' But they would never talk in detail about it."

The race had received coverage on Sunday night's network news broadcasts, a rarity for a NASCAR event. On NBC Dick Schaap commented, "The speed, stakes, and the risks are so great, tempers can and do suddenly flare." The race, he said, "produced an incredibly dramatic finish and an explosion of tempers." Apparently taking his cue from Kitty Allison, Schaap then reported that Donnie Allison had been the one exchanging blows with Yarborough. Over on ABC, Al Ackerman proclaimed that the race had been decided by "a deliberate crash at 200 miles per hour."

Monday's newspapers gave the Daytona 500 unprecedented real estate: first page of sports, six columns, above the fold was the norm. And most didn't run pictures of the race winner. They ran pictures of the fighters. Aroused by what they were seeing on their TVs and in their morning papers, people began to clamor for a real, live taste of the action. The phone lines for the ticket office at the Charlotte Motor Speedway (CMS) were jammed even though the World 600 was three months away. "We're getting an unusual number of calls from people who say they've never been to a major race before," the CMS ticket manager said. "But now that they've seen the spectacle at Daytona, they want to see a race in person."

So much ado about scuffling presented Bill France with a dilemma.

As a promoter, he saw the value in any kind of publicity, but as the son of the man who'd founded NASCAR, he didn't want to chuck the hard work his father had put into making the sport respectable in exchange for a short-term bump in media attention and ticket sales. "When you're promoting races or you're running NASCAR, you need to be at the edge of the cliff all the time," says Wheeler. "That's what makes people want to buy tickets. You need to stand at the edge of the cliff; you just don't want to fall off." So France knew he had to do something to counter the impression that he was running an anarchic sport without completely discouraging future acts of lawlessness that might land his drivers' faces on the front page of a sports section or two. Public penalties were rare in NASCAR. Any trouble was usually dealt with behind closed doors, where a stern admonition from France, or from Big Bill before him, to "cut that crap out" usually did the trick. This one was different, though, because the crap had been nationally televised. So France summoned Cale Yarborough and the Allison brothers, plus a track worker who had been in the infield during the fight, to his office on Monday. The drivers repeated the same arguments they had made on Sunday, and then finally, after nearly two weeks in Daytona Beach, they went home.

Hoss Ellington was a man of his word. Cale Yarborough had asked him for a ride home the day before the 500. Ellington's kids often swam and played with Yarborough's at motels on the road, and Hoss's wife was friendly with Betty Jo Yarborough. To Ellington, the fact that Yarborough ran into his driver on the last lap, tore up a $60,000 race car, and cost him the biggest win of his life didn't change the fact that he had made a promise to a friend. Still, he knew giving Yarborough a lift home might not sit well with his driver or his crew, so he made it a point not to hide it from them. "It's a damn shame this wreck happened," Ellington told them after the race, "because I told Cale and Betty Jo I'd take them home."

One crew member threatened to quit, as did Allison. Says Ellington, "I said, 'Well, I feel bad about this, guys, don't get me wrong, but I made a promise before this race even started that I'd take him home. I'm as good as my word. I wasn't in either one of them damn cars. Had nothing to do with that damn wreck. And it ain't got nothing to do with me taking a man and his wife home.'"

After Yarborough finished giving his side of the wreck and fight to France, he and his wife piled into Ellington's van. The trip was awkward, to say the least. Hoss sat up front with a member of his crew, while Cale and Betty Jo sat in the back. Around Savannah, Yarborough said, "Hoss, you want me to drive?"

Says Ellington, "I looked back at him and said, 'Cale *can* you drive?'" Eventually, he relented and gave Yarborough the wheel, but he made sure to point out the ice on the road: "I told him not to get onto the grass, that he had trouble driving on the grass."

"I don't know whether Hoss changed his mind after that or I changed mine," says Allison, "but things were definitely different between us."

The Kyle fever that had a hold on so much of the stock car community continued unabated even after Petty returned to his job as tire carrier and gopher on his father's team. The ABC News national broadcast following the Daytona 500 briefly mentioned Richard's win and then devoted several minutes to a feature on Kyle. "Maybe I'm bragging a bit," Lee Petty told Al Ackerman, "but he's a chip off the ol' block. In fact, he's got the second chip. I've taken the first chip with Richard, and Richard chipped him off."

Lee then suggested that his grandson retire and become "the only undefeated race car driver in the world." Kyle, looking a bit uncomfortable in a blazer, said, "I don't think I want to do that."

So what did Kyle want to do? Well, he wanted to make a name for himself, but he was smart enough to know that wasn't going to happen.

"I want to race as Kyle Petty if everybody will allow me, not as Richard Petty's son," he said. "As far as all the assets I have, my situation is ideal. Being Richard Petty's son is not ideal. From the identity standpoint, I'd be better off as Kyle Jones. But I like being Richard Petty's son."

What Kyle wanted to do was largely a moot point anyway, since as long as he was a part of Petty Enterprises, his fate rested with Richard and Lee. The King's win in the 500 was vital: STP would be back on the hood for the next race, and any worries the crewmen had about their jobs or their paychecks were allayed. And the win rejuvenated Petty. No one was talking about how frail he looked or whether he'd make it through the year in one piece. He'd driven a grueling 500-mile race against the strongest field ever assembled and come out on top. But he was forty-one and clearly on the downhill side of his career, which made Kyle's win so significant for the operation. There was a successor in place, one who looked just like his old man, talked just like his old man, and, thank God, drove just like his old man.

For the ARCA race, Kyle—who, like Richard twenty years earlier, had started going to business school three nights a week—negotiated his own sponsorship deal with Valvoline. He clearly wasn't going to need to rely on his entrepreneurial skills going forward. Finding a sponsor was going to be as easy as answering the phone when it rang. "With 10 laps to go in [the ARCA] race, two potential sponsors were already talking," reported Petty Enterprises business manager Bill Frazier. "When I got back to the motel, I had a bunch of telephone messages that resulted in at least four more legitimate offers." The most fervent suitor was STP, which was anxious to get Kyle into the fold and to sever his association with Valvoline, one of its chief rivals. "Once the Pettys decide which way Kyle is going, they have promised us first crack at sponsoring him," an STP exec told the *Atlanta Constitution*. "I don't know when that will be—a week, a month or whenever. But we will be ready."

And it wasn't just sponsors doing the wooing. Promoters were dying to have the Kyle Show come to their tracks. Rockingham, North Carolina, which was host to a Grand National race on March 11, and Atlanta, which had one the following week, both made pitches to Richard. Humpy Wheeler wanted him for the World 600 on Memorial Day weekend, so much so that he was willing to pony up $25,000. "Some guy in California even wanted Kyle to drive a Corvette in a race there," Frazier said.

Richard was reluctant to rush Kyle into a Grand National car, not because it wasn't safe, but because it wasn't cheap. "If a sponsor will come up with $200[,000] or $300,000, we will build Kyle his own race car," Richard said. "But if that doesn't work out, I might even farm him out for a few races. If someone comes up with enough money to run a NASCAR Grand National or an ARCA race or any type of race, then we will look at it."

It's easy to be cynical about the way Kyle was being shopped, but he was in an unprecedented situation. Drivers simply didn't enter the sport to that kind of fanfare. It didn't happen that way. "You may be talking about a $10 million man," Buddy Baker said. "The Pettys are handling him just like a Sugar Ray Leonard."

Of course, Sugar Ray Leonard had almost as much experience behind the wheel as Kyle, and that was going to have to be addressed at some point. "It will take four or five years for Kyle to be a steady Grand National contender," Junior Johnson said. "When he goes to Darlington and some other tracks, he is going to find a whole new deal. Take Darrell Waltrip. People forget that Darrell had years of short-track experience before going Grand National, and it took him three or four years to make it then. If Petty doesn't run the short tracks, he never will be an effective driver. Racing who he did and racing against the Pearsons, the Yarboroughs, the Bakers, the Allisons, and, well, his daddy, you are talking about two different worlds."

Johnson was right, and Richard knew it. Following his son's win he said, "Kyle has won a trophy, kissed a beauty queen, and met the press. Now he has to learn how to drive a race car." They could have sent him out to compete in some more ARCA races or on any one of the short tracks in the Carolinas, where he could get the seat time he needed. But the lure was too great. Not the money—though the $25,000 was nice—but the lure of believing that he was *that* naturally gifted, that he could repeat what he had done at Daytona.

They took Humpy's deal. Kyle's second race would be the World 600 in May.

On Bill France's agenda Tuesday, the day after he sent the combatants home, was watching videotape of the race and fight, which was a much bigger production than it sounds. No one in the NASCAR offices had a VCR, so France and Bill Gazaway had to go across International Speedway Boulevard to the offices of the Motor Racing Network, where they set up a makeshift screening room in the office of broadcaster Jack Arute. "He was trying to be serious, but he couldn't help himself," says Arute. "He was smiling, because he knew it was something people were going to talk about."

The punishments were handed down that evening. All three drivers would be fined $6,000, with the proviso that $1,000 would be returned following each of the next five races so long as they kept out of trouble. It was a cagey move by France. Six thousand bucks was a lot of money—half the Daytona 500 field made less than that in the race—so he gave the appearance of coming down hard on the ruffians. But by giving most of the money back, France was ultimately administering little more than a slap on the wrist.

Had France stopped there, the issue might have died. But he and Gazaway ruled in no uncertain terms that the wreck was Donnie Allison's fault. "In reviewing the television tapes, Donnie Allison went down onto the apron, resulting in Yarborough's car going into the grass. In doing so, Donnie Allison acted in a manner contrary to the best interests of the sport," Gazaway said. "Again, a race leader cannot run anywhere he pleases on the race track." Allison was given six months' probation. The additional penalty, coupled with having a very big finger pointed at him, didn't sit well with Donnie or with his brother. "It's unreal," Bobby said. "I am shocked by the amount of the fines and the unfairness of the whole thing. I don't see how Donnie can be blamed for the wreck. He was leading the race and can use up all the track he wants. He didn't have to give anything to Yarborough, and didn't, but Cale just ran over him."

Bo Grady, a friend of Donnie's who worked on his short-track car, was the most indignant member of the Allison camp. "I'm not believing that," he said. "Six months' probation? You don't get that for killing someone."

Yarborough, meanwhile, felt vindicated. The way he saw it, he was being fined solely for the fight, and a thousand bucks was pretty good value for getting a pop at Bobby Allison. "I'm glad NASCAR has taken its stand," he said. "I think they clarified it pretty well. It's always been a gentleman's agreement that you can use all the racetrack you want when you are out front, but you don't ever leave a man without an escape route. When a man gets alongside you, you don't try to put him out of the racetrack. That's what happened to me. If I had been behind him, he could have gone anywhere he wanted. I would have finished second. But I got beside Donnie fair and square. He moved down on me and I moved down with him as far as I could go. My left side tires were off the track and I was running the left side on the dirt when he finally hit me the first time. We were side-by-side then.... When he saw me down low, here he came with me. I went low as far as I could go, and I wasn't about to drive out in Lake Lloyd."

His ruling handed down, France, a man whose word on a subject was usually the last, considered the matter closed. Asked if he was worried about the wreck, the fight, or both spilling over into subsequent races, he said, "It better not. It was a big race, and those guys came down here to race...and they carried it one step beyond. It's over now.... We do not anticipate any more trouble."

But not even Bill France always got what he anticipated.

Chapter Nine
Round Two

Sunday, March 4
Race 3: Carolina 500
Rockingham, North Carolina

THANKS TO the weather—perhaps Big Bill France climbed on top of a press box and prayed for a storm—the second race on the 1979 schedule, the Richmond 500, was snowed out and rescheduled for the open week following the Carolina 500. That meant the fight would remain topic A for seven more days, providing the kind of buildup that Don King would have loved.* Indeed, spectators heading into Rockingham were greeted by a billboard that read, WELCOME, RACE FANS, TO ROUND TWO.

---

*At the first Daytona 500, Big Bill France and his cronies learned that a little controversy goes a long way in keeping a story alive. At that race, in 1959, Johnny Beauchamp and Lee Petty crossed the finish line in such close proximity that it was virtually impossible for the naked eye to separate them. Beauchamp was declared the winner, but Petty drove his car to Victory Lane. France issued a nationwide call for any photos or film that might shed some light on the matter to be sent to the NASCAR offices. They spent three days—perhaps dragging their feet a little to keep the story in the sports pages—poring over the evidence before reversing themselves and declaring Petty the winner.

The Rock was a tough track to drive. Originally built as a flat one-mile track in the mid-1960s, it had been reconfigured as a banked, D-shaped tri-oval. Because of the high sand content in the soil in that part of North Carolina, the asphalt used to pave the track was especially gritty, and it ate up tires. Rockingham stood in sharp contrast to Daytona—in terms of both the track and the surrounding town. Rockingham is a tiny burg of less than 10,000 people about halfway between Charlotte and Fayetteville, down near the South Carolina border. Which is to say, it's in the middle of nowhere. The closest thing to a tourist destination is Pinehurst No. 2, the golf course twenty-five miles up the road that has hosted two U.S. Opens and a Ryder Cup. So during their stay in Rockingham, drivers had to make their own fun. One way they did that was to roast one of their own the week of the spring race, and in 1979 it was Buddy Baker's turn to sit on the dais.

It wasn't easy to find someone who didn't like Baker, so a large crowd of fans and drivers showed up, including both Allison brothers and Cale Yarborough.* Two of Baker's friends, Buck Brigance and Jim Hester, were dressed as mountain men, replete with overalls, floppy hats, and shotguns, to keep order and stand guard over the guest of honor in case he decided to make a run for it. Yarborough took the stage, eyed the shotgun-toting hillbillies, and said, "Where were you guys when I needed you in Daytona?" He then surveyed the room and cast his eye on the Allisons, who were sitting in the front row. "You know," Yarborough said, "looking out and seeing Bobby and Donnie in the audience, I have something I'd like to do before I get to Mr. Baker. I would like to apologize to the Allisons for the fight. It was an unfair fight. I used both hands."

---

* Being a straight-out-of-central-casting gentle giant, Baker was a fine roast target. To a point. Steve Waid of *Grand National Scene* was supposed to hit Baker in the face with a lemon meringue pie. Waid's pal Tom Higgins of the *Charlotte Observer* told him, "Unless you want to be embarrassed, you better leave that pie the way it is." Waid wisely took his advice.

With that, the brothers shot out of their seats, and for a brief second it looked like everyone in the auditorium was going to find out the hard way whether or not the hillbillies' shotguns were indeed loaded. But none of the combatants could keep a straight face, and everyone had a good laugh, making it clear that although no one should expect the Allisons and Yarborough to become fast friends, they could certainly put any residual resentment over what happened at Daytona behind them. The détente continued when Donnie Allison was seen having a beer with Busch Clash mastermind Monty Roberts, whose status as an employee of the company that sponsored Yarborough's car should have made him the enemy. "We have disagreements," Monty said, "but we are friends."

When qualifying started at 3:00 p.m. on Thursday, Bill Gazaway was noticeably absent. Earlier that afternoon NASCAR's director of competition had abruptly left the track and hopped on a private plane bound for Daytona.

Bobby Allison turned the fastest lap, followed by his brother and Yarborough, meaning they would start the race in the exact same positions they'd been in when Bobby triggered the wreck that sent them all sliding through the muck in Daytona. Buddy Baker was fourth. "What a hell of a place to begin the race," he said. "It's like having a choice between smoking a cigar in a dynamite factory or carrying a tube of nitroglycerin on a roller coaster. You could get blown away either way." Baker's tongue was in his cheek, but the light mood in the garage didn't last long. Shortly after qualifying ended, the reason for Gazaway's absence became apparent. NASCAR was announcing a change in the penalties.

As promised, the Allisons had lodged a formal appeal of the sanctions Bill France had handed down. They were given a hearing on February 26 at a motel near the Atlanta airport. The night before, Donnie Allison received a cryptic phone call. A man who refused to identify himself told him that NASCAR was in possession of a video-tape of the wreck shot by a Florida TV station. The footage, shot from a different angle than the CBS race coverage, seemed to back Allison's claim that Yarborough had initiated the contact. "Make them show you the tapes," the caller told Allison. "Make them show you the tapes."*

The hearing was held in front of a three-man committee comprising NASCAR field director Lance Childress, Riverside Raceway president Les Richter, and president of Dover Downs International Speedway John Riddle. The first order of business was to discuss the penalties for the wreck. Since Bobby was only appealing a penalty for fighting, he excused himself. The mood in the room was informal; no lawyers were present, and the proceedings were not recorded.

The VCR was cranked up, and just as Donnie's Deep Throat had told him, one of the tapes showed Yarborough turning into Allison while he was still on the track, which seemed to contradict his argument that he had been forced down onto the apron before there was any contact. "Why haven't we seen this before?" Childress asked. If the footage didn't completely exonerate Allison, it certainly implicated Yarborough. After an hour and ten minutes, Allison was excused. The committee members shut off the VCR, had lunch, and talked things over. Says Riddle, "It was obvious that the only real solution was to cut the baby in half." Allison's six-month probation was chopped to three, and Yarborough was given a three-month probation of his own.†

"I thought we did well," says Riddle, "because they were all mad at me."

* * *

---

* Allison still doesn't know who the caller was. For a time he suspected it was Jack Arute, which makes sense, as Arute was in the room when France and Gazaway looked over the videotapes. However, to this day Arute denies making the call.

† Bobby, who spent only ten minutes in front of the panel, lost his appeal. He never had much of a chance, given that the whole world had seen pictures and/or video of him fighting Yarborough.

The wreck and fight in Daytona offered NASCAR fans a chance to live up to their reputation for unmatched loyalty and zeal. *Stock Car Racing* got an unprecedented amount of mail, as did *Grand National Scene*. One reader called Donnie's actions "disgusting," but most agreed with the Canadian gent who distilled the wreck and NASCAR's decision to penalize Allison down to two words: "pure bullshit." No one was entirely certain how fans were going to treat the drivers, especially after a few prerace cocktails. The depths to which a drunken sports fan could fall had been demonstrated the night a week earlier when someone had chucked a liquor bottle onto the court during the ACC basketball tournament in Greensboro. To be safe, L. G. DeWitt, the president of the Rock, hired extra police to sit in the grandstands and observe the crowd of 44,000—a speedway record—with binoculars from towers.

Reaction to the drivers as they were introduced was mixed. Yarborough was booed, and the Allisons were cheered, but the ovation they got was no match for the one reserved for the grand marshal, Kyle Petty. He performed his duties—riding around the track in the back of a convertible in an STP jacket, while looking mildly embarrassed at the fuss being made over him—then made his way to the pits, where he became likely the first grand marshal in the history of the esteemed position to perform menial tasks such as carrying tires during the race. His dad, who had seen plenty of fenders banged in his day, wasn't sure what to expect when the green flag flew. "There'll be no love taps out there," Richard said. "There'll either be a whole lot or nothing."

There was a whole lot.

The Carolina 500 consisted of 392 laps. Nine of them were peaceful. Yarborough pulled into the lead almost immediately, but going into Turn 3 on the tenth lap, Donnie got inside him. The roles were reversed from the last lap at Daytona, but the result was the same: Yarborough moved down and hit Allison, and both cars ended up in the fence. This time they weren't a mile in front of their closest pursuers. The wreck touched off a pileup that collected several of the fastest cars: Petty, Darrell Waltrip, Buddy Baker, Dale Earnhardt, and Ricky Rudd. Neil Bonnett, who was driving a second Hoss Ellington car, couldn't avoid the mess either, meaning that in the last ten laps of Grand National racing, Hoss had seen three of his cars totaled in wrecks involving Yarborough.

Allison and Yarborough both had the same initial reaction, one shaped by the fact that they were on probation and they wanted to see their $1,000 checks again: *Hey, man, it was an accident.* If anyone was in the right, it was Allison, who was minding his own business when Yarborough hit him. But controversy of any sort was the last thing he needed, and he wasn't about to start pointing fingers. Instead, he was content to write it off as just one of them racing deals.* He found a phone in the garage and called Bill Gazaway, who was up in the tower, to tell him it was an accident. Allison's car was done, but Yarborough's was fixable. He blew an engine fifty laps later, and as he watched his crew put a new motor in the Oldsmobile, he echoed Allison's sentiment that there was no malicious intent. "What happened was totally unrelated to anything else that has happened between us," he said. Allison's final assessment was: "I don't blame Cale for anything. We just went slidin' and everybody ran over everybody. There's no hard feelings."

He was clearly speaking for himself.

The fact that Allison and Yarborough swore that they didn't mean to take out most of the contenders provided little solace to Baker and Bonnett, who both ended up in the hospital getting foot X-rays. In the ambulance on the way to the hospital, they tried to reconstruct

---

* The NASCAR phrase "Just one of them racing deals" translates roughly to "Shit happens." The word "deal" itself has no set definition. It can be used to describe just about any noun. In rare cases, it actually means a business agreement, an explanation of which might begin, "The deal with that deal…" Usually, though, it means "that thing." On one memorable occasion, it was used in place of "hot dog cart." A few crewmen were screwing around with half a stick of dynamite and happened upon a cart in the middle of a field. When explaining what happened next, one of the crewmen told me, "We lit it and threw it up under that deal."

the origin of the wreck, but neither had seen much except tire smoke. Others, though, had no trouble identifying the culprit. Petty sounded like he was trying to tie what was left of his stomach in knots, his syrupy voice wavering with rage. "If they keep driving like that much longer, I'm gonna start fighting," he said. "Donnie got under Cale. Outmaneuvered him. Then Cale turned left—and Donnie was sittin' there. Deliberate? Yeah. He had control of the steering wheel. How deliberate I don't know. It was a misjudgment in driving, and I made one too, for being so close. They should put 'em on top of the trucks and let 'em watch other people show 'em how it's done." He might not even have been the hottest Petty. Maurice got into an altercation with Bill Gazaway's brother Joe, a NASCAR official, in the pits following the wreck, which led to a two-week suspension. "Chief just pushed the wrong cat," said Richard later. "That's all."

But the most enraged driver had to be Waltrip, whose white hat was nowhere to be seen. As he watched his crew give Wanda the mother of all nose jobs (they performed a hoodectomy and removed the front fender, too), he looked like he would have gone after Yarborough if the opportunity had presented iteself. "It was the stupidest thing I ever saw. He drove over the man's hood is what he did," Waltrip said. "They ought to pull his butt out of the car and beat the hell out of him.... There should be one driver on probation after today, and it ain't Donnie Allison. The other one ought to be up there," he said, pointing at the stands, "learning how to drive."

One of the few fast cars to get through the wreck unscathed was Bobby Allison's. When he saw his brother and Yarborough start to spin, Allison took his Ford down onto the grass and floored it. David Pearson also made it through safely and led for 119 laps, but he blew an engine just past the halfway point. Three laps later Allison took the lead from Benny Parsons and looked like he was going to drive away from what was left of the field. But there was one driver hanging around who had a car that was strong enough to keep up with Allison: rookie Joe Millikan, a former floor sweeper at Petty Enterprises.

Millikan was a well-fed twenty-nine-year-old who wasn't used to wrestling a Grand National car for almost four hours. "My back was killing me, and I wasn't doing the car justice," he'd say later. Luckily for him, thanks to round two there were plenty of guys in the garage with nothing to do. Around lap 240 Millikan got out of his Chevy during a pit stop and turned it over to a relief driver: his old boss, Richard Petty.* The King had just about everything he needed to reel in Allison — a solid car and years of experience on the track. Although he'd already shipped his gear back to Level Cross, he had Buddy Baker's helmet and one of Millikan's old uniforms. But he didn't have his shoes.

The evolution of the driver over the past three decades has been pronounced. He's become less shaggy, more presentable to sponsors, and, for the most part, more at ease in front of a camera. His sunglasses have become much fancier, his caps are less boxy, and his helmet no longer looks like something the Great Gazoo would wear. But perhaps the most notable advance has been on his feet. Drivers today wear state-of-the-art kicks designed specifically for racing. They're heat-resistant but thin enough to let the driver feel the pedals, and only a handful of companies make them. Petty and his cronies, though, had to look no further than the local Payless to get their gear. They drove in everything from Hush Puppies (Bobby Allison) to Converse running shoes (Yarborough) to wing tips (Dave Marcis). Dale Earnhardt wore snappy yellow and blue sneakers that matched his uniform, while Neil Bonnett drove in casual shoes with thick soles that looked like something he stole from his grandfather's closet. "I don't just wear them to race," Bonnett said. "I wear them everywhere except to church." He loved them so much he bought them in bulk

---

* The driver who starts the race is the one who gets the points and the check.

at a discount store near his home in Hueytown. David Pearson raced in a pair of $60 patent leather loafers he had originally intended to wear as dress shoes, only to discover he didn't like the color. They had replaced a pair of alligator loafers he'd worn in 116 straight races; Pearson had resoled the right one fifty times before his wife finally had them pewtered.*

The key was to find something with a thick enough sole to keep the right foot—the one that works the gas—from blistering. Benny Parsons wore work boots; he gave tennis shoes a try but wound up with a blister on his heel the size of his fist. Petty also drove in work books, and to give himself added protection, he glued rubber to the right sole. But he had sent the boots home with the rest of his stuff after the crash, meaning that when he got into Millikan's car, he was wearing his cowboy boots.

Petty was two laps behind Bobby Allison when he took over, but he got one back when Allison ran out of gas. Allison's radio wasn't working—he wasn't aware that it was Petty chasing him now, not Millikan—and he missed the sign Bud Moore put out telling him it was time to pit. Allison had to coast all the way around the track. Petty got around Allison again to get back onto the lead lap and was closing in on him when the discomfort in his feet became unbearable. "I wasn't used to the car," he said. "I got blisters on my hands and on the heels of my feet because I had to drive in my street boots....I would have stayed in the car, but I couldn't see hurting myself with someone else's car." With thirteen miles left, he got out of the car, and Millikan got back in. The driver change did away with any chance that Allison would be caught. "I really do think if I hadn't made the stop to get Joe back in the car, we could have beaten Allison," Petty said. Instead, Millikan was denied the chance to become the first rookie since 1974 to be credited with a win.

Talk in the garage after the race, however, had nothing to do with

---

* Not bronzed. Pewtered.

Allison's victory, Millikan's aching back, or the King's toasted feet. The story was what had happened on the tenth lap. Petty, who finished thirty-second, was among the many who believed that suspensions were in order, but he realized it was unlikely that NASCAR would keep two of its most popular drivers—both of whom had loyal sponsors—away from the track. "Suspensions? Yeah, why not? But NASCAR officials didn't see it," he said with a wink. "Know what I mean?"

He was right. Bill Gazaway said that he wasn't even going to look at film of the incident "unless I happen to be watching TV and it comes on."

Standings After the Carolina 500

1.	Darrell Waltrip	472
2.	Cale Yarborough	444
3.	Bobby Allison	431
4.	Donnie Allison	398
5.	D. K. Ulrich	395
...		
13.	Richard Petty	314

Chapter Ten

Round Three

Sunday, March 11
Race 4: Richmond 400
Richmond, Virginia

BEFORE HE flew to Richmond, Bobby Allison made a quick stop in Atlanta to appear at a press conference alongside Zell Miller, whose duties as lieutenant governor included officially designating the week of the upcoming Atlanta 500 as "Race Days" in Georgia. Donnie Allison was noticeably missing from the festivities. He had previous engagements, but his absence gave birth to rumors that he was lying low because he feared for his safety. The *Atlanta Constitution* broke a story earlier in the week that he had received a warning in the mail, scrawled on tablet paper, from a Cale Yarborough fan, whose lack of social graces was matched only by his lack of command of the English language: "You'd better look out for a Coke bottle through your winshield or somthing like that when you race at Atlanta." The missive bore an Atlanta postmark.

Ed Hinton of the *Atlanta Journal* had been approached with the story of the letter by the promoter of the Atlanta International Raceway, who claimed that he had found it in the garbage near Hoss Ellington's garage stall in Rockingham. Finding the whole story a little too neat—the promoter of an Atlanta track fortuitously finding a letter postmarked in Atlanta two weeks before a race in Atlanta—Hinton had passed.* But after the story broke, Hinton contacted Donnie, who denied that he was hiding. "I don't know where they get those stories—in the bars, or where," he said. "But as for any of that business about that letter keeping me out of Atlanta, that's a bunch of bull. I don't want a bottle through my windshield or Bobby's or Cale's or anybody else's. And I'll tell you what: If something is thrown at any of us, and we find out who it is, Cale and Bobby and I are all going to be fighting—but not against each other. We'll be on the same side."

Donnie knew that bad blood was nothing new in NASCAR. For proof of that, he only had to look as far as his brother, who had spent the better part of a decade cleaning Petty Blue paint out of dents in his fenders. But that rivalry, like most, simmered. It didn't rear its head every week, because you couldn't just put someone into the fence every time you got mad at him. The sport was described by Petty as "a live-and-let-live kind of deal." Said the King, "I'd hate to see us get to the place where if I crash you last week, it's for sure you're going to crash me this week." But that's exactly what fans were banking on, and that's exactly why the press box was flooded with out-of-towners. Bloodlust had gripped the sport. Papers in Houston and Jacksonville didn't send writers to see if Waltrip would hold on to his slim lead in the points race. They sent them to see if Donnie was going to get back at Cale for getting back at Donnie. And Richmond was a good place for it to happen. Banging was inevitable. The track is barely half a mile long and not especially wide, meaning that even if a driver decides he wants to steer clear of conflict, there's little room to hide. Said Bobby Allison, "Every time we go to Richmond we're wary of tempers flaring."

Only one driver was even remotely happy that the ill will was still

* "If you were writing a novel and you wanted a death threat from a Georgia redneck, that would be the letter," says Hinton.

lingering in the air: Darrell Waltrip. On his last trip to Richmond, in the fall of 1978, he had spun out leader Neil Bonnett nine laps from the end of the Capital City 400 and gone on to win. Bonnett had responded by ramming Wanda on pit road after the race and then trying to get at Waltrip in Victory Lane. NASCAR gave both drivers thirty days' probation, but Waltrip paid a far more severe price than Bonnett in the court of public opinion. He was booed lustily after the race, and the incident was routinely held up by Waltrip haters as further evidence of his moral turpitude. But no one was looking to dredge up that old story, not with the prospect of round three. "It's a hell of a break for me," Waltrip said. "I wasn't really looking forward to coming here."

Eager though he was to have things return to normal, Cale Yarborough wasn't about to hold his tongue. If anything, on Friday he seemed to be spoiling for a fight. He had been given a stall in the corner of the garage, isolated from everyone else, meaning that if he wanted casual chatter without having to walk across the garage to seek it out, he was going to have to settle for his crewmen or members of the press, several of whom were lurking near his car. As he talked to a couple of reporters, he took exception to the way his fellow drivers had reacted to the "racing incident" he had triggered the previous Sunday. In a clipped voice he said, "What happened at Rockingham could have happened to anybody. The real problem at Rockingham was two big mouths that started more trouble than anything else — Jaws One and Jaws Two."

He was referring to Petty, who didn't appreciate being dissed (or lumped in with Waltrip, for that matter). "Consider the source," Petty said. "Consider the source."

The back-and-forth only whetted the appetites of the fans. One Richmond writer suggested that tickets would be "as hard to come by as gold-filled chickens' teeth." Track officials announced that they were releasing 8,000 tickets on Saturday morning at 8:00. By 7:00 people were already lined up in the snow waiting for a crack at them. They might not have been so eager to brave the elements had they known that there was a movement afoot to bring the feud to an end through diplomacy. With some coaxing from Hoss Ellington, who was perhaps the most innocent victim in the whole wreckfest,* Donnie and Yarborough finally sat down face-to-face. For thirty minutes they hung out in the back of the NASCAR trailer. When they emerged, they were all smiles. "We talked about what good friends we've been all these years," Yarborough said. "We talked about everything—about bird hunting, deer hunting, coon hunting, about what a good pair of coon dogs I've got. It turns out Donnie doesn't have a good coon dog. I just might give him one."

But if the main combatants had agreed to a truce, word of the cease-fire didn't make it to the front. Junior Johnson was in the garage launching broadsides at Petty and Waltrip, who he felt had gone too far with their rebukes of Yarborough in Rockingham. Johnson claimed that Waltrip had "wrecked himself" by trying to speed through the crash instead of avoiding it. And he used an old defense attorney's trick to paint the King as an unreliable witness. "Petty's not god," Johnson said. "He's just another race car driver. He lied about Donnie getting alongside Cale in the first turn [at Rockingham]. He didn't get under him until they were going into three. A man that would tell a lie about one thing would tell a lie about another."[†]

Yarborough and Donnie planned to celebrate the thaw in their relations by having dinner together Saturday night, but their racing responsibilities forced them to cancel. When Allison finally left the track, he seemed also to leave behind the sense of peace that had been forged there. When he got back to the Holiday Inn, he began to agonize. The knock on Donnie had always been that he wasn't like Bobby, that he wasn't intense enough, that he didn't care enough about racing to put

---

* The value of his cars torn up in the two wrecks was around $120,000, and the damage to the second car from the Rockingham wreck kept him from being able to enter Neil Bonnett in the March 18 Atlanta race, as he had planned to do.

[†] Johnson also accused Waltrip's owner, Bill Gardner, of instructing Waltrip to wreck Yarborough in Rockingham after Wanda was repaired.

himself in the Mayo Clinic with stomach problems. But Donnie was fine with that. He believed there was more to life than racing, that it wasn't a life-or-death proposition. And now, wouldn't you know it, that's just what everyone seemed hell-bent on making it—literally, if the yokel letter writer from Atlanta was to be taken seriously.

He decided he had to talk to someone. He picked Hinton, who, as a writer, was the closest thing to a neutral party he was going to find. As Hinton headed into the Holiday Inn, Allison emerged from the shadows. "I don't know what to do," Allison said softly. "I've never been through anything like this before in my life. I don't know how to handle this."

"It'll die down," Hinton told him. "Everybody will go away as soon as you don't wreck each other."

Allison seemed relieved, but he was understandably still a little freaked about what might happen the next day.

Nothing happened.

Okay, stuff happened. But it wasn't the kind of stuff that was going to please sports editors, and it certainly wasn't the kind of stuff that was going to please the fans who were freezing their asses off in the hope that there might be some carnage in the offing. It snowed again Sunday morning and didn't stop until two hours before the green flag. In a repeat of Rockingham, the Allisons were cheered during driver introductions, while the three-time defending champ was given the Waltrip treatment. The race started under gray skies, as pole sitter Bobby Allison pulled away from the pack. Yarborough, who started ninth, was playing it safe and stroking. "I wanted to stay out of the crowd and take no chances of getting into any more trouble like that, and then make my move when the field got strung out and the traffic was thinner," he said. And Donnie Allison, who started eleventh, had handling problems from the start. His brother put him a lap down early in the race, and Yarborough got around him shortly thereafter. The pass was clean and uneventful, as Donnie, realizing he was no match for the leaders, pulled to the side and let Yarborough go.

And that's when people started leaving.

To the chagrin of many, the Richmond 400 was, according to Petty, "the cleanest race I ever saw." There were two caution periods for a total of ten laps. The first yellow came out on the second lap, when Dale Earnhardt hit a slick patch and spun, and the second flew when Baxter Price spun just after the midway point. There was one lead change in the race that was the result of a pass, not a pit stop: Yarborough got around Bobby on lap 225, and he gradually built a comfortable lead, winning by a cozy six-second margin. The closest thing to drama came with three laps left when Waltrip, who was one lap down, tapped Yarborough's bumper while fighting off Benny Parsons for third place. "He almost spun me out," said Yarborough. "I don't know what his problem is."

After the race, Bobby stood in the muddy infield talking to the press. One of the newbie reporters pointed out that it had been an exceptionally clean race. "Does that disappoint you?" Allison shot back. Yarborough was also short with the media. "Now I mean this," he said. "This press conference is going to be the last time I'm going to say anything about all that other mess. So there's no use in people asking me anymore. Like I told Bobby and Donnie, as far as I'm concerned, it's like all that stuff never happened." Yarborough was then asked by one of the regular beat writers what he thought of all the new faces in the press box. "I hope," Yarborough said, "that they'll now become interested in racing."

Standings After the Richmond 400

1.	Darrell Waltrip	637
2.	Cale Yarborough	624
3.	Bobby Allison	611
4.	Donnie Allison	536
5.	Joe Millikan	530
	...	
10.	Richard Petty	469

Chapter Eleven

Wild and Young, Crazy and Dumb

Its peace seemingly restored after Richmond, NASCAR moved the following week to Atlanta and then to North Wilkesboro, North Carolina, where Bobby Allison beat Richard Petty in a race that was, like every other sporting event that weekend, overshadowed by what was happening in Salt Lake City. On Saturday, March 24, in the first of the day's two NCAA basketball national semifinals, Michigan State sophomore Magic Johnson put up a triple double (29 points, 10 rebounds, 10 assists) in the Spartans' 101–67 undressing of the tournament's hopelessly overmatched Cinderella team, Penn. The Michigan State fans at the Special Events Center were so dismissive of the Quakers that they spent much of the game taunting fans of undefeated Indiana State, which was playing DePaul in the second game. "We want the Bird!" the Spartan fans chanted, to which the Sycamore fans responded, "You'll get the Bird!" (Many, with one finger, gave the State fans another kind of bird as well.) They all got their wish. Playing with a broken left thumb, Larry Bird had 35 points, 16 boards, and 9 assists in a 76–74 win, booking Indiana State's spot in Monday's championship game.

If the fans were thrilled about the prospect of a Bird-Magic matchup in the final, the people who inhabited the Manhattan offices of the National Basketball Association were ecstatic. The NBA was in trouble, and the Fifth Avenue suits knew it. The league had already decided to hire an outside PR firm—necessitating the quadrupling of the NBA's meager PR budget of $125,000—to deal with a litany of image problems, many of which had been spelled out the week after the Daytona 500 in a *Sports Illustrated* story titled "There's an Ill Wind Blowing for the NBA." Attendance in the big four markets—New York, Los Angeles, Chicago, and Philadelphia—was down from the previous season by an average of 24 percent. Jerry West, the coach of the Lakers—one of the league's best teams—lamented, "People I talk to around Los Angeles all tell me that there isn't a great deal of interest in either the Lakers or the NBA." And national TV ratings, never too good to begin with, were off by 26 percent. "Those twin indicators of public appeal—attendance and television ratings," wrote *SI*, "are disappointing, raising serious questions about the future of the sport."

The playoffs were just around the corner, but instead of drumming up interest in the NBA, the advent of the postseason only invited more criticism. At the start of the 1979 playoffs, the *Charlotte Observer* ran a column by *New York Daily News* columnist Mike Lupica* under the headline NBA'S PLAYOFFS BEGIN, BUT DOES ANYONE CARE? The piece centered on a ho-hum Friday night game between the Lakers and the Seattle SuperSonics aired by CBS—a game the network's Charlotte affiliate did not, as was its policy, broadcast. That was nothing new. The CBS affiliate in Atlanta, home to an NBA team since 1968, hadn't shown NBA games for five years.

In a way, the NBA had the same problem as NASCAR in the late 1970s: when it came to TV, it was largely relegated to the land of misfit sporting events. "CBS has been properly criticized for treating its telecasts as little more than a bridge between a refrigerator race and a golf tournament," wrote *SI*. Indeed, when CBS wasn't showing NBA

---

* In his pre-TV, pre-novel days, Lupica was something of a boy wonder in the newspaper business. In 1977, at age twenty-five, he had become the youngest sports columnist for a New York paper. That didn't stop the *Observer* from mistakenly calling him *Ron* Lupica in the byline.

Finals games on tape delay, the network was often trying to force the NBA to alter its schedule to allow more popular sports to be shown in choice time slots. As a result, Game 3 of the 1976 NBA Finals in Phoenix between the Suns and the Boston Celtics tipped off at 10:30 on a Sunday morning so that CBS could show the Kemper Open golf tournament in its entirety. Still, the outrage in Phoenix was mild at best, and it came mostly from members of the clergy.

But unlike NASCAR, the NBA had occasionally enjoyed prime-time exposure, and when it did, the results were abysmal. In the fall of 1978 *Variety* published the ratings of the 730 shows that appeared in prime time from September 1, 1977, through August 31, 1978. Four of the top five were sporting events, led by the Super Bowl. The highest-rated NBA broadcast, the deciding sixth game of the Celtics-Suns series, was tied for 442nd with *Peter Lundy and the Medicine Hat Stallion* (Leif Garrett as a Pony Express rider in pre–Civil War Nebraska), *The Hostage Heart* (terrorists in the OR!), and *Country Night of Stars* (Eddy Arnold!).

College basketball had proven only slightly less unappealing to television viewers. The 1978 NCAA title game between Duke and Kentucky was tied for 216th with *The Laughing Policeman, Battle of the Network Stars,* and *Hanna-Barbera's All-Star Comedy Ice Revue.* But the Magic-Bird game changed all that, even though as a game, it was nothing special. Bird was frustrated by his thumb injury and a stifling Michigan State matchup zone. He finished just 7 of 21 from the floor, and the Spartans were never really threatened in a 75–64 win. But the meeting of the sport's two brightest stars still pulled a 24.1 rating and a 38 share, numbers that had never been approached before and haven't been since.

That's just what the NBA was banking on. In May, Magic declared himself eligible for the 1979 draft under the league's hardship rule and was subsequently taken by the Lakers with the first pick. Bird's rights had been shrewdly snapped up by the Celtics a year earlier, meaning that they'd both be in the league in the fall of '79, which is why the NBA was optimistic that people might actually start paying attention to pro basketball.* In his column ripping the playoffs, Lupica wrote: "Hopefully this will be the last NBA season to be covered with such tedium and disgust. Players like Larry Bird and 'Magic' Johnson...can begin to change things next season. But for now, the NBA playoffs, once so special, are nothing more than a sideshow for a faltering circus. The circus will still be playing in June. By then, no one outside of two cities will care."

Marketing players is nothing new. There have always been superstars. But in the late 1970s and early '80s, they became something bigger. They became personalities. The biggest sports star in the mid-'70s was probably Cincinnati Reds third baseman Pete Rose. When would a kid in Topeka ever see Pete Rose play, let alone listen to him talk? Sure, he'd hear about him. But actually lay eyes on him? The All-Star Game. Maybe once or twice a season on *Monday Night Baseball*. The playoffs, if the Reds had a good year. Past that, Rose was just a face on a baseball card, a guy to be read about in the sports pages, that dude who warbled embarrassingly alongside Vic Tayback in a commercial for Aqua Velva.

But the '80s brought about new means by which Rose and his cohorts could infiltrate their fans' lives. Cable TV meant a wider audience for games and highlights. In 1982 *USA Today* hit the shelves. Computers meant players had their own personalized video games, such as Dr. J and Larry Bird Go One on One. Magic and Bird had their Converse Weapon deals; Jordan shilled his Air Jordans. And the process fed on itself. The more we saw of Bird—hey, there he is selling Chardon jeans or playing H-O-R-S-E with Michael Jordan in a McDonald's commercial—the more famous he got, which meant we saw even more of him. Being a superstar was no longer the pinnacle of athletic achievement. No, in the 1980s you had to be a megastar.

_____

*LA got the pick from New Orleans as compensation for the Jazz signing Gail Goodrich in 1976 and then won a coin toss with the Bulls for the top pick overall. Boston was able to draft Bird with the sixth pick of the '78 draft because of the NBA's arcane "junior eligible" rule, which was taken off the books shortly after the Celtics landed Bird.

No sport thrived more in that new era than pro basketball, which rode Bird and Magic—and Jordan a few years later—to unprecedented heights. In 1979 just six of the NBA's twenty-two teams averaged 12,000 fans per game, and the average attendance was 10,756. In 1989 twenty-one of twenty-five teams were pulling in 12,000 people a game, and the average had climbed to 15,073, an increase of 42 percent—by far the largest increase of the four major sports.* As for the second indicator of public appeal, TV ratings, the NBA was the only sport to see its viewership rise between 1979 and 1984. Which explains why CBS, which nearly dropped the NBA in 1978 in the middle of a contract that paid the NBA $11 million a season, signed a four-year, $173 million deal with the league seven years later.

Of course, all that success can't be laid at the Converse-clad feet of Bird and Magic. But the NBA's growth showed that hitching its star to larger-than-life personalities—especially Bird, who gave the NBA what it so sorely needed, a Great White Hope that its fans could relate to[†]—was a viable growth model, especially if the sport in question had a lot of room to grow.

A sport like NASCAR.

There was remarkable overlap in the life stories of Larry Joe Bird and Ralph Dale Earnhardt. Many of the similarities were superficial: The sandy hair. The beady blue eyes. The mustache. The twang in the voice.

---

*Baseball attendance rose by 27 percent over the same period, the NHL was up by 17 percent, and the NFL held steady.

[†] The subject of race in the NBA wasn't danced around by blacks or whites. "This is something we must no longer whisper about," Denver general manager Carl Scheer told *Sports Illustrated* in 1978. "It's definitely a problem and we, the owners, created it. People see our players as being overpaid and underworked, and the majority of them are black." His sentiments were echoed by Seattle forward Paul Silas, a black player who was the president of the NBA Players Association: "It is a fact that white people in general look disfavorably upon blacks who are making astronomical amounts of money if it appears they are not working hard for that money."

The *I'm having the time of my life because I'm so damn good at what I do* smirk. But their paths to stardom also had a lot of similar landmarks.

Bird was a self-described "hick from French Lick," a factory town in southwestern Indiana, a place where everyone was obsessed with one sport—basketball. His early life had been bumpy. He'd had a difficult relationship with his father, a Korean War vet who had killed himself when he couldn't adjust to life back in the States. Then he'd married early and dropped out of college for a year, which he spent working as a garbageman.

Earnhardt was a "linthead." That's what everyone from Kannapolis, North Carolina, was called, on account of the Cannon textile mill that dominated the town's otherwise unremarkable skyline. Without the mill, there wouldn't have been a Kannapolis. It was carved out of what had been a cotton plantation northeast of Charlotte in the first decade of the twentieth century by James William Cannon, who needed a place to house his workers and their families. Cannon-opolis, as it was originally called, was organized in a series of grids, with the street names in each grid sharing a theme. Earnhardt's family lived in an area known as Car Town, at the corner of Sedan and Coach.

If basketball was made for Indiana, short-track auto racing was made for North Carolina. The soil—a thick red clay that packed just right—made a perfect racing surface. Tracks sprang up all over the Charlotte area, where every neighborhood had at least one or two shade-tree mechanics who turned wrenches on their cars after work or on the weekend. Ralph Earnhardt was one, at least until he quit his job at the mill and started racing full-time in cars he built in the cinder block shop in his backyard. His middle young 'un, as Dale's mother called him, was Ralph's biggest fan, and Dale often found himself drifting into the same kind of dazes that made Larry Bird such an average student. "I can remember being in school," Dale said in 1979, "counting the seconds ticking off the clock until class was over and I could go home and help him in the racing shop."

*　　*　　*

Ralph Earnhardt was a stoic man, described by one friend as "taciturn to a fault."* He was devoted to his family, so much so that he passed on a Grand National career in favor of dirt tracking in the Carolinas so he wouldn't have to be away from his wife, Martha, and their three kids. And he steadfastly refused to put the family in debt by borrowing money to fund his racing. That necessitated a conservative on-track style. He'd lay back and keep his car out of trouble, not showing his hand until he absolutely had to. It kept the repair bills down, and it won him a lot of races to boot: he was the 1956 NASCAR Sportsman champion. As good as he was at driving a car, Ralph might have been even better at putting one together.† "He never worked on the car at the track," says Humpy Wheeler. "He was always perfectly prepared. Everyone else would be working, and Ralph would be leaning against his car, smoking a cigarette."

Eventually, Dale got sick of counting down the seconds left in the school day, so he dropped out at fourteen. "It was the only thing I ever let my daddy down over," Earnhardt said in 1987. "He wanted me to finish. It was the only thing he ever pleaded with me to do. But I was so hardheaded. For about a year and a half after that, we didn't have a close relationship."

He got a job as a mechanic at Punch's Wheel Shop in Concord, a gig he gave up in 1973, when he was twenty-two, to have a go at a racing career. When Earnhardt handed in his notice, Punch Whitaker's immortal reply was "You're going to starve, boy." In retrospect, ol' Punch was wide of the mark. But for a while it looked like he had gauged the situation perfectly. Dale was, by his own admission, "wild and crazy, young and dumb." His favorite movie was *Animal House,* which apparently inspired

---

* Ralph was played by J. K. Simmons in *3,* the ESPN movie about Dale's life, which pretty much tells you all you need to know about Ralph.
† He built cars for other drivers, too, most of whom were racers. "Ralph was well-known for building engines for cars that would transport liquids other than gasoline," said his friend Marshall Brooks.

Earnhardt as much as it entertained him. To wit: One late night Earnhardt and a friend, a motorcycle shop owner named Marshall Brooks, were cruising Kannapolis in a truck that Brooks used to haul bikes. The truck had a loudspeaker, the kind of toy that made Earnhardt's eyes light up. He suggested that they go and harass his brother-in-law. They parked outside the house and ordered the inhabitants to come out with their hands over their heads, but they got no reaction. Dejected, Brooks took Earnhardt home, but as he made his way back to his place, he noticed several flashing lights in his rearview mirror. The house hadn't belonged to Earnhardt's brother-in-law after all, but rather to Clifford Cook, a lawman who was none too amused. With some sweet-talking, Brooks was able to convince Cook not to haul him down to the slammer. Brooks confronted Earnhardt over the prank the next day. "He was sitting on the floor in the middle of the shop," said Brooks. "When he saw me pull up, I saw him cock his head sideways, and that little grin came out. He thought it was the funniest thing in the world."

So it should come as little surprise to learn that Earnhardt had been married at seventeen, divorced at nineteen, and remarried at twenty. By the time he quit Punch's shop, he already had three kids. A fourth, Dale Jr., would be born within a year, and his second marriage would end shortly thereafter. His family, he said, "probably should have been on welfare.... For our family cars, we drove old junk Chevelles, anything we could get for $200."

As his career progressed, Dale and his father slowly reconciled, largely through time spent together in the shop. Ralph began playing an active role in Dale's blossoming driving career. They built a go-kart, and Dale started driving on dirt. Then on September 26, 1973, Ralph died.

As Dale Earnhardt became more famous, the circumstances surrounding his father's death were romanticized. The most common story to evolve was that he was tuning a carburetor in the backyard when he suffered a massive heart attack. In some versions of the tale,

Dale was the one who found the body. In reality, Ralph had a heart attack, and Martha found him on the kitchen floor. Dale was gutted. "I didn't know which way to turn, what to do, where to go for help and advice," Dale said in 1979. "I was helpless. I tried to go hunting. I couldn't. Everywhere I looked, there he stood, gun in hand. I sold his bird dogs." When he was working on his car, he found himself talking to Ralph, asking how to fix that carburetor or what gear he should be using. "Sometimes, late at night, I would sit down and cry for an hour without stopping," he said.

After Ralph died, Martha gave Dale his cars. And at that point, there was no more wavering about how committed Dale was to racing. He was in it for good. "Daddy had begun to help me," Earnhardt said in 1987. "Then he died. It left me in a situation where I had to make it on my own. I'd give up everything I got if he were still alive, but I don't think I'd be where I am if he hadn't died."

Ralph's death pushed Dale into a world he was destined to conquer, but one he might not have seemed ready for at the time. He didn't look like he belonged. For starters, there was his getup. Says Darrell Waltrip, "Dale was always saying, 'I need to get a break. I need to get a break. I got to get off these dirt tracks. I can't ever make it if I just run dirt. I don't want to end up like all these other guys, spending my whole life running on short tracks and dirt tracks. I want to be out there with you.' I kind of looked at him like, *Good luck*. Because he was rough. He had a scruffy old mustache, and he always had on a dirty T-shirt and a pair of high-water pants, a pair of Hush Puppies. Always wanting to borrow something. If you looked at him and said, 'Will this guy ever make it?' You'd probably have said, 'Nah, I don't know. Questionable.'"

Lou LaRosa, who'd later build engines for Earnhardt, remembers seeing him drive at Metrolina Speedway in Charlotte. "He was no great driver," says LaRosa. "He wasn't a superstar. Only time you heard of Dale is when he flipped the son of a bitch in Atlanta."

The son of a bitch in question was a Chevrolet belonging to man named Johnny Ray. They hooked up right around the time Earnhardt was at his lowest. He'd wrecked everything his dad had left him and was forced to go to Robert Gee, his second ex–father-in-law, with his hat in hand.* Gee put him to work in his shop, doing things like painting cars orange in an unventilated room. Earnhardt would leave at the end of the day looking like the world's most avid University of Tennessee fan, but in exchange for the work, Gee let Earnhardt drive his Sportsman car.

Late in 1976 Gee convinced Ray to put Earnhardt in a Grand National car for the fall race in Atlanta. Aware that Earnhardt's reputation might kill the deal, Gee agreed to fix any damage Earnhardt might do to the car. Waltrip kept his car at Gee's shop, and Gee told him about the arrangement. "I said, 'Well, you might as well get ready to be fixing that thing, because you know Dale is going to tear it up,'" says Waltrip. "Because he was reckless. He just drove like an idiot—run over people, run over anything. He had one speed, and it was like a bull in a china shop. No finesse. Just throw it in there and hope it sticks.

"So anyway, at Atlanta, I come off of Turn 2, the caution lights come on, and I see a car flying through the air, bouncing, rolling, tumbling down the back straightaway. Get down there, and guess who it was: Earnhardt, in Johnny Ray's car. Tore it all to pieces. Totaled it." The wreck was so bad that Richard Petty radioed to his crew, "I think they just killed Ralph Earnhardt's boy."

Earnhardt's driving style had just as much to do with his situation as it did with his naturally aggressive personality. Stroking in a one-time deal wasn't going to do him any good. He needed to get noticed, and being conservative wasn't going to do that. But if you put him in a situation where he didn't feel like he had to drive the wheels off the car, he could put his natural gifts on display. One day in 1978 NASCAR

---

* Gee was Dale Earnhardt Jr.'s grandfather; his daughter Brenda is Junior's mom.

historian Greg Fielden was watching him turn practice laps at Myrtle Beach Speedway, a little old oval with ivy on the wall. Every time Earnhardt went past Fielden, he'd clip a piece of ivy. The groove wasn't that close to the wall; Earnhardt was just doing it for practice, or fun. Awed by the display of precision, Fielden asked, "Are they paying you to clip that ivy off the wall?" Then, says Fielden, "he gave me that possum-eating shit grin and said, 'You noticed that, huh?'"

As freakishly gifted as he was, Earnhardt never forgot who he was. Bird was the same way, which went a long way toward explaining his popularity. When he was presented with the 1984 NBA Most Valuable Player Award at a black-tie affair, Bird accepted it in a bowling shirt. A 1981 *Sports Illustrated* profile noted that aside from basketball, "the rest of his pleasure comes from winning, mowing his lawn, drinking beer, hunting squirrels, fishing, playing golf, and being with friends and family." The same could be said about Earnhardt, except he was partial to chopping wood, not mowing the lawn, and his preferred quarry was deer, not squirrels. He was easy to relate to. People wanted to be like him, the guy who drove his car hard and reckless and knocked the hell out of whoever got in his way. "You have a tremendous amount of transference at the racetrack," says Humpy Wheeler. "People subconsciously become the driver of that car. And here's a kid who came from the bottom, worked hard for everything he got, and didn't have any airs about him. Truck drivers, dockworkers, welders, and shrimp-boat captains loved that. He was everything they dreamed about being."

So all those fans sat in the stands worshipping him because he seemed like the kind of guy they could kick back and go hunting with. And he was. Late in the '79 season, he was driving a beat-up Chevy pickup truck in Charlotte when he saw something in the back of the truck in front of him that piqued his interest: a big, dead deer. He followed the driver to a gas station, then approached him. "I see you've got blood on your shoes," he said. "You either been fighting or hunting." Earnhardt then demanded that the stranger, Frankie Fraley, take him hunting the next morning and show him where he'd bagged the buck.

He and Fraley eventually became such good friends that Earnhardt made Fraley join his race team, even though Fraley, who built mobile homes and raised dairy cows, hated racing. The lengths to which Earnhardt would go to hunt were astonishing. Stalking a stranger on the road was nothing. He'd come to Fraley's at three in the morning to help him milk the cows so he'd have time to hunt. "He'd show up in the milk barn with donuts and Coke," says Fraley. "He'd say, 'We're not having milk.'"

One year Fraley held a dirt bike race on his property, and he got Earnhardt to come out and serve as the honorary starter. Earnhardt waved the flag and then hopped on a four-wheeler, telling Fraley he wanted to go find a good vantage point to watch the race. When it ended two hours later, Earnhardt was nowhere to be seen. Trophies were handed out. No Earnhardt. Finally, around dusk, he appeared, carrying a rifle. Despite the fact that it was a Sunday, which meant no hunting, he thought the race might provide him with an opportunity too good to pass up. "I thought those motorcycles running around would run some deer across," he said.

"Whatever he was doing," says Fraley, "he'd be thinking about hunting."

And God help the man who went hunting or fishing without Earnhardt. In 1989 Neil Bonnett broke his sternum, so he sat out the fall race in Charlotte. Bonnett and Fraley decided to take advantage of Bonnett's time off by launching a boat on the pond on Earnhardt's property and doing some fishing. When Earnhardt got home from the track, he was incensed that his friends were having fun without him. He demonstrated his displeasure by firing several shots across their bow with a high-powered rifle.

That was Earnhardt. Just a guy who'd rather be hunting.

He had the makeup to be NASCAR's megastar, its Bird, and the time was right. But there was one more thing. He had to start winning.

Chapter Twelve

Diamonds As Big As Horse Turds

Sunday, April 1
Race 7: Southeastern 500
Bristol, Tennessee

DALE EARNHARDT's 1979 ride was procured at the end of a very strange 1978. In May he made his fifth career Grand National start, in Will Cronkrite's car in the World 600 in Charlotte. Earnhardt hadn't been Cronkrite's first choice. Humpy Wheeler, always looking for a way to drum up publicity at his home track, convinced Cronkrite to give the seat to Willy T. Ribbs, a twenty-three-year-old Californian who happened to be black, which made him something of a novelty in NASCAR. Ribbs certainly had the bona fides—he'd cut his teeth driving in Europe, where he'd won the Formula Ford series championship in his first year. He also shared Wheeler's knack for promotion, possibly to a fault, which became apparent two days after Wheeler introduced him to the press as "what we promoters have been waiting for since Wendell Scott."*

---

*Scott remains to this day the only black driver to win a Grand National race. His life story was told in the 1977 film *Greased Lightning,* with Richard Pryor as Scott.

Late in the evening, Ribbs was spotted by the Charlotte cops going the wrong way down a one-way street in a Charlotte Motor Speedway pace car. His racer's instincts getting the better of him, Ribbs tried to outrun the police and wound up near Queens College, in an upscale part of town. He ditched the car and hightailed it into a gym, where he picked up a basketball and was casually working on his jump shot when the cops happened upon him. Ribbs insisted that he was a student, a defense that might have flown better had Queens College not been an all-girls school that was, in the words of one of the arresting officers, "lily white." When Ribbs was booked, he didn't call a lawyer or Wheeler. No, he called a writer, Tom Higgins of the *Charlotte Observer*. "I'm fine," he told Higgins. "I just thought you'd like to know about me getting nabbed."

A few weeks later Ribbs was a no-show at a couple of practice sessions, and Wheeler and Cronkrite pulled the plug on the experiment. "There could be rednecks with deer rifles out in that infield," Wheeler told Ribbs. Cronkrite gave the ride to Earnhardt, who finished a creditable seventeenth—ahead of both cars entered by Rod Osterlund.

Osterlund was yet another owner with deep pockets who was new to the game. He was from Northern California, where he'd made his fortune in real estate. Like Bill Gardner's pinochle game, Osterlund's introduction to racing was nontraditional. His daughter Lana went to high school with three guys—Dave D'Ambrosio, Jeff Prescott, and Doug Richert—who liked to work on cars and race them at tracks in the San Jose area. "He got interested in who his daughter was hanging out with," says D'Ambrosio. "Then got interested in the racing part of it."

Osterlund wasn't the kind of man who half-assed things. Before long he decided that he wanted to build a real team, one that could be competitive at the sport's highest level. In the summer of 1977 he decided to move the operation, including Richert and D'Ambrosio, to North Carolina. So what if they were still in high school. "Our parents saw how dedicated we were to it, and there was a lot of infrastructure," says D'Ambrosio. "It was the same group we had been running with for the last three or four years. There was a comfort level involved. Rod made sure we were taken care of." They loaded up a truck and trekked across the country, with Richert celebrating his seventeenth birthday on the highway in the middle of Texas. Osterlund also brought along Roland Wlodyka, a thirty-eight-year-old contractor who had done some work for Osterlund and also did a little driving. When they arrived in Charlotte, D'Ambrosio and Richert moved into a fifth-wheel trailer parked at an amusement park near the South Carolina state line. After six months they moved it to the parking lot outside the shop, which was near the Charlotte Motor Speedway. "We'd get up, go have breakfast at the Pit Stop Grill, come back across the street, work, work, work, then go back to the trailer and go back to sleep," says D'Ambrosio. "We didn't make any money—I think it was $123 a week—but everything was paid for."

Osterlund's ownership style was Steinbrenneresque: he had a checkbook and a pen, and he wasn't afraid to use them. He built a shop; poached some talent from DiGard, including Nick Ollila; and hired veteran engine builder Ducky Newman and his protégé, Long Island native Lou LaRosa. The team manager was Wlodyka, whose brashness would make him Billy Martin in this New York Yankees analogy. "Roland had a Northern California smart-ass attitude, like he was trying to convert the good ol' boy network," says Ollila. "He assumed they were all stupid and since they spoke with a southern drawl they couldn't add or subtract, and therefore he was going to be smarter than them. He alienated so many people. He would say it to people's faces, the Pettys and the Pearsons: 'You guys are a bunch of dumb-ass rednecks.'"

Wlodyka also drove for a spell, and he spread about as much joy on the track as he did in the garage. He didn't have much experience, but that didn't bother him. "Roland was braver than Dick Tracy," says LaRosa. "Not a great driver, but fearless." When it became apparent late in the 1977 season that there was more to driving than possessing a square-jawed resolve, Osterlund hired Dave Marcis, an old schooler from Wisconsin who was best known for finishing second in points in 1975 and for driving in wing tips.*

In the eyes of Osterlund and Wlodyka, at least, Marcis's problem was that he wasn't enough like Dick Tracy. Marcis was getting decent results—he finished the '78 season with twenty-four top 10s in thirty starts—but he wasn't winning any races. (Even in his best season, when he finished runner-up to Petty in '75, he won only once.) Osterlund began making noise about dropping him for the '79 season. He took a list of potential replacements to Cale Yarborough in the fall of '78 and asked him whom he should hire. Osterlund might have been hoping that Yarborough would say, "Hell, I'll race for you." Instead, Yarborough picked the most inexperienced driver on the list: Ralph Earnhardt's boy.

Dale Earnhardt had another benefactor, longtime family friend Humpy Wheeler. Wheeler leaned on Osterlund to give Earnhardt a shot. That might have been enough to convince Osterlund, but just to be safe, Wheeler relied on something that tends to be more effective than a persuasive argument: cash. Five grand got Earnhardt a seat in a second Osterlund car in the November Atlanta race, the next-to-last event of the season.

But first Wheeler wanted to get Earnhardt in the Sportsman race at Charlotte in October. Osterlund relented, putting him in a car that Marcis had totaled a few weeks earlier in Darlington. "It was twisted every which way," says LaRosa. Richert, working with brothers Jim and Bill Delaney, took the frame off the junk heap and fashioned the mangled Grand National vehicle into a Sportsman car; LaRosa built the engine. Earnhardt finished second and would have won were it not for problems with the clutch.

Marcis couldn't help but notice the attention being lavished on

---

* Not necessarily in that order.

Earnhardt. "I think the jealousy was there already, or the animosity," says LaRosa. Late in the Atlanta race, Marcis, who was making his 310th career start, gave Earnhardt a rap. The rookie code held that Earnhardt take the contact and like it, but Earnhardt wasn't the type to stand on ceremony. He popped the veteran back. If Marcis was expecting Osterlund to reprimand Earnhardt, he was disappointed. After the race no one said a word about the contact. Marcis finished the race third, one spot ahead of Earnhardt, but he didn't need any help reading the writing on the wall. He drove the season finale, then quit. Earnhardt would be Osterlund's driver in 1979.

Hiring Earnhardt guaranteed one thing: Osterlund and Wlodyka wouldn't be able to complain that their driver wasn't aggressive enough. In January of '79 they took a car to Daytona for testing. It was a Buick with a square back, which made it about 4 miles per hour slower than the Oldsmobiles most drivers were using. But the idea was that it would handle better in the draft, which would make up for the lack of pure speed. After a few practice runs by himself, Earnhardt was disgusted with the results. LaRosa tried to tell him that he shouldn't worry, that when he ran with other cars, his times would pick up. Earnhardt was having none of it. "Put a smaller spoiler on it," he said.* Still slow. So the spoiler got gradually smaller, until Earnhardt finally told LaRosa to take the damn thing off.

"Dale, you can't run without a spoiler," LaRosa told him.

"Who's driving the son of a bitch, me or you?" Earnhardt said.

Off came the spoiler.

"He went through the tri-oval about sideways," remembers LaRosa. "You heard the engine roar, then get quiet when he came off the gas. He came into the pits white as a ghost and said, 'Put the spoiler back on.'"

---

* A spoiler is a metal strip on the trunk that keeps the back end of the car on the track. A small spoiler reduces drag and makes the car faster, but it does so at the expense of stability.

Earnhardt obviously had the nerve, and he had the desire. He was driving well in spells, but his aggressiveness was leading to a lot of mistakes. He slipped the clutch and broke the transmission in Riverside. He got pissed at his crew, revved his motor, and broke the engine in Daytona. He ran too hard on a slick track and spun out on the second lap in Richmond. He ran out of gas in Atlanta. And he was used to driving a Sportsman car, which was lighter and handled differently than a Grand National car.

Yeah, he had the nerve, and he had the desire. What he needed was someone to guide him through this new world.

If there was ever a car whisperer, it was Jake Elder. "Suitcase Jake," he was called, on account of his penchant for blowing into town, instantly improving the fortunes of a race team, and then leaving as suddenly as he had arrived. He was shrouded in an air of mystery, and not just because of his peripatetic ways. Elder had a third-grade education and was illiterate, which ruled out keeping notes on setups. Instead, he carried two tape measures—one for short tracks, one for longer tracks. On the side opposite the ruler he made a series of marks with a felt-tip pen that corresponded with various points on the car. No one was sure exactly how the system worked, but Elder would unroll the tape measure, hold it up against the car, and tinker with the body a little. The end result would be a perfect setup. Elder had a few other tricks. Like every crew chief, he'd lie down on a creeper and slide under the car to check out the setup. Unlike every other crew chief, he'd then slide under an adjacent car and check out *its* setup. Then another, and another, as far down the garage as he could make it until someone noticed him.

"Jake was a simple man," says LaRosa. "If he told you something, it was true. He didn't get paid to read or write. He got paid to make that race car go fast." And he did. Elder won championships with David Pearson in 1968 and '69, but he was best known for mentoring green drivers.

"The reason I had success early on is that Jake could make a car drive right," says Darrell Waltrip, who worked with Elder in the mid-1970s. "I've driven cars that didn't drive right. That just scares the hell out of you. You don't know if it's you, you don't know if it's the car, or you just don't know if you can't do this. Because if you've never been in a car that drives right, you say, 'Man, this is scaring the hell out of me. I can't do this. These things will hurt you. I'm going to wreck this thing.' And that's what Jake could do for everybody that he ever worked with: when you got in that car and you went around the racetrack, you drove the car — the car didn't drive you. I'd get in some other people's cars, and man they'd dart and dive all over the place — scare the heck out of you. And I'd say, 'Forget speed — the car's not going to go fast if you can't drive it. But you can really drive it fast if it handles right and drives right.'

"And that was what he was good at. Could he do anything else? No. But he could look at a race car and tell you what was wrong with it. He could look at the suspension, or he could look at the toe, or he could look at the body — he just had a sense about him. He knew a race car from one end to the other."

In December 1978 Osterlund announced that he had hired Elder, but as was Suitcase Jake's wont, he backed out of the deal the same day and took a job under Herb Nab on Buddy Baker's crew. He reconsidered in the spring of '79, dumping Nab and signing with Osterlund. When the deal was announced in Atlanta, Elder showed that he hadn't moved past his fear of commitment. "I made a mistake [in December], now I want to give Osterlund a shot," Elder said. "If after two months we can't get along, then I'll leave."

Even a two-month marriage seemed optimistic. Working for Osterlund — who was based in California and traveled to only about a quarter of the races — really meant working for Wlodyka, which was proving to be a less-than-attractive proposition. Marcis laid into Wlodyka after he quit, and Ducky Newman had harsh words for the operation when he jumped ship in January to go build engines for Benny Parsons. "The money was better, but the real reason I decided to leave Osterlund is because I couldn't get along with Roland," said Newman. "If we'd had a good crew chief things might have been different."

In the other corner was Elder, himself a perennial no-hoper in the Boss of the Year competition. "Oh, man, he was a nut," says Waltrip. "He had to do it all himself. And that's probably some of that insecurity from not being able to read or write. He couldn't work with people. He had to do it himself. He didn't want anybody helping him. He didn't trust anybody, for one thing. He worked himself to death, because that's all he knew how to do. He couldn't communicate with other people because he didn't know how. He had paychecks in his pocket from when he worked at Holman Moody that he had never cashed."

"Jake could be psychotic at times," says Ollila. "Then the next day we'd be at the Derita Grille, eating lunch together like nothing had happened." Those meals were occasionally eventful. "We'd be at the restaurant, and we'd have our menus out," says Ollila. "I knew he couldn't read. He'd look at me and say, 'What are you going to get?' So I'd point at something I knew he hated, like liver and onions, and say, 'I'm going to get that.' So when the waitress would come, he'd point to that. Then his dinner would come, and he'd say, 'Damn you, you know I hate that shit. Why'd you point that out?'"

Elder's my-way-or-the-highway routine might not have flown with the crew, but it worked wonders with the drivers. Earnhardt — whose nickname early in his career was Ironhead, a play on his father's nickname, Ironheart — occasionally tried to buck him, and when he did, Elder wasted little time forcefully reminding "the boy," as he called him, that he was the boss. But for the most part, they worked well together. In their second race, Earnhardt finished a career-best fourth at North Wilkesboro. Says LaRosa, "If you ask me the one thing that made Dale — Jake Elder settled his ass down and helped refine him as a driver. He was going to be a good driver no matter what, but Jake helped him hurry up and get there sooner."

Waltrip puts it more simply: "Jake made my career, and he made Dale's, too."

There was a palpable sense of inevitability lingering over the Earnhardt team in the garage the day before the Southeastern 500. The writers who followed the circuit were by now pretty sure that Earnhardt had the talent and the equipment to win a race—even though no rookie had done so since 1974—so they started paying attention to him. Gene Granger of *Grand National Scene* was hanging around the Earnhardt stall, observing the ball breaking (Ollila was taking heat for being Swedish) and pondering aloud what it would be like when Earnhardt won a race: "He'll be saying, 'I'm not going to talk to you. You haven't written anything about me.' I'll bet he'll crack up the press."

If he was going to win, Bristol was as good a place as any to start. It's barely half a mile long, and it's banked more steeply than Daytona—36 degrees—so it rewards a driver who can bang a little and isn't afraid to stand on the gas. Buddy Baker qualified on the pole for the 500-lapper, but when he and Yarborough took each other out—Yarborough's third wreck in seven races—it became a two-car race for the final 235 laps: Earnhardt and Waltrip. Neither could get around the other when the green flag was out, so when the yellow flag came out on lap 473, both men knew that whoever got out of the pits first was going to win. It was Earnhardt. With each lap he pulled away a little more from Waltrip, who got a bad set of tires. "I really had to make an effort not to let myself get over-anxious," Earnhardt said. "The last 15 laps, I worked to make every corner count."

The win changed a lot of lives. As payment for various bets, Earnhardt shaved his mustache, and Doug Richert quit smoking. But more significantly, it put the team in NASCAR's Winner's Circle program, which meant they'd get a bigger chunk of the purses for the rest of '79 and all of '80. So while the oversize check Earnhardt received in Victory Lane was for just $19,800, the win was worth, all told, around $200,000. "When we qualified ninth for this race, we didn't win tires or nothing," said Elder. "Now we can go out and buy all we need."

There was no reason to think this wasn't the start of something big. "Stick with me," Elder told Earnhardt after the race, "and we'll both be wearing diamonds as big as horse turds."

Standings After the Southeastern 500

1.	Bobby Allison	1,146
2.	Darrell Waltrip	1,132
3.	Cale Yarborough	1,028
4.	Benny Parsons	978
5.	Dale Earnhardt	975
	...	
8.	Richard Petty	939

Chapter Thirteen

Pearson's Kerfuffle

Sunday, April 8
Race 8: CRC Chemicals Rebel 500
Darlington, South Carolina

DARLINGTON IS located a few miles north of Florence, South Carolina. To get there from Charlotte, you drive south for about an hour and a half on Highway 151, a road named in different places for two local major league baseball players: Bobo Newsom and Van Lingle Mungo.* The pace of life was pretty slow. In setting the scene for the Rebel 500, ABC's Jim McKay said of Darlington, "Population 7,500. They grow tobacco and cotton and soybeans around here, and on Saturdays some of the good ol' boys go down to the barbershop to watch some haircuts."

---

*Mungo and Newsom, who had two of the greatest names in baseball history, both played for the Brooklyn Dodgers in the 1930s, but they never overlapped. Newsom is best known for being a four-time All-Star. Mungo is best known for being smuggled out of Cuba in a laundry cart by Dodgers officials after he was caught in flagrante delicto with a dancer by her butcher knife–wielding husband.

The idea for putting a superspeedway in such a rustic setting first came to Harold Brasington, a local businessman and occasional driver, in 1933 after he returned from Indianapolis, where he watched Louis Meyer win the Indy 500. Not surprisingly, Brasington had a little trouble getting the project off the ground. Given the ramshackle state of stock car racing at the time, there was no way to justify building a huge track in rural South Carolina in the middle of the Depression. But after the war — and after Bill France Sr. brought some order to the sport — Brasington finally pushed forward with his plan. He purchased some land from a poker buddy, Sherman Ramsey, who sold it with one caveat: that the minnow pond on the corner of the property not be disturbed.

When baseball stadiums were built in the early part of the twentieth century, they tended to be constructed in developed areas, leaving their architects at the mercy of existing streets and buildings. Hence the ridiculously odd shape of, say, Cleveland's League Park* and the nooks and crannies of Boston's Fenway Park. Ramsey's request left Brasington in a similar bind, so one end of the track had to be narrower than the other. The result was a quirky racetrack with character and a charm sorely lacking in so many of the cookie-cutter tracks that have sprung up over the past fifteen years.

Getting Darlington Raceway built was no easy task. Brasington did much of the work himself, bulldozing the dirt into mounds for the banked turns. He worked around the clock and even on Sundays, which, according to one local, "brought rebuke from his church." Unbowed by the congregation's collective stink eye, Brasington finished his mile-and-a-quarter, 25-degree-banked, egg-shaped track in 1950, and the first race was held on Labor Day. Seventy-five drivers showed up, and not one of them knew what they were getting into. Up to that point, NASCAR had run twenty races; eighteen had been

---

* The right field fence was just 290 feet from home plate, but it was 461 feet to center field.

on paved tracks, and only the two Daytona Beach races had been on a course of more than a mile. A steep, long, asphalt track was new on all three counts. The biggest problem presented by Brasington's beast — which would soon earn the ominous appellations "the Track Too Tough to Tame" and "the Lady in Black"* — was tire wear. For years "grand theft Goodyear" was a Darlington tradition: desperate crew members would head into the infield mid-race and pinch tires from spectators' cars. (The trick was to find a spectator who had already passed out; they put up the least fight.) The inaugural 400-lap race was won by Johnny Mantz, an Indy car driver who equipped his 1950 Plymouth with harder truck tires. Mantz was slow — he started forty-third — but he avoided the blowouts that plagued every other car in the field. He won by 9 laps and led for the final 351.

The other thing that made Darlington such a challenge was its racing groove. The track was narrow, and the fastest line required that a driver scrape up against the wall coming out of Turn 4, which left the car with a "Darlington stripe" on the passenger side door.† "I put more effort into doing well here than I do anywhere else because it's always considered to be a drivers' racetrack," Darrell Waltrip told ABC before the Rebel 500. "You feel like, *If I'm going to be a great race car driver or if I am of great race driver quality, then I have to excel at Darlington.*" And Waltrip had excelled: he had a win and four runner-up finishes at the track heading into 1979.

With just over 100 of the 367 laps remaining in the Rebel 500, only three cars were on the lead lap: Waltrip, Richard Petty, and pole sitter Donnie Allison. There hadn't been many wrecks, but in her typical fashion, the

---

* For years drivers had to watch a movie before they could race on the track. The flick was similar in tone and production values to those gorefests they show in drivers ed. "They showed about a hundred wrecks," says Ricky Rudd.
† The track was reconfigured in 1997. What are now Turns 1 and 2 were then Turns 3 and 4.

Lady in Black found other ways to vex the big names. Bobby Allison cut four tires before his engine finally blew after 246 laps, relegating him to a twenty-sixth-place finish. Cale Yarborough kept running out of gas and was three laps down. And David Pearson cut a tire and went a lap down, but his car was still strong. He was hanging with the leaders, trying to force his way back onto the lead lap. Pearson was in a frantic duel with Yarborough's lapped car. A wreck looked inevitable, but Pearson finally got around Yarborough, prompting Jackie Stewart, the three-time Formula One champ who was calling the race for ABC's *Wide World of Sports* with McKay, to drop some Scottish lingo on his viewers: "I'm afraid Cale's got himself passed by David Pearson there in that little kerfuffle."

"Would you care to explain that Scottish expression you just gave us?" asked McKay. "A kerfuffle, my boy?"

"A kerfuffle is much the same as getting your foot in the wrong side of the bed when you're trying to get out in the morning. A kerfuffle is a Scottish habit. And James, a lot of things have happened over in this country that the Scots have been a part of."

For Pearson, the kerfuffles were only beginning.

David Pearson was cool. Really cool, in just about every way you could imagine. He looked cool: he was well over six feet tall, was part Cherokee, and had rugged good looks, so he could tick the boxes next to tall, dark, *and* handsome. He acted cool—so cool that you tended to forget he was a forty-four-year-old grandfather. He smoked cigarettes, and even if you don't buy that smoking makes a man look cool, you have to agree that smoking *while driving a race car* does, at least a little. Pearson insisted that his car have a working lighter, lest he crave a butt during a caution period.

Most of all, though, Pearson was cool under pressure.

On the last lap of the 1976 Daytona 500—which until 1979 had set the standard for final-lap hijinks in a major race—he passed

Richard Petty for the lead heading into Turn 3, only to have Petty retake it coming off Turn 4. Petty, however, had to dip down low to get around Pearson, and he couldn't hold the line. His right rear fishtailed, tapping Pearson's front left and sending Pearson into the wall and down into the infield. Petty then overcorrected, which sent him nose-first into the fence and back down the track as well. He wound up one hundred yards ahead of Pearson's car, spitting distance from the finish line. But Petty stalled in the wreck and couldn't get his engine refired. Pearson had the presence of mind to mash the gas and the clutch as soon as he started spinning, so his engine never stopped. When his mangled Plymouth settled, he dropped it into first gear and sputtered across the finish line, taking the checkered flag at 30 miles per hour.

Throughout the entire episode, Pearson was on the radio with one of his crewmen, Eddie Wood, giving him a play-by-play: "I got him," followed a few seconds later by "He's under me," and then "We hit." Then, as his car was still spinning backward, Pearson asked Wood, "Where's Richard?" the same way he might have asked where his pack of smokes was. And to talk to Wood, Pearson had to key a switch on his shoulder harness, which meant he was wrestling the car to a stop, keeping the engine running, and getting it back into gear with one hand. It was like smoking, drinking a cup of coffee, and doing a crossword puzzle all at once.

"He wasn't excited; he wasn't angry," says Wood. "He was just matter-of-fact. *Where's Richard?* I told him Richard was stuck, and he said, 'I'm coming.' So I look up, and here he comes."

Pearson was Petty's greatest rival, the Salieri to his Mozart—just as talented but constantly overshadowed. Pearson didn't seek out the press, because he didn't want his lack of education to show. Born in Spartanburg, South Carolina, he dropped out of high school at sixteen to start working at the local mill, where both his parents worked the second shift. He liked to tell people that he got his education at

WMU, Whitney Mill University, with a degree in "skinning quills, pushing a broom and running an elevator."

If Pearson was self-conscious around strangers, he made up for it when surrounded by friends. He had a wry sense of humor that occasionally bordered on sadistic. Jack Arute once interviewed Pearson at a benefit race. When asked what charity he was racing for, Pearson said, "Well, Jackie, as a result of being around you so much during the past few years, I think I'm going to give what I win to The School for Mentally Retarded Announcers." He was a good-natured ballbuster and an inveterate prankster, with a special knack for automotive mischief. While riding shotgun with Whit Collins, the director of racing operations for his sponsor, Purolator, Pearson hammered Collins about how dirty his car was. Collins finally took the bait and pulled it into a car wash — at which point Pearson lowered the driver's side window, soaking Collins. Pearson was laughing so hard he couldn't get the window back up. On another occasion, he was riding with a friend who was pulled over for going 87 miles an hour. When the police officer approached the car, Pearson feigned relief and told him, "I'm glad you stopped us. I've been trying to get him to slow down ever since we left Savannah." The cop wrote a ticket, which carried a fine, but Pearson's flustered buddy was $10 short. "Shoot, lock him up if he can't pay the fine, officer," Pearson said. "I'll go on without him. A man that wants to drive like he does ought to carry enough money to pay the consequences, don't you think?"

Early in 1978 he bought a sixty-eight-acre farm outside Spartanburg that came with an old country store, which Pearson converted into a trophy room/clubhouse. Busch gave pole winners beer taps as prizes, and Pearson put his in his rumpus room. "I don't drink beer," he said, "but a lot of my buddies do, and that'll be a good place for them to sort of drop by and hang around." His mother, Lennie, lived nearby, in a house around the corner from the mill, and in Jim Hunter's 1980 biography of Pearson, *21 Forever,* the Silver Fox reported, "Miss Lennie is just as apt to get a switch after me today as she was back when I was growing up."

She had ample cause to, as Pearson's love of mischief dated back to childhood. He also loved racing and was able to combine his two loves one year in the soap box derby, when he won, but he was disqualified for having illegal steel-geared wheels. When he was working at the mill, he still made time to work on a car in the garage under "Miss Lennie's" house, using parts scavenged from the junkyard. He raced a little around Spartanburg and finally made the jump to Grand National cars at age twenty-five, in 1960, even though he didn't really want to. Two locals had started a David Pearson fan club and went on the radio to raise money for his racing expenses. "I didn't have any choice but to go along with it," Pearson said. "I didn't know who to give the money back to."

He ended up being named Rookie of the Year — he put his '59 Chevy on the pole in Sumter, South Carolina, and nearly won the race, one of his three top 5 finishes — but he collected only $5,030. Pearson ran a few races at the start of the 1960 season, but he was in danger of going bust until he got an offer to drive a car in Charlotte prepared by Ray Fox, one of the best wrenches in the game. Fox, like Bobby Allison, had had a brief but successful run working for Carl Kiekhaefer. In 1956, his only year with Kiekhaefer, Fox's cars won twenty-two of twenty-six races and he was named NASCAR's Mechanic of the Year. Pearson jumped at the offer. For once in his life, he was in a ride that allowed him to be patient, but he inexplicably drove like a madman. Starting from the third spot, he took Fox's Pontiac down onto the dirt apron in the first turn of the first lap of the 600-mile race to get past pole sitter Richard Petty. Driving the car like he stole it wasn't a sound game plan, but it worked. Pearson pulled away from the field, building up a four-lap lead, which came in handy when he blew a tire as he took the white flag. Pearson pulled down onto the apron and tooled around the track at 40 miles per hour, winning by two laps over Fireball Roberts. Pearson's take was $12,000. The next day he paid $5,000 in cash for the house he and his wife, Helen, had been renting.

He beat Fireball again at Daytona that July, which caught the attention of Cotton Owens, who gave him a full-time ride. Pearson won the 1966 championship with Owens, then moved to Holman Moody, where he won two more.* He left Holman Moody shortly after Ford pulled out of the sport in 1971, and in '72 he latched on with Wood Brothers. He won the pole at Darlington his first day in the car and lapped the field in the Rebel 400 that Sunday.

Glen Wood's early biography mirrors David Pearson's, with one difference. Like Pearson, Wood was from a small southern town: Stuart, Virginia, a sleepy hamlet of less than 1,000 people named for a Confederate general that to this day is twenty-five miles from the nearest McDonald's. Like Pearson, he quit school at age sixteen to work in a mill, in Wood's case a lumber mill, which gave him the nickname "the Old Woodchopper." Like Pearson, Wood dabbled in cars whenever he could and was mesmerized by the speed demons who came to the tracks near his home. Wood's favorite was Curtis Turner; whenever Pops was nearby, Wood would drive the lumber truck to the track to watch him. And like Pearson, Wood eventually started racing his own car, taking it to local tracks and struggling through some lean times. Wood's first race was in 1950 at the Morris Speedway, between Stuart and Martinsville. He crashed out of the heat race and tore up his '38 Ford. Unbeknownst to him, the housing bent and broke the axle, which busted the gas spout. Wood finally realized something was wrong when, as he towed the car home to Stuart, the Ford burst into flames. Wood had to pull the tow chain apart with his bare hands.

---

* For a variety of reasons, Pearson ran only four full seasons in his career. He won the title in three of them.

"We couldn't afford to lose both cars, or we would have been walking home," he said.

That one difference between Pearson and Wood was a big one. Whereas Pearson had the requisite need for speed, Wood, in his own words, was "not what you call a speed demon. I just don't like fast driving that much." Which, no matter how you cut it, is kind of a problem for a race car driver. Still, Wood averaged half a dozen starts a year and won four times before getting out of the car for good in 1964 and focusing his attention on running the team.

Wood Brothers was a loose collection of family members — Glen, his brothers Leonard and Delano, his sons Eddie and Len — and a few locals, most of whom were moonlighting. Scheduling was always a problem — they were at the mercy of one guy's cotton crop — and without the resources to run a full schedule, the Woods usually limited themselves to about twenty-two races a year. Although they'd never won a championship, they came into the 1979 season with eighty-two wins, more than any other team except Petty Enterprises.* Glen was the face of the operation, but Leonard was the brains.

Leonard Wood was one part Robert Carradine in *Revenge of the Nerds,* one part David Carradine in *Kung Fu,*† and one part MacGyver. His tall, angular frame and his horn-rimmed glasses made him one of the most recognizable men in the garage, and he also stood out as one of the more introspective, cerebral people in the sport. He worked on every aspect of the race car — the engine, the chassis, the body, the tires — and he did so tirelessly in the cinder block shop the Woods built on the banks of Poorhouse Creek.‡ (Unless it was Sunday. A

---

* Pearson's 1973 season, his second with the Woods, was ridiculous. He won eleven times in eighteen starts, including one stretch where he won nine of ten and came in second in the one race he didn't win. But since he sat out ten races, he finished thirteenth in the points standings.

† The contemplative part. Leonard didn't go around kicking people.

‡ The shop's proximity to the creek led to a problem: water moccasins. A particularly large one was once discovered in the dyno shop. Leonard originally thought it was an air hose.

devout Presbyterian, Leonard avoided working on Sunday whenever possible.) He once worked straight through dinner—which his wife, Betty Mae, put on the table every night at six o'clock sharp—because his watch had stopped and he somehow missed the fact that the sun had gone down. (Betty Mae finally called him at seven.) When he wasn't working on a car, chances are he was thinking about working on a car. "He thinks all the time, except maybe when he's asleep," Pearson once said of Leonard. The most widely told story about Leonard was that he actually kicked a crewman out of the hotel room they were sharing because the poor guy's presence interfered with Leonard's ability to think.

"I can't ever remember racing when my mind wasn't on it at least 50 percent, trying to come up with a new way to run better or figure out how somebody else is beating you," Leonard said in 1974. "I think if you concentrate on what you're doing hard enough, you can come up with something better than those who don't concentrate at all. I don't know how much thought the others put into it, but I put a lot."

Most people in the sport dreaded the cross-country hauls to California. Wood loved them, though, because the open road was a great place to be alone with his thoughts—so long as someone else was behind the wheel. "I have asked some of the boys to drive the tow truck at a time when I had a lot of thinking to do," he said. "When I'm trying to come up with something on the race car or the engine, I can't concentrate and drive at the same time. Take those trips to Riverside, California. That's about three days of thinking right there."*

Wood had been thinking about cars for most of his life. He spent

---

* The thinking paid off: the Woods won seven times with twenty-four top 5 finishes in forty-three starts at Riverside.

much of his time in school drawing cars or carving them out of wood blocks and selling them to his classmates for 50 cents. (The cars had seats, metallic paint jobs, and hood emblems—always Ford.) He built a foot-long '49 Ford with a working steel suspension, and his prized creation was a go-kart with a washing machine motor that he built when he was fourteen. It could go 30 miles per hour, and Wood hung on to it well into adulthood because, he said, "I'm right proud of it."

He began working on race cars a year later, when Glen started driving. (Leonard never considered getting behind the wheel. "I've always felt driving was too dangerous," he said.) His career was interrupted in 1957, when he was drafted into the army and sent to serve a two-year hitch in Germany, building transmissions for military vehicles. Bored with the challenge that presented, Wood set to building a working model of an Indy car. Powered by a model airplane engine, the eighteen-inch, ten-pound car was hooked up to a cable and ran in circles, but the bumpy ground caused it to jump all over the place. So Wood found a German cobbler, got some sole rubber, and fashioned a set of springs. "I'd trim the rubber out perfectly round and glue two pieces together for one wheel," he explained. "I put them together with metal discs and inserted ball bearings." The car ran so fast that the sole rubber couldn't take it: the springs tore apart, flew through the air, and hit an officer.

Leonard was always on the lookout for anything that would give him even the slightest advantage—like pit stops. Most Grand National teams paid little attention to them, which made no sense to Leonard, given how much time cars spent getting serviced. So he set about speeding up the entire process—choreographing the movements of the crew members to avoid collisions and improving the tools his team used. He built a jack that could get the car off the ground faster, he improved the pneumatic wrenches used to change tires, and he rounded the studs on the tires so the nuts could be threaded faster. The Wood crew became so quick that Ford sent them to Indianapolis in '65 to work in the pits for Jimmy Clark, a Scot who was driving for

Lotus-Ford.* It was an interesting meeting of brogue and drawl. The Woods were apprehensive — "Well, you don't just walk in and start pitting another fellow's car. I mean, you just don't do that...giving orders," Leonard said — but everyone got along swimmingly. Clark's two pit stops lasted 44.5 seconds, the fastest stops Indy had ever seen, and he won by two laps.

By the 1970s the Woods had sliced even more time off a pit stop. In 1977 the *Washington Post Magazine* raved, "They make a practice, even an art, of fueling their race car, changing two tires, wiping the windshield and sending the driver on his way with a drink of water and a kind word — all in fifteen seconds or less." During one memorable stop — one that lasted 12.7 seconds — Leonard, who changed the front tires, left a thumbnail under the front fender. That didn't bother him. To the Woods, pit stops were a matter of pride.

On lap 302 of the Rebel 500, Neil Bonnett hit the wall, bringing out a yellow flag and the final round of pit stops in the 367-lap race. Pearson was still a lap down, which meant he was going to have to beat the leader, Waltrip, out of the pits to have any real chance of winning the race. He pulled the Mercury onto pit road, and the elaborate dance began. Delano Wood was the first over the wall, carrying the jack out into the middle of the pit so he'd be in position to hoist the right side into the air as soon as Pearson stopped. Delano furiously pumped the jack, and once the car was off the ground, the tire changers removed the spent right tires, and two new Goodyears went on in their place. Then Delano dropped the jack, and Pearson took off, which created a problem: it was supposed to be a four-tire change. Pearson never saw

---

* It wasn't the only time Ford sent the Woods on the road. In 1966 Glen went to the 24 Hours of Le Mans as a guest of the factory. Fearing escargots, pâté, and any other food he didn't see in the diners of Stuart, Glen took his own grub to France: pork and beans and Fritos.

the crewman loosen the lugs on the left side because Glen, who had come over the wall to clean the windshield, blocked his view. Pearson made it to the end of pit road before the left-side tires came off and the car came to a halt, sparks flying from its undercarriage. One tire went bounding through the pits and almost brained Hoss Ellington, who didn't see it coming but heard it as it whizzed past his ear. Pearson tried to move the car, but when he hit the gas, the one rear wheel just spun in place. In the booth Jackie Stewart had worked himself into a right lather: "This is the Wood Brothers, perhaps the most experienced pit crew in the world! Something has very, very strangely happened to the car of the great-grandfather of motor racing, David Pearson. The Silver Fox is now spinning his wheels, literally, as, my goodness, two wheels have fallen off!"

A few laps later Pearson, who had already changed out of his racing suit and into a smart maroon shirt, explained what had happened to ABC's Chris Economaki: "I didn't know they was gonna change all four tires. Of course they usually tell me, but that time I guess I was so interested in beating Darrell out of the pits that I didn't hear them. When they let the jack down, that's the signal to go.... They were hollering for me to *whoa*. I thought they were saying *go*."

At that point a light rain began to fall in Darlington, which brought out a caution flag and allowed everyone to catch their breath, while giving Jim McKay an opportunity to display his marvelous gift for extemporization. "Gee," he said to Stewart, "we got up this morning, it was beautiful, someone said zero chance of rain. And it began to change, slowly, but then I guess there was a reason Mr. Shakespeare from your island, Jackie, referred to this month as capricious April."* Then McKay finished his riff with an announcement that succinctly

---

*It was T. S. Eliot, not Shakespeare, and he called April cruel, not capricious. But cut McKay some slack. Most NASCAR press boxes don't keep a copy of *Bartlett's* on hand.

illustrated where, to ABC, NASCAR stood in the sporting spectrum: "We're going to stand by here, see what happens. Right now we're going to go back to the Oriental world of self-defense," at which point the picture cut to a martial arts ring behind a title card that read: THE FELT FORUM, WORLD PROFESSIONAL KARATE CHAMPIONSHIP, MIDDLEWEIGHT DIVISION, LOUIS NEGLIA VS. BUTCH BELL.

When the rain let up and ABC returned from the kicking, there were thirty-nine laps to go and three cars on the lead lap: Waltrip, Petty, and Donnie Allison. The possibility of more showers meant that every lap had to be run all out, because in the event of rain, the winner was going to be whoever was out in front when the skies opened up. With nine laps left, another tire got loose on the track, this one from the car of Butch Hartman, who happened to be driving down the front stretch at the time. That brought out the yellow flag and set up the most frenetic trophy dash the Lady in Black had ever seen.

The green came out with five laps to go and Waltrip in front. Petty got around him in Turn 3 as the cars made the gentlest of contact, and the King held the lead for the next lap. Three to go. Waltrip got inside Petty just past the start/finish line, but Petty regained it going into Turn 3, only to see Waltrip pull back to the inside and go to the front in Turn 4. Petty, unbowed, nipped in front of Waltrip at the start/finish line. To make things even more interesting, Allison materialized out of nowhere to make it three-wide down the front stretch. Officially, since Petty led when the lap started as well as when it finished, there was no lead change. In reality, the lead had switched hands four times in thirty-three seconds. Two to go. No passes. Last lap. Waltrip got inside Petty in Turn 1, then Petty got him back at the end of the backstretch by driving hard into Turn 3. He didn't know it, but he was playing right into Waltrip's hands.

Before Waltrip became a regular on the Grand National circuit, his home track was Nashville Speedway. As it was at Darlington, the natural line at Nashville was up around the wall. "It was a very similar banking kind of track, where you ran in low, went up and almost touched the fence, and then came off the corner," says Waltrip. "I would run a different groove than anyone else, and it scared the hell out of them, because I'd go in and drive underneath them in the middle of the corner. Well, you're not supposed to be able to do that. But I'd just always had a knack for cutting a car under and getting by a guy."

So Waltrip made his pet move. He jerked the wheel hard—it wasn't so much a lane change he was making as it was a left turn—taking Wanda across Allison's grille and inside Petty. You make that move on Van Lingle Mungo Boulevard, and you'll find yourself pleading with a South Carolina state trooper not to write you a ticket. Somehow Waltrip made it stick. Allison was able to get next to Petty and engage him in a battle for second, which gave Waltrip a relatively easy ride to the checkered flag, after seven lead changes in the final three laps.

Upstairs, the Wee Scot, who had seen his share of races, was breathless. "I can't remember ever seeing the end of a motor race, Jim, being as exciting as that!" said Stewart. "Never have I seen a finish with so many passes on such a short track in such a short time."

Waltrip was giddy, as he had every right to be. He had outdueled the King, who several years earlier had put Waltrip in his place by saying, "When he wins at Darlington, then he'll be a real race car driver." And he'd done it cleanly. "Our cars got together a few times there near the end," Waltrip said. "But when they did, he'd wave at me and I'd wave at him, and we'd go at it again."

After he had finished his postrace interviews, Waltrip made his way back up to the press box. Surveying the moonlit track, he raised his arms and serenaded the Lady in Black: "I'll see you in my dreams."

Before he left the track, Pearson talked to Leonard Wood. Neither man mentioned what had happened in the pits. They agreed to talk early in the week about their next race, in Martinsville. The incident would provide some laughs, giving what is still one of Waltrip's favorite gags: singing "You picked a fine time to leave me, loose wheel" to the tune of Kenny Rogers's *Lucille*. But there was also something slightly moribund about it. It wasn't quite Willie Mays fumbling around in center field, but it was unsettling to see Pearson screwing up such a basic task in front of a national TV audience. "I just hope he doesn't let this thing force him to retire," said Petty. "He's not washed-up or through by any means."

Three days later Pearson got a phone call from Glen. He was fired.

Standings After the CRC Chemicals Rebel 500

1.	Darrell Waltrip	1,317
2.	Bobby Allison	1,236
3.	Cale Yarborough	1,178
4.	Donnie Allison	1,142
5.	Benny Parsons	1,138
6.	Richard Petty	1,114

Chapter Fourteen

Old Chow Mein

Sunday, May 6
Race 10: Winston 500
Talladega, Alabama

LIMOUSINES ARE a rare sight in a NASCAR garage—the preferred mode of transportation being more Schwinn than Rolls—so when a stretch job pulled into the Talladega Superspeedway as teams prepared for practice, heads turned. It rolled to a stop near the Wood Brothers stall, and after a minute one of the back doors opened. Out popped David Pearson. The newly unemployed Silver Fox surveyed the bemused faces in the garage and asked with a sly grin, "Now, does this look like I'm doing too bad?"

Pearson had flown himself to Talladega in his Aztec—in addition to a country store, the farm in Spartanburg had an airstrip—and two friends had surprised him with the flashy ground transportation. One of the first people to greet Pearson's limo was Leonard Wood. The two had a friendly chat, and although it was clear that Pearson was serious when he said he bore no ill will toward the Woods, as details of their parting emerged, it became clear that the divorce had been messy.

The day after the Darlington fiasco, Pearson had talked to Glen Wood, who'd complained that the driver wasn't trying hard enough. "I told him he had lost some of his enthusiasm," Wood said a few days later. "He was laying back more so than before. He said he wasn't afraid of the car. In my opinion, he is afraid of the car at Talladega and Daytona. When I was racing and they went to the big tracks, I no longer cared to run up front so I quit driving.... He twice quit at Talladega, and last year part of the crew almost quit because of the way he was driving. When he got a lap or two down he'd quit. Races are won from that far back all the time." Wood also criticized Pearson's driving in the '79 Daytona 500, in which he'd been caught up in a wreck while running far back in the field: "You can't win if you don't stand on it." Pearson didn't appreciate the lecture — "I'm too old to be treated like a kid," he said — and when one of Wood's business partners called later that day, Pearson told him how close he had come to quitting while being reamed out by Wood. That revelation got back to Wood, and it sealed Pearson's fate. Wood called two days later and cut him loose.

Pearson and the Woods had been together since 1972 — a remarkably long NASCAR marriage — so they were due for a change. Animosity had been building through the early part of the year. In Bristol Pearson suggested that the Wood Brothers pit crew wasn't as fast or consistent as advertised. There was bickering in Atlanta, when Pearson told some writers that "Leonard wouldn't admit it if he makes a mistake." His brother took umbrage at that. "Leonard works around the clock," Glen said. "You know David was always one of the first to leave the track. Instead of working out the problem, he'd say, 'We'll get it tomorrow.'"

After Glen Wood let him go, Pearson was hounded everywhere he went by well-wishers: the regulars at Jimmy's Restaurant in Spartanburg, the guy who sold him a new lawn mower. All had the same question: "What are you going to do now?" Pearson's standard answer was that he didn't know, and he wasn't going to rush into anything. Pearson was only forty-four, certainly not over-the-hill. He had options. Short-track owners were offering show money, and Humpy Wheeler was desperate to get him in the field for the World 600 on Memorial Day—in part because he wanted a strong field, and in part because he was sitting on fifty billboards touting Pearson that had been ordered months earlier.* Pearson had a shop out behind Miss Lennie's house where he worked on his Ford Fairlane. Until the right Grand National offer came along, he was content to bide his time racing it on short tracks near home, which meant he'd have more time to spend with his wife, Helen, and his peach trees, his three-acre lake, his new lawn mower, and his loyal German shepherd, Bullet. "I want to keep racing, but not in junk," he said. "I may be done. I don't know right now. If a good offer came along, I'd be interested in talking about it. But I won't go looking for a ride, and any ride I take would have to be a good one."

Pearson wasn't the only one goofing around in a fancy mode of transportation. Following Saturday's final practice session, the press box was full of writers slaving over their copy for the Sunday papers. The box provided an excellent view of the airfield beyond the backstretch, which is where all eyes turned when the din of a small plane became audible over the clacking of typewriter keys. The scribes watched with an increasing sense of dread as the Aerostar rose from the runway and made a line right at them. Just when it looked like it might be time to dive under a desk, the plane rose and cleared the roof by a hundred feet, though it seemed like ten. "Who the hell was that?" one frazzled writer asked.

"That was an Alabama kamikaze pilot on his 150th mission," said one who'd seen a similar stunt before.

It was Bobby Allison.

Confronted the next day, Allison admitted to being an Alabama

---

*Pearson was in the midst of an incredible streak: he'd won the pole for eleven straight races at Charlotte Motor Speedway. Wheeler's billboards read: BUSCH PUSH FOR THE POLE: CAN CALE BEAT THE SILVER FOX?

kamikaze pilot. "Yep. That's me. Old Chow Mein," he said, also confessing to some strange flying habits in his younger days. "Maybe we'd throw a cat out with a parachute tied on its back. One of them even came home, parachute and all. But most found new homes."*

Old Chow Mein was taking the Aerostar on a quick hop to Birmingham, where his eighteen-year-old son, Davey, was racing that night in a Chevy Nova he had built from the shell of a car his uncle Donnie had given him. Davey took his first checkered flag, and the next morning in the garage Bobby was showing the kid off like the proud papa he was. It was just another sign that Allison's luck was changing. For once he was catching breaks. Despite all the banging he'd done at Daytona, he'd still finished eleventh. Then he'd avoided the carnage and won in Rockingham. Three weeks later, at North Wilkesboro, his suspension had broken as he took the checkered flag, causing his right front tire to fold back under the car. After a victory lap accompanied by sparks and smoke, Allison had to ditch the car in the pits and walk to Victory Lane. It was the kind of thing that, two years earlier when he had been mired in a sixty-six-race winless streak, would have happened with five laps to go. Through nine races in '79 he had two wins and three second-place finishes, and that elusive first championship seemed a real possibility.

Allison had every reason to expect he'd be strong at Talladega, too. Until the wreck he'd caused took him out of contention in the 500, he had been pretty stout at Daytona, and Talladega is a similar course, just a little bigger. The track has a checkered history, and the fact that it is located on land that once belonged to Creek Indians has led to the birth of some rather wild explanations for all the bad mojo. Some say it can be traced to a Creek chief who was killed in a horse racing accident, while others claim a disgruntled medicine man placed a hex on the land while being driven out by white men. Another tale holds that the curse dates to 1813, when Andrew Jackson boldly put down

---

* PETA wasn't founded until 1980.

an Indian uprising in the area. And some—obviously influenced by *The Amityville Horror, Poltergeist,* and too many episodes of *Scooby-Doo*—believe that the track's woes are the result of its being built on an ancient burial ground.

Hokum or not, there was no arguing the fact that some weird stuff had gone down at Talladega. Located fifty miles east of Birmingham, the track was built by Big Bill France on what had once been an air force landing field, a bit of trivia that was eventually incorporated into the track's supernatural backstory: the military, the story goes, had to shut the place down because planes kept crashing with no explanation. The 2.66-mile tri-oval opened in the fall of 1969, and it quickly became apparent that the track had been born under a bad sign. The steep banking—33 degrees in the turns—led to speeds that taxed both the drivers (they were nearly blacking out from the g-forces) and the cars (the tires would blow apart after four or five laps). Bobby Allison suggested to France that to maintain a safe speed, the drivers should start on foot, but then he reconsidered. "I take that back," Allison said. "The track is so rough we'd probably trip and fall before we got to the first turn." A short-lived drivers union had been formed that August,* and Talladega provided the Professional Drivers Association (PDA) with a cause to take up. Richard Petty called a meeting of the PDA, and when Big Bill France tried to follow, Cale Yarborough blocked his path and reminded him what "drivers only" meant. After discussing their options—risking their lives, driving at slower speeds, or going home—the union members decided to walk. In an effort to prove that they were overreacting, the fifty-nine-year-old France got behind the

---

* A few years earlier Curtis Turner had tried to unionize the drivers. Turner went into debt building the track at Charlotte and tried to arrange a loan from the Teamsters in exchange for getting his fellow drivers to join that union. Bill France Sr. vowed that he would "plow up my racetrack and plant corn on the infield before I'll let the Teamsters union or any other union tell me how to run my business." France also decreed that no union driver would ever compete in a NASCAR race, a policy he said he'd enforce "with a pistol."

wheel of a car and turned a few laps himself. He filled out the field for the race with lower-level journeymen, and caution flags were thrown every twenty-five laps so they could change tires.

That was nothing compared to the string of oddities that plagued the place in the next decade. Larry Smith, the 1972 Rookie of the Year, was killed in an innocuous-looking crash in '73, supposedly because he had cut the lining out of his helmet so it would fit over his long hair. The next year, several cars were found to have been sabotaged—sugar was put in gas tanks, tires were cut, brake lines were severed—in the middle of the night before the race. In the spring of '75, Richard Petty's brother-in-law Randy Owens died when a pressurized water tank exploded in the pits. That fall, Grant Adcox withdrew from the Talladega 500 after his crew chief died of a heart attack in the garage. His spot in the field was given to the first alternate, Tiny Lund, who was fatally injured in a fiery crash on the seventh lap. And in 1977 the mother of driver David Sisco was killed in the infield when she was struck by the mirror of a passing truck.

The creepiest incident, though, didn't involve death or mayhem. In 1973 Bobby Isaac, who had won the championship in 1970, was cruising down the backstretch when a voice told him to "get the hell out of the car." Isaac, not unreasonably, pulled into the pits, got out of the car, and announced he was quitting, effective immediately.

Although race car drivers are a superstitious lot, most of them tend to brush the curse aside. Bobby Allison scoffed that Talladega was nothing compared to the eerie sixteen-room house he'd lived in as a kid: it was haunted, it had secret passageways and a mysterious room hidden behind a false wall, and none of his friends would come over to play. Petty admitted to having once been scared by ghost stories told by his uncle Roy, but, he said, "when I grew up that stuff quit bothering me." And Waltrip rationalized, "Heck, man, it's so frightening in my car that a ghost wouldn't dare hang around."

Even without otherworldly interference, Talladega is a scary place. The cars draft in tight packs at high speed; if one gets out of shape, there's not much time for the others to react. A field-thinning, multicar wreck has become such a common occurrence that it's been given its own name: the Big One. Since drivers are usually a lot more cautious in the early laps, the Big One usually comes late in the race.

But not always.

As requests went, this one was pretty odd. Four laps into the Winston 500, Dave Marcis was sitting behind the wheel of his Chevrolet, minding his own business and pondering the wreck he had just been involved in, when a face appeared in the driver's side window. It was Cale Yarborough. He was hysterical, and he had a question. Would Marcis mind looking to see if Yarborough's legs were still attached to the rest of his body?

The trouble had started when Buddy Baker had cut a right rear tire and got sideways, triggering a massive chain reaction. Yarborough was in Baker's wake and ended up airborne for what he said seemed like "several minutes" before touching down and sliding over the infield grass. When the car came to rest next to Marcis's, Yarborough got out to inspect the damage. But just because he had stopped moving didn't mean the wreck was over. D. K. Ulrich* was running way back in the pack, and as he came around to the front stretch where the Big One had started, he ran over some debris and flattened all four of his tires. Here's the thing about 33-degree banking: if you're not going fast, you'll slide down the track, and if you have four flat tires, you're not going to go fast. So no matter how hard Ulrich yanked the wheel to the right, his car kept sliding down toward the infield. It collided with Marcis's car, which slid into Yarborough and pinned his legs between his car's left front wheel and Marcis's bumper. After a few seconds Yarborough was able to slither free, but he couldn't feel his legs—and

---

* Yes, D. K. Ulrich is related to Skeet Ulrich. He's the actor's stepfather. Skeet, who briefly worked on D.K.'s team as a teen, is also Ricky Rudd's nephew.

he certainly wasn't going to look down, lest he be confronted with the sight of a couple of stumps where the tree trunks that had carried him on so many wild adventures had been. "I just knew they were cut off," Yarborough said. He was more scared than he'd ever been, which, given the fact that his life up to that point had been one near-death experience after another — the pilot-less plane ride with Wib Weatherly, the bear wrestling, the failed parachutes, the lightning strikes, barring Big Bill France from that drivers' meeting — was saying something.

Marcis was stunned and a little confused by Yarborough's request, and when he finally figured out what Cale was talking about, he assured Yarborough that he was still in one piece and stayed with him until the ambulance arrived. Yarborough was taken to the infield medical center, where he convalesced for an hour and a half before limping out under his own power. But his day was over, and so was any notion he was entertaining of winning a fourth straight championship. He had the skills; he had the car; he just didn't have the luck. In ten races he had wrecked four times, run out of gas at least half a dozen times, and been roughed up by a former water boy — one whose supply of good fortune seemed limitless.

Bobby Allison had no right to escape the Big One, but he did his best Moses imitation and emerged unscathed. "There were four or five cars wrecking in front of me and four or five wrecking behind me," he said. "Then, suddenly, I had a nice wide-open channel right through the middle when a couple cars went high and a couple went low. The Good Lord drove the car for me."

The man upstairs had no such love for contenders Richard Petty, Darrell Waltrip, Dale Earnhardt, and Benny Parsons, though. They were among the seventeen cars that got caught up in the wreck. Earnhardt's car was bent so badly that it wouldn't fit on the truck. When Nick Ollila went to the truck to get a cutting torch, Jake Elder flew into a rage. "Jake got so upset because we were going to have to cut the car, he picked up a jack handle and was going to hit me over the head with it," says Ollila. "The truck driver grabbed him and dragged him off to the side and held him down."

Petty and Waltrip were able to continue, but only after their crews had refashioned new noses for their cars out of duct tape. Donnie Allison, always a threat on a superspeedway, fell a lap down getting his car repaired and dropped out for good when his engine gave out. That meant that Bobby had only one car to be concerned about: the one being driven by his protégé.

Firing David Pearson in the middle of the season left the Wood Brothers with little time to find a replacement. Since the season had already started, they weren't going to lure a big name away from an established operation. The best available man was Neil Bonnett.

Bonnett was from Birmingham, where he had worked as a union pipe fitter, a job that entailed walking a six-inch beam fifteen stories above city streets. He eventually came to the realization that if he was going to have a job that required him to risk life and limb, he should at least pick one that was a little more fun. He'd been dabbling in short-track racing and decided that if he was going to be serious about it, he needed to go where the action was: Hueytown. Bobby Allison was happy to let Bonnett help out around the shop. The two were similar — pragmatic and cerebral, with a quick wit and a quick temper. Allison flew the Aerostar all over the country to race at small tracks in between Grand National events, but he still couldn't make every event he wanted to. When he had to turn down promoters, he sent Bonnett in his place.

Bonnett ran a few Grand National races in his own car before Nord Krauskopf, who'd won the '70 championship with Bobby Isaac, hired him in '77 to drive a car with Harry Hyde as the crew chief. But halfway through the season, Krauskopf pulled out of racing. Hyde was able to convince his old — and rich — friend Jim Stacy to buy out Krauskopf. Stacy pumped a quarter of a million dollars into the operation, and Bonnett put the car on the pole for Stacy's first race.

Of all the flush new owners, Stacy was easily the most mysterious.

Kentucky-bred but based in Scottsdale, Arizona, he was an eighth-grade dropout who had owned his own construction company at nineteen, building tunnels, bridges, roads, and dams. He smoked fat cigars, so they called him "Boss Hogg" when he was in the garage, which wasn't often. "He does most of his business from an airplane," one team member noted. And sometimes those business dealings were shady. In November 1978 he was mired in a lawsuit concerning a loan — unrelated to racing — that required him to appear in court in Concord, North Carolina. Two Cabarrus County sheriff's deputies were having breakfast at Stacy's hotel, the Holiday Inn. As they walked through the parking lot to their car, they stopped to admire Stacy's Cadillac limo. Then one of them noticed something odd: wires under the car. Taking a closer look, they discovered eight sticks of dynamite — each eight inches long and two inches in diameter — connected by wires to the battery and the exhaust pipe, so that when the car moved, the dynamite would go off. A bomb squad from Fort Bragg dismantled the bomb and detonated the blasting caps in an empty field near the hotel. "I feel fine, because it didn't work," said Stacy, who vowed to keep using the limo.

As deep as his pockets were, Stacy didn't realize how expensive racing could be. Bonnett was running well — he won two races in 1977 and had seven top 5s in '78 — but he wasn't always getting paid on time, and the team fell apart after the '79 Daytona 500.* Rescued by the Woods, Bonnett found himself in the awkward position of succeeding a living legend. He said all the right things — "I'm the weak link in this chain. I'm a new driver in a new car, and I'm not David Pearson" — but comparisons were inevitable, especially at Talladega, one of the tracks that led to Pearson's falling-out with the Woods. If there was any doubt that the car Leonard Wood prepared was strong enough to run up front at a superspeedway, it was done away with

---

* Stacy was last seen in 2002 trying to turn Elvis Presley's Circle G Ranch into a $500 million Elvis theme park and convention center.

when Bonnett put the Purolator Mercury on the inside of row two. He made it through the Big One scratch-free, and with forty laps left he had opened up a fifteen-second lead on Bobby Allison.

Then his engine blew up. "Boy, that was fun while it lasted," he said.

With Bonnett gone, Allison could have stopped for some barbecue and still won with ease. He won by nearly two laps over Waltrip, who expended so much energy wrestling his jerry-rigged car that he took his postrace Gatorade with a straight oxygen chaser. "The car drove like a tank after the crash," he said. Like Wanda, the nicest thing anyone could say about Petty's car after the wreck was that it was drivable. But the King latched onto the bumper of Buddy Arrington, who was driving an old Petty Enterprises Dodge, and was pulled to a fourth-place finish.

After the race Allison returned to the scene of Saturday's aerial crime, the press box. With his son Davey by his side, he joked, "It's also especially nice to win this one because now I can go home tonight and not be the only winner in the house."

As Allison walked down the stairs of the press box, his path was blocked by two kids. One handed him a program, which Allison grabbed and began to autograph. As he signed his name, he said something, and when he didn't receive a reply, he looked up to see the boy saying something to his friend in sign language. Without saying another word, Allison returned the program and, realizing the boy's friend didn't have anything for him to autograph, took off his hat, signed it, and put it on the kid's head. Allison had seen his son win his first race, made two fans for life, and inched closer to Waltrip. It was the end of a very good weekend.

Standings After the Winston 500

1.	Darrell Waltrip	1,662
2.	Bobby Allison	1,581
3.	Richard Petty	1,459
4.	Joe Millikan	1,397
5.	Cale Yarborough	1,377

Chapter Fifteen

Bring on the Dancing Bears

Sunday, May 27
Race 13: World 600
Concord, North Carolina

I⊤ HAD been more than three months since Kyle Petty had driven a race car. The Kylemania that had gripped the stock car world had waned in his absence but not completely subsided, which was why, on the morning of May 15, a crowd—writers and photographers included—assembled at Charlotte Motor Speedway to watch one of the most boring aspects of stock car racing: practice. CMS is a mile-and-a-half oval located just north of town. It's fast, but not nearly as fast as Daytona, which meant that for the first time in his driving career, young Mr. Petty was going to have to do something other than put the gas on the floor and keep it there.

Since winning his first race in Daytona, Petty had returned to his relatively mundane life. In April, *People* magazine did a short feature on him, becoming approximately the 2,143rd publication to call him "a chip off the old engine block." Past that, there was little glamour. He and Pattie were living at the farm outside Level Cross. She was still teaching school, and he was drawing a meager check as a mechanic on his father's team. Their most substantial source of income came from the Southern Pride Car Wash that Ron Bell had given them as part of a sponsorship deal. Once a month they'd go into town and pick up their cut. In quarters.

Kyle was still driving his father's old Dodges, but unlike the car he'd taken to Victory Lane in Daytona, they weren't navy blue, there was no eagle on them, and Valvoline's name was nowhere to be seen. The cars were Petty Blue and STP red—a provision of the lifetime deal he had signed with his dad's sponsor. Kyle would pull into the pits, and Richard—shirtless in the heat, wearing a white cowboy hat and sunglasses, and chomping on a small cigar—would stick his head in the window and give a few pointers. On his eighth lap Kyle tapped the wall in Turn 2. On his twenty-fifth, he hit the wall hard coming off Turn 4. "Came in way too low," said his father, watching from pit road. Kyle tried to spin it down onto the grass, but he overcorrected and ended up in the wall. As Richard casually walked across the grass that separates the pits from the track, Kyle waved that he was okay.

The car was a different story. Richard thought it severely damaged, so they loaded it up and made the two-hour drive back to Level Cross. He wasn't optimistic that the Dodge could be fixed quickly; the King's Grand National effort was still priority one, and Petty, who had five races in five weeks, was in the thick of the points race. He was in no position to divert any resources to Kyle's car. But back at the compound, Steve Hmiel and Robin Pemberton were able to get the car repaired, so they took it back to Charlotte the next morning.

Richard watched the second session with Humpy Wheeler, who was a close friend of the family and also wanted to check on his investment. From their bench in the garage, they watched Kyle until he got through the first turn, at which point they lost visual contact. But they had both been around the track enough to be able to tell what was going on by the sound. Things got quiet, which meant he was out of gas. Then a squeal. "We knew he was sideways," remembers Wheeler. "Then things got quiet, and that's when you really know something bad's going to happen. And then we heard the boom."

Petty looked at Humpy matter-of-factly and said, "Well, let's go see how bad it was." They got in a car and drove over.

"It was a hell of a wreck," says Wheeler. "The car was busted in half. He lost it coming out of two and hit the inside wall backwards, something you don't want to do." Kyle had skidded about 750 feet, backed into a steel gate, taken a two-foot chunk out of a concrete retaining wall, flown 150 feet through the air, and had his fuel tank ripped out of the car and go flying down the track. Pattie got the news as she taught at Hasty Elementary School, but aside from a banged-up knee, Kyle was fine. The car, however, was totaled, and any notion the Pettys or Humpy had about Kyle driving in the World 600 was forgotten. "Sure, it takes a load off me for the 600," said Richard. "I'd have been thinking about Kyle and looking for him, no doubt about it."

A few days later things got worse for Humpy. His deal to get David Pearson into the field fell through. Wheeler had convinced Hoss Ellington to prepare a second car and settled on an appearance fee with Pearson. But when Wheeler found out that he wasn't getting an exclusive engagement—Pearson was racing in a short-track race at nearby Concord Speedway the night before the 600—he substantially cut back his offer, and Pearson backed out.

Racing at Charlotte meant being at home all week, which meant one thing: parties. The most legendary bashes were thrown in the 1960s by Curtis Turner, who'd have a couple of hundred folks out to his sprawling ranch house. Pops's bar was lit by fluorescent lights, which cast everything—including the paintings of nude women on the wall—in a purple glow, and he had not one but two jukeboxes to keep the music—mostly country, with the occasional Motown hit thrown in—pumping until the sun came up.

The social event of race week '79 wasn't nearly as debauched, but it was a good time nonetheless. It was a party in honor of Dale Earnhardt at Sgt. Pepper's lounge in Kannapolis. About two hundred people showed up on Thursday night for what Benny Phillips of the *High Point Enterprise* described as "a promenade of life, a celebration, a roof-raising and the office Christmas party mixed and stirred well." Earnhardt had done his part to fatten the Sarge's coffers when he was younger — "You could tell by the way he knew his way around," noted Phillips — but he returned a different man. Even those who swore they'd never doubted that he'd make it — like his mother, Martha, who was on hand — had to be surprised at how quickly he'd made the transformation from hungry struggler to consistent check casher. Since the win at Bristol, he'd had an eighth-place finish at Martinsville, a fourth at Dover, and a fifth at Nashville. Now he was coming back to a track he was famil- iar with. He failed to qualify in the first round, when the top 15 spots were set, but in the second round on Thursday afternoon he had the fastest time — and second-fastest overall — meaning that he would start sixteenth. Earnhardt told the well-wishers at Sgt. Pepper's, "We're fly- ing now. We're ready for Sunday, and I don't think it will take me long to work my way to the front." It was hard not to believe him.

Relatively early in the evening, the bash ground to a halt. The lights came up, the music stopped, and the pouring of drinks was halted. After asking for a moment of silence for his father, Earnhardt received a plaque from the city fathers. Then he proposed a toast. "Most of all I want to thank my mother and sisters, especially my mother, for sticking behind me through the tough times before I got to where I am today," he said. "Martha Earnhardt, my mother, is the greatest supporter a son could have." The partygoers gave her a standing ovation, and then the lights went back down, the music started back up, the booze flowed, and the party continued well on into the night.

The biggest race in the United States in 1979 took place, as it had since 1911, at the Indianapolis Motor Speedway on the Sunday before Memorial Day—the same day Humpy Wheeler held his 600-miler. Indy had the advantage of years of tradition and a field full of names that were familiar to even casual fans thanks to ABC's tape-delayed prime-time broadcast, which had given birth to a holiday weekend tradition—trying to make it through the day without finding out who won the race, so the show would not be spoiled.

But the champ car world wasn't without its problems. In 1978 Dan Gurney had sent a state-of-the-sport report to his fellow team owners. The missive, which became known as the Gurney White Paper, laid out a series of grievances with the United States Auto Club (USAC), which sanctioned open-wheel racing in the States. Purses were too small, the promotion was too passive, and the owners didn't have enough say in matters that concerned them. "USAC for instance negotiates with TV as though it had the TV rights which in fact, if it came to a showdown, would turn out to be ours. (The car owners and teams)," Gurney wrote. He suggested the owners band together into something they'd call CART (Championship Auto Racing Teams), which would share power with the USAC. The USAC, not surprisingly, said, in effect, *Thanks, but we're going to go ahead and hold on to our power.* So a handful of teams went ahead and formed CART and put together their own schedule for 1979. But they also planned on running at Indianapolis, which was still a USAC-sanctioned event. In his white paper Gurney wrote, "It appears that a 'show down' with the Indianapolis Motor Speedway is or should be the first target. They are the ones who can afford it."

He got his showdown, all right. The USAC promptly rejected the 1979 Indy 500 entries of six CART teams. CART took the USAC to court, arguing that it was violating the Sherman Antitrust Act, and successfully won a temporary restraining order allowing the six to compete. But that was just the beginning of the farce. After the first of the two weekends of qualifying, the USAC "clarified" a rule dealing with the cars' engines, which prompted the owners of eight cars that failed to qualify to protest, on the grounds that the clarification essentially meant that the qualifying had been held under two different sets of rules. And to top it all off, an owner named Wayne Woodward filed a suit after his car was disqualified because he'd broken a rule having to do with a turbocharger inlet pop-off valve. All thirty-three drivers who qualified were served subpoenas to testify, and some of them were not happy about it. A. J. Foyt told the deputy who served him exactly where he could shove the papers, and Danny Ongais nearly ran his server over with a bicycle. Judge Michael T. Dugan II issued bench warrants for the pair. Ongais quickly showed up, apologized, and was sent on his way. Foyt, however, had gone to Louisville for a day at the horse races. His lawyer called him at Churchill Downs and told him to get back to Indy if he valued his freedom.

In a bizarre hearing Foyt, who'd never been the apologizing type, told Dugan what was on his mind. "Well, I don't have much to say," Foyt told the judge. "But when you are in a group of people and somebody shoves a bunch of papers in your face, you ought to know who they are. I don't appreciate it at all." After Foyt told Dugan that he didn't feel he had done anything wrong, Dugan threatened to hold him in contempt. "Mr. Foyt, do you understand that you are subject to the same service and process like any other ordinary citizen here in Marion County?" Dugan said.

"Right, your honor," Foyt said. "But, you know, I come here to race, not to be served subpoenas." Satisfied that Foyt wasn't going to get any more remorseful than that, Dugan cut the Texan loose. Woodward was denied his motion to stop the race, an extra round of qualifying was added for the disputed cars, and the Indy 500 eventually went off as scheduled and without incident.

But the whole episode exposed a fundamental weakness in open-wheel racing: it was run in a way that fostered bickering. The Indy debacle made a pretty strong case that Big Bill France had been right when he and Bill Tuthill had decided back in 1947 that the best way to run a racing series was to set it up as a dictatorship. Yes, the country had been founded on the principle that all voices should be heard. But when it came to running a racing series, sometimes you needed a guy who wasn't afraid to announce to dissenters that he had a gun and knew how to use it, as France had done when the Teamsters had tried to move in back in 1961. No one ever threw the Sherman Antitrust Act in the face of someone like that.

The litigation also underscored the extent to which the Indy 500 dominated the open-wheel landscape. It was so much more significant than any other race that whoever controlled Indy effectively controlled the sport. It didn't take a Machiavellian mind to see how one might stage a power play: use the 500 to hold everyone else hostage. That's precisely what happened in 1994, when Tony George, whose family controlled the speedway, announced that anyone who wanted to run in the Indy 500 had to do so under his new rules. He formed his own circuit, the Indy Racing League, which competed directly with CART. The schism doomed open-wheel racing, which was having enough trouble surviving in its battle against an increasingly popular NASCAR when it was unified. As a sport divided, it stood no chance.

While the Indy boys were dodging subpoenas and explaining themselves to judges, the Grand National crew was preparing for plenty of good fun in Charlotte. A race at Humpy Wheeler's track was always an event, a chance for Wheeler, who had gotten his start as a promoter at age nine when he'd sold tickets to a bicycle race, to demonstrate his Barnumesque bent. There was nothing he wouldn't try once in the name of entertainment. One year a writer in the press box made a snide crack that the only thing missing from the show was dancing bears. The next year? You'd better believe there were dancing bears.

Wheeler's best-known production was at the fall race in 1977, which was run not long after Cale Yarborough gave Darrell Waltrip the nickname "Jaws" following a run-in during the Southern 500. To commemorate the feud, Wheeler commissioned a friend who was a commercial fisherman in South Carolina to catch a shark. The guy showed up with a 150-pound blacktip, which Wheeler hung from the back of a wrecker. At the time Yarborough was sponsored by Holly Farms chicken, so Wheeler put a dead, bloody chicken in the shark's mouth, drove it around the track, and parked it in the garage. The crowd loved it. Those within smelling distance were less amused.

Wheeler's shows didn't always go off without a hitch. One year, during a tribute to America's farmers, a goat got loose on pit road. And at the fall race in 1986, Wheeler decided to break the record for the world's largest marching band. He assembled 5,000 high schoolers in heavy wool suits, but — just as it did at Daytona on the morning of the 500 in 1979 — his internal weather radar let him down. A warm front came in, forcing the kids to march in 85-degree heat. They set off in opposite directions and were supposed to meet at the start/finish line. About halfway a few dropped from the heat. Wheeler's producer asked him what they should do. "The show must go on," said Wheeler. Then a few more dropped. Then a dozen. Then came a new order: "The show must be stopped!" A hundred of them were treated at the infield medical center.

The '79 festivities were tame by comparison. Willie Nelson was the grand marshal, and the three-hour prerace production featured skydivers, hang gliders, cloggers, disco dancers, and — because no Wheeler show was complete without some sort of pyrotechnic display and/or show of force — artillery fire.

Another Charlotte tradition was the candy-apple red and white Wood Brothers Mercury sitting on the pole. David Pearson had put it there twelve races in a row at the track, and Neil Bonnett, who had won at Dover the week before, made it thirteen. Richard Petty started second, and defending World 600 champion Darrell Waltrip, who had had engine trouble in Dover and surrendered the points lead to Bobby Allison, was third. But one of the strongest cars in the early part of the race was Donnie Allison's. He and Hoss Ellington had shelved their plans to run a full slate and compete for the championship after ten races. The stress on a small operation of getting a car ready every week proved too difficult. As Petty was showing, a win in the Daytona 500 was the kind of thing that could kick a team to life, which Ellington's crew desperately needed. And the driver-owner relationship was still strained over Hoss's post-Daytona chauffeur routine. Donnie took the Chevy to the lead seventy-six laps in, but for the third straight race he blew an engine.

The first 341 laps of the 400-lap race featured sixty lead changes, but as the field was culled, Waltrip emerged as the driver to beat. He took the lead with 59 laps left, leaving Earnhardt and Petty to engage in a furious battle for second that thrilled the baking spectators almost as much as it thrilled Waltrip, who was able to stretch his lead to a comfortable five seconds as Earnhardt and Petty fought each other. If Earnhardt's car looked like it was being driven by a man who was holding on for dear life, that's because it was. As the race passed the four-hour mark, Earnhardt couldn't keep his Oldsmobile down on the low groove. He simply didn't have the strength. He could barely keep his head up; other drivers noticed he looked like a bobblehead doll. "That's a pretty good sign when someone has about had it," said Yarborough.

Petty, by contrast, was putting to rest any notion that his stomach ailment was going to cause him any lingering problems. He was clearheaded enough to formulate a strategy and physically strong enough to put his car in a position to carry it out. The plan he came up with was to do to Earnhardt what Waltrip had done to him in Darlington. He was going to let Earnhardt take his car high up into Turn 3 on the last lap and then make a hard left and cut underneath him. It worked like a charm, and he edged Earnhardt to the line for second. "You can say we're never too old to learn something in this business," said Petty.

With his win, Waltrip regained the points lead, thanks to Bobby Allison's engine troubles and twenty-second-place finish. Petty had also sent notice that he was going to be a factor in the championship race. But all anyone wanted to talk about was the guy who came in third—his rivals included. Petty hopped out of his car, went straight to Earnhardt's blue and yellow Oldsmobile, stuck his head in the window, and said, "Where you been, boy?" Buddy Parrott, Waltrip's crew chief, stomped his foot on the pavement in the garage and said, "That boy there is as tough as this asphalt right here." Even Waltrip, who enjoyed few things more than talking about himself, couldn't help but yield the spotlight. "When all the others go by the wayside, he'll be the one I have to fight," he said.

In the garage Martha Earnhardt watched her son, surrounded by a throng of a hundred bodies. A few were media members, but most were autograph seekers. "I never thought it would be like this so soon," Earnhardt said. "I was absolutely awed by the crowd when I was introduced before the race. I think all of my hometown was here. We didn't win, but I think they know we were here."

Oh, they knew. A movement was clearly under way. Earnhardt's win at Bristol had been historic, but it was something most fans had only heard about; they hadn't seen it. But this performance, this duel with the winningest stock car driver who ever lived, happened in front of thousands of people. So what if he didn't win? He showed that he could hang, that he belonged. Martha watched as the throng fussed over her son. "I think Ralph really believed someday Dale would do something like he did today," she said. "In fact, a lot of times I wonder that Ralph might well know what's going on."

Standings After the World 600

1.	Darrell Waltrip	2,066
2.	Bobby Allison	2,013
3.	Cale Yarborough	1,897
4.	Richard Petty	1,887
5.	Dale Earnhardt	1,756

Chapter Sixteen

Gassed

Wednesday, July 4
Race 17: Firecracker 400
Daytona Beach, Florida

As HE watched the mangled car of rookie Gene Rutherford being towed through the Daytona Speedway garage after qualifying for the Firecracker 400, Richard Petty couldn't help himself. "Hey," he called out. "Is Kyle driving for you boys, too?" After the wall-kissing session in Charlotte, the Pettys decided that the best course of action for Kyle's Grand National career was to have him stick to what he knew: Daytona. He entered another one of the cars from Richard's suddenly dwindling stable of old Dodges in the Firecracker 400, the track's annual Fourth of July race. The car was painted blue and red, with Lee Petty's old number, 42, stenciled on the side. That came courtesy of Marty Robbins, who was turning out to be quite a pal to Kyle. First he'd put in a solid wingman performance when Kyle had brought Pattie to meet him in Nashville a few years earlier, and now he was

214 • MARK BECHTEL

letting Kyle race with his grandfather's old number.*

Kyle practiced okay, turning laps within 1 mile per hour of his dad. But when it came time to qualify, the results were all too familiar: he got the car too high, didn't back off, spun it out, and put it into the wall. Richard consoled Kyle, telling him how he had wrecked so frequently when he was starting out that he carried a hammer under his seat so that when he crashed, he could jump out and break something on the car to make it look like it wasn't his fault. He also told him to load the car up and send it home. "You have just earned yourself a place on my pit crew come Wednesday," the King said.

If there was an upside to it all, it was that Richard no longer had to consider the question of what to do with all those leftover Dodges he had lying around. "It doesn't look like we're going to have to worry about that any longer," he said. "Kyle has pretty well taken care of the Dodge crop."

The latest crash was frustrating, but Kyle had made progress since Charlotte. Richard had realized that more than anything, Kyle needed seat time, so he'd sent him to an ARCA race at the five-eighths-mile Nashville Speedway in early June. Lanny Hester, the track promoter, was elated to welcome Kyle. His nineteenth birthday was on Saturday, June 2, the day before the race, and Pattie and his mother, Lynda, flew in for a party thrown by Hester at the track that afternoon. Hester had arranged for a car for Kyle to drive, but when he took it on the track for shakedown, the brake pedal fell off—never a good sign. After consulting with Richard, who was in College Station, Texas, for the Grand National race, Kyle informed Hester that he was going to pass on the ride and go back to Randleman. It proved to be a wise choice; the guy who ended up driving the car hit the wall after the gas pedal stuck.[†]

---

*Robbins, a pretty fair superspeedway driver—he finished fifth at Michigan International Speedway in 1974—took number 36.

[†] The clutch worked fine, though.

A week later Kyle was at the road course in Riverside, California, for a 200-mile Grand American race run the same day as the Grand National NAPA Riverside 400. He was in a '78 Pontiac owned by a couple of locals and sponsored by a towing company. This time all the pedals worked. Kyle qualified twelfth and got up to fourth place before he noticed transmission fluid in the cockpit. Pretty soon he couldn't shift out of third gear, and he had to purposely spin the car out to slow it down. His day was over. "I was driving it," Kyle said. "I guess I was responsible for what happened to it." Still, it was another decent performance on a long track. The time had come to get him some real Saturday night short-track experience.

Bub Moody was having a good time exercising his authority. The chief steward of Caraway Speedway was standing in the back of a pickup truck, addressing the field for the night's 100-lap main event—a field that, in addition to Kyle Petty, included future NASCAR drivers Sam Ard, Jimmy Hensley, and Morgan Shepherd.* Bub spoke passionately in a slow, deep drawl that one onlooker said brought to mind "a combination Barney Fife/worked-up camp meeting evangelist." This particular sermon focused on conflict resolution: "If there's a protest after any of these races, I don't want nobody bringing any woman they might have in the pits with 'em along to the hearing afterward. All of us hear enough of that female chin music at home and I ain't gonna listen to none of it from the sidelines tonight."

It was June 23, an off weekend for the Grand National circuit, so Richard Petty was on hand, soaking in the fumes and waxing nostalgic. "The sights, the sounds the scents are all the same," he said. "Racing on this scale is still pretty rustic. And still a lot of good fun."

---

* Ard was the 1983 and 1984 Busch Series champ, Hensley was the 1992 Rookie of the Year, and Shepherd became the second-oldest race winner in 1993, when he won the last of his four races at age fifty-one.

The last race of the night didn't go green until 10:30. Kyle, who qualified seventh in a Nova, was spun out on the fourth lap by another newbie, Harry Lee Hill. The car was still drivable, but the contact left him a lap down. Fifteen laps later, Kyle mixed it up with Satch Worley on a restart. Kyle maintained that Worley got too high and came down on top of him, but the vet — who backed into the inside retaining wall, ending his night — wasn't having any of that. "The biggest thing that happened is he's racing in the wrong class," said Worley. "Beginners should start at the beginning and not in this class of racing. I had been watching him, and he was all over the track. I was running with the leaders, and he wasn't going anywhere. It sure messed up my car, and it's one of those things that sometimes happen in racing. But the point is, he is not gifted enough to be running in our division. He's being put out there."

Kyle realized that there were going to be drivers who resented him. They were racing for their dinner money, while he was getting guaranteed show money from the promoter, meaning he'd outearn most of them no matter how he drove. Lee would go along on most trips, his job being to make sure the promoter didn't back out of the deal. They wouldn't unload the car until the dough had been handed over to him. It was usually a thousand dollars, and Lee liked it in a sandwich bag or an envelope for easy handling. If they were slow producing it, Lee would make the whole gang — Kyle, Pattie, Steve Hmiel, and Robin Pemberton — sit on the truck until they got paid.

Lee Petty loved his grandson. He also loved a good payday.

"When we went to a short track, especially a dirt track, the locals weren't thrilled," says Hmiel. "It was like, *This kid's getting a lot of deal money. This kid's coming in here with his big truck.* So the dirt racing, they'd certainly run into you. Kyle did a good job with it all. I don't know that the other team people were ever our friends, but he did a great job with the crowd." And he was getting experience. Even if it wasn't in top-notch equipment — "The car was junk," says Pattie — he was at least turning some laps. But he was still a long way from where he wanted to be.

Despite the return of all the major players from the Daytona 500, the Firecracker 400 played to a much smaller crowd. Only about 35,000 fans were on hand for the race. For one thing, Independence Day fell on a Wednesday. For another, even though the race started at 10:30 in the morning, it was hotter than hell in Daytona — 104 degrees on the track when the green flag flew.

What was really keeping people away, though, was the fear that they'd get stranded on the highway. The country was in the midst of its second energy crisis of the decade. Americans had long been warned about their dependence on foreign oil, but the release of the movie *The China Syndrome* in March, followed twelve days later by the meltdown at the Three Mile Island nuclear facility in Pennsylvania, pretty much cooled people to the notion of alternative fuel sources for a while. But the summer of '79 was not a good time to be at the mercy of oil producers. The Iranian Revolution, which came on top of strikes by the country's oil workers in late 1978, put a huge dent in supply. The United States was used to importing 750,000 barrels a day from Iran, but the country had cut its production to 250,000 barrels a day by early 1979. The shortage left motorists on edge. OUT OF GAS — WILL ROGERS NEVER MET AN ARAB, read one sign at a station in Iowa. Long lines at the pump led to measures such as even/odd-day rationing based on license plate numbers. Some areas instituted maximum purchases — sometimes as low as $3 — while others allowed refills only on tanks that were at least half-empty, to keep away "tank toppers." The situation was so bad by late June that Congress considered shutting down all gas pumps the weekend before the Fourth. Things weren't terrible around Daytona; the speedway released a list of twenty-four area stations that would have gas. But the trick was getting there from someplace like, say, Birmingham, when virtually every station in Alabama was closed.

And even if fans could get gas, a trip on the interstate wasn't exactly a Sunday drive, thanks to a wildcat strike of independent truckers, who were protesting escalating diesel fuel prices, the 55 mile per hour speed limit, and restrictive weight limits on their loads. The strikers were serious about keeping trucks off the road—windshields were busted; trucks were firebombed—and they didn't care about collateral damage. Sniper fire at moving rigs killed a trucker in Alabama and wounded a fourteen-year-old boy in Arkansas. Nails sprinkled on heavily traveled roads had caused huge traffic jams in Alabama and North Carolina. National Guardsmen were called out in at least ten states, and three states, including Florida, declared a state of emergency.

As the nation's highways were turning into the Thunderdome, President Jimmy Carter was in Tokyo at an economic summit. He had planned to take a short vacation in Hawaii following its conclusion, but as *Air Force One* left Japan on June 30, Carter received a call from his pollster Patrick Caddell, who briefed him on the deteriorating situation and told him, "You have to come home." Two weeks earlier Carter had concluded negotiations with the Soviet Union on the SALT II arms control treaty, and the previous fall he had brokered the Camp David Accords between Israel and Egypt. But those foreign policy achievements weren't enough to make Americans overlook the fact that they were spending more and more of their time waiting in line for the chance to be gouged for a few gallons of gas. Carter's approval rating was in the low 20s, worse than Richard Nixon's during Watergate. So Carter canceled his vacation and retreated to Camp David, where he began work on a speech on energy—the fifth of his presidency on that topic.

Before long the president realized that there wasn't much he could say that hadn't been said in the previous four talks. "It just seemed to be going nowhere with the public," his wife, Rosalynn, said. Carter changed tacks, broadening the focus of his address. Spurred by a memo from Caddell that described a national "malaise," he invited dozens of Americans from various walks of life—politicians, professors, preachers—to Camp David and sat on the floor taking notes as they told him what they thought was wrong with America. (Arkansas's boyish governor, Bill Clinton, told him, "Mr. President, you are not leading this nation—you're just managing the government.") After more than a week, Carter—over the strenuous objections of Vice President Walter Mondale, who threatened to quit—delivered what became known as his "malaise speech" (though he never uttered the word). He spoke of a threat to the country, one that "is nearly invisible in ordinary ways. It is a crisis of confidence. It is a crisis that strikes at the very heart and soul and spirit of our national will. We can see this crisis in the growing doubt about the meaning of our own lives and in the loss of a unity of purpose for our nation." Carter accepted his share of the blame, but not all of it. "Too many of us now tend to worship self-indulgence and consumption," he said. "Human identity is no longer defined by what one does, but by what one owns."

The speech, more sermon than policy discussion, was initially well received, but within days public opinion turned. There was something to be said for candor, but as it turned out, suggesting to the American people that there was something wrong with them, or that they were in some way responsible for their dire situation, was pushing it. Carter's approval rating edged back downward, and, worse, he was now associated with a message of pessimism—one that would hound him throughout his reelection campaign in 1980.

The good news for Carter was that the public didn't hold him completely responsible for the energy crisis. The weekend before the holiday, the Greater Miami Jaycees held a seven-hour call-in, inviting people to vent about the situation. A spokesman for the Jaycees reported that blame for the shortage was "running about 50-50 between the government and the oil companies." The callers offered a variety of suggestions for keeping consumption down: a four-day workweek, a four-day school week, an investigation into "where the government is hiding the oil," and mandatory jail terms for drivers caught speeding.

That presented NASCAR with a bit of an image problem, as the sport would pretty much cease to exist if speeding were removed. The cars got around four or five miles to the gallon, which hardly sent the message that the sport was doing its part in the conservation campaign. And in a 1976 study of gas-guzzling pastimes, auto racing ranked seventh.* "A man parked in a line waiting to get a limit of 10 gallons of gasoline and listening to a 500-mile race on his radio could begin to hate the sport in a hurry," said Cale Yarborough.

During the previous energy crisis, in 1974, NASCAR had cut the length of all its races by 10 percent. Bill France decided against shortening any races in '79, but the teams wouldn't be guzzling quite as much gas: NASCAR's fuel provider, Union 76, cut its supply by 20 percent from the 1978 season. A few drivers tried to do their part. Richard Petty dispensed advice to motorists via newspaper columnists, telling them that although drafting allowed racers to ease off the throttle, hitching your car to someone's bumper on the interstate was a bad idea. "There are certain race drivers I would not consider drafting with," he said. "I don't know them that well, and I certainly don't know the strangers I'm behind on the highway."

The trick, according to the King, was to apply steady pressure to the accelerator, which made the difference on both the track and the highway. "Smoothness does it," he said. "That's the key to driving race cars faster than the next cat, and smooth driving is the key to more miles per gallon.... The cat who can run three or four extra laps with his car before he has to make a pit stop for gas is the one who's likely to win the race." And, he noted, if you had access to a top-notch racing

---

* The study took into account everything associated with the sport—fuel used by the race cars as well as fans, transporters, etc. Number one on the list, by the way, was vacations.

team, it might be a good idea to have them take a look at your Dodge Dart. "I try not to slow for curves on the racetrack or on the highway," he said. "I have my passenger car set up to handle real good in curves and corners."

Petty's Oldsmobile was handling pretty well at Daytona, but not as well as Buddy Baker's Gray Ghost, which was on the pole for the Firecracker 400, just as it had been for February's 500. And it was beset by ignition problems, just as it had been in February, but this time it was the real deal. Baker dropped out after fifty-seven laps, but at least he could take solace in the fact that he wouldn't have to spend any more time sitting in his car, which was kind of like sitting in a pizza oven. There was no reprieve from the heat. Darrell Waltrip kept sticking his arm out the window in an effort to cool off, but the air he was bringing in was no relief. He said it was like "working around a blast furnace in a steel mill."

The temperature also made it more difficult to draft. A driver couldn't simply tuck in behind a car and stay there, because if he didn't get his nose out into the fresh air, his engine would overheat. The field was strung out, and after Baker dropped out, four drivers began to pull away: Neil Bonnett, Dale Earnhardt, Benny Parsons, and Waltrip.

That Bonnett was still in the race was a sign that it might have been his fate to win. He escaped two major catastrophes in the first ninety laps. Twenty laps into the race a car spun out in front of Waltrip and Bonnett. Waltrip slammed on his brakes, and Bonnett, who was right behind him, had no choice but to get off the gas and veer left. The car did a one-eighty, and Bonnett went sliding down the grass on the back-stretch, backward. Eventually, the front end started to come around, and when it did, Bonnett dropped it into third gear and floored it. "One of the damnedest jobs of driving you ever saw," he said. "I had both my eyes closed." His second break came when Bobby Allison T-boned the sliding car of Terry Labonte, sending Labonte's bumper on a journey that took it through the air, onto Bonnett's hood, and off his windshield before it finally flew over his roof. Bonnett never slowed down, and his car suffered no damage.

Any chance Waltrip had of winning was lost when he made a green-flag pit stop just before a caution period, which allowed the leaders to pit under yellow and left Waltrip a lap down. Earnhardt stayed on the lead lap, but, as he did in Charlotte, he had trouble handling the heat. Late in the race he got woozy—"My brain wouldn't work," he said—and brushed the wall, so he wisely backed off. That left Bonnett and Parsons to duel for the win. Bonnett took the lead with twenty-seven laps left and held on to it as he took the white flag. Parsons was trying to set him up for a slingshot pass, but he was slowed down just enough by two packs of slower cars—packs that Bonnett expertly slalomed through—that he was never able to get close enough to make his move.

Bonnett wasn't able to enjoy the spoils of victory, the hugs of one chesty Winston Girl notwithstanding. As he launched into his postrace speech in Victory Lane, the heat finally caught up with him. He turned as white as the one-lap-to-go flag, his legs went rubbery, and he got light-headed. An official took him by the arm and led him to the infirmary by way of the garage, which looked like a triage area. Waltrip—whose fourth-place finish, combined with Allison's early departure, meant that he added 92 points to his lead—was prone on a workbench, his shirt and shoes off and an oxygen mask on his face. Parsons was on the bench next to him. His foot was so badly blistered that when he saw a crewman with an artificial right leg walk by, he said, "That's just what I need now." Chuck Brown sat on the ground with a wet towel on his foot as he pondered his shoe, the sole of which had become a gooey mess.

Waltrip eventually got up and moved into the drivers' locker room, where he promptly submerged himself in a tub of ice water. Nearby Richard Petty, who had finished fifth, was changing. He was one of the few drivers who didn't look like he had just run two marathons in a winter coat. "Boy," Earnhardt said to him, "you're the toughest old man in the world."

Standings After the Firecracker 400

1. Darrell Waltrip   2,720
2. Bobby Allison   2,587
3. Richard Petty   2,522
4. Cale Yarborough   2,500
5. Dale Earnhardt   2,342

Chapter Seventeen

Rising Again

Monday, July 30
Race 19: Coca-Cola 500
Long Pond, Pennsylvania

IF ANYONE could have used some time away from the track, it was Cale Yarborough. Sure, he'd won two races, but all anyone seemed to remember about his season was that he'd fought Bobby Allison and that he'd nearly turned a routine check of his car into an impromptu leg amputation. His twentieth-place finish in the Firecracker 400 left him in fourth place in the standings. Nobody was talking about whether he'd win a fourth straight championship. Now the talk in the garage centered on his relationship with his owner: there were strong rumblings that Yarborough and Junior Johnson were on the outs.

As luck would have it, the schedule offered Yarborough a break. There was only one race, in Nashville, between Daytona and the 500-miler at Pocono International Raceway. Yarborough spent a large chunk of the downtime on a working vacation in Hollywood, where he filmed a cameo for the TV show *The Dukes of Hazzard*. The producers had originally offered the part to Richard Petty, but the King had turned them down. "It's not that I've got something against good ol' boys," Petty said. "I guess I'm still sort of one myself. Their people contacted us, but we couldn't get together on the money." So Yarborough was recruited instead.

The show, which was based on the 1975 movie *Moonrunners,* had made its debut in January 1979 as a midseason replacement on CBS. *Flying High*—a Connie Sellecca vehicle about three flight attendants—tanked, so the network stuck *Dukes* in its Saturday night time slot. The premise was simple: two bootlegging cousins drove around the backwoods of Georgia in a car that had a giant rebel flag painted on the hood. It was a massive hit, proof that the country had, against all odds, become a place where people would rather watch two flannel-wearing southern boys outsmart some really stupid local lawmen than watch Connie Sellecca and two other hot stewardesses do *Charlie's Angels* at 35,000 feet.

America's tastes had certainly changed.

In 1920 H. L. Mencken published an essay called "The Sahara of the Bozart,"* which laid out the curmudgeonly columnist's view of the post–Civil War South: "It is almost as sterile, artistically, intellectually, culturally, as the Sahara Desert. There are single acres in Europe that house more first-rate men than all the states south of the Potomac; there are probably single square miles in America." Mencken went on to decry the "unanimous torpor and doltishness, this curious and almost pathological estrangement from everything that makes for a civilized culture," and suggested that if a tidal wave were to wash the whole region away, no civilized person would notice.

And this from a man who lived in Maryland, just on the other side of the Potomac.

Ouch.

---

* "Bozart" is a play on "beaux arts."

When he wrote the essay, Mencken had never been to the South; a friend and editor told him it would be a good idea to keep it that way for "two or three years." (The reaction in Dixie was predictable. In Arkansas a campaign was undertaken to implore the state's congressional delegation to have Mencken deported.)* When Mencken did venture down south, his firsthand impressions were little better. In 1925, while covering the Scopes monkey trial in rural Tennessee, Mencken referred to the locals as "yokels," "halfwits," and "buffoons" living in a region he dubbed the "Coca-Cola belt."

Not every northerner viewed the South with such unabashed derision, nor did Yankees pay much attention to how life was lived in the Land of Cotton. It's not that southern culture wasn't embraced; it was barely acknowledged, let alone examined. "The American South has existed largely as an imaginary landscape in the nation's popular arts," historian Allison Graham wrote in her essay "The South in Popular Culture." Meaning that in movies, southerners were almost always one-note characters, bumpkins who were generally harmless and maybe good for a laugh. The tendency to oversimplify applied to historical representations as well. Antebellum southerners all seemed to live on plantations where the men wore bolo ties, the women wore hoop skirts, and the slaves wore smiles that were completely at odds with their lot in life.

The picture provided by television wasn't much better. As TV was becoming a viable medium for delivering national news in the 1950s and early '60s, the enduring images coming out of the South were of governors in schoolhouse doors and fire hoses turned on demonstrators. The picture painted of southerners on shows such as *The Beverly Hillbillies*—slack-jawed, unwashed mouth breathers, who, though

---

* The attitude of the Arkansans would eventually shift from hatred to pity. A decade later, when Mencken wrote that Arkansas was the "apex of moronia," the state legislature passed a motion to pray for Mencken's soul. Said an ungrateful and unmoved Mencken, "My only defense is that I didn't make Arkansas the butt of ridicule. God did."

they had no hope of fitting into polite society, were at least harmless, decent people — didn't seem quite so bad.

But as the '60s wore on, the South's image softened. The Civil Rights Act of 1964 and the Voting Rights Act of 1965 went a long way toward eradicating the nastier aspects of southern life. As more blacks registered and voted, a new guard of young, progressive politicians was installed in local offices and statehouses. Race relations in the South, so long the area's chief source of embarrassment, became less volatile, especially when compared to what was happening up north and out west. Riots in Philadelphia and the Watts section of Los Angeles in 1964 and 1965 were followed by troubles in Cleveland, Newark, and especially Detroit, where five days of rioting in the summer of 1967 led to forty-three deaths and two thousand buildings being burned down. The days of Yankees being able to look down their noses at their overall-wearing neighbors were over. The rubes weren't the ones torching their cities; that was happening in places run by what Alabama governor George Wallace called the "pointy-headed intellectuals."

One of the more interesting explanations for the South's progress on race was offered in, of all places, *Ebony,* which devoted an entire 1971 issue to the region and declared that it had cleaned up its ways because it had become "too busy to hate." Indeed, the 1960s and '70s were a time of unprecedented economic development in the South. After decades of seeing its population shrink, the South grew by 12 million people in the '70s, a jump of 21 percent, and the size of its workforce increased by one-third. Attracted by the untapped resources and the mild weather, businesses — some from the North, many from overseas — moved into the Sun Belt. A study in the mid-'70s ranked the states by their business climate: Texas was first, followed by Alabama and Virginia, with both Carolinas and Arkansas also in the top 10. In his 1975 book, *Power Shift,* Kirkpatrick Sale declared that "the pleasant little backwaters and half-grown cities [had changed] into an industrial and financial colossus."

For the first time in more than a hundred years, the South had become a relevant voice in the national discussion. It was forging its own identity and asserting itself, and its contributions to culture—including stock car racing, the one sport it called its own—were being noticed north of the Mason-Dixon Line. It was happening slowly, but it was happening.

Then came the 1976 presidential election.

From its inception, Jimmy Carter's candidacy seemed something of a lark. For starters, he was a southerner, and no one from the Deep South had been so much as nominated by a major party since before the Civil War. And he wasn't even a famous southerner. Unlike George Wallace, whose ultraconservative message found an audience among disenchanted northerners, Carter—a peanut farmer who had in 1970 been elected governor of Georgia—was anonymous outside the Peach State. At the beginning of 1976, his national name recognition was 2 percent.* When he announced to his family that he was running for president, his feisty mother, Lillian, asked, "President of what?"

But as the Carter campaign gained momentum and the prospect of a southern president began to look like a real possibility, the national curiosity about Carter Country turned into a full-blown case of *Hey-look-at-this-itis*. Writers descended on the South. *The New York Times* ran a weeklong series devoted to the South in February 1976. *Time* sent seventy staffers down to Dixie to collect material for an entire issue dedicated to the region—replete with a piece on stock car racing—that ran six weeks before the election.

Carter's victory over Gerald Ford in November of '76 only hastened what one observer dubbed "the Reddening of America." With

---

*Some quick math: Georgia's population was about 4.6 million. The population of the United States was 203 million, meaning about 2.2 percent of Americans lived in Georgia. So a name recognition of 2 percent means that even some people in his own state didn't know who Carter was. And Carter had been on the cover of *Time* in 1971. *That* is anonymity.

one of their own now the most powerful man in the world, "southerners no longer felt ashamed of their region, no longer were blackballed as bigoted, retrograde, out of step," historian Bruce Schulman wrote in *The Seventies: The Great Shift in American Culture.* "On the contrary, their culture—at least the Seventies version of it—became increasingly popular in the very places where it had been most disdained."

The increase wasn't entirely due to curiosity about the new commander in chief. The post-Watergate landscape bred a strong distrust of The Man, and southern culture has long been infused with a rebellious, antiestablishment streak. The new American heroes of the mid-'70s were antiheroes. "The same distrust of the powers that be that undermined traditional sources of authority and fractured public life also spurred creative, personal, highly charged art that addressed just that discontent," Schulman wrote. "The decade's most potent and memorable cultural projects raised an upturned middle finger at conventional sources of authority." That was evident in films featuring morally ambiguous protagonists, such as *Taxi Driver*'s Travis Bickle (played by Robert De Niro) and *Chinatown*'s Jake Gittes (Jack Nicholson). It also showed up on TV. According to Bo Duke, the blond cousin played by John Schneider, the Dukes of Hazzard were raised "never to turn their back on somebody who needs help fighting the system."

But nowhere was the antihero trend more apparent than in music. Spearheaded by Willie Nelson, Waylon Jennings, and Merle Haggard—who wasn't kidding when he sang, "I turned 21 in prison"—the outlaw movement brought country music to a national audience. In 1960 there were eighty radio stations in the United States dedicated to country. By the mid-'70s, there were more than a thousand. *Newsweek* and *Time* ran cover stories on the crossover appeal of country artists, whose songs routinely topped both *Billboard*'s Hot 100 and the country chart. (Among the people who were listening to country, according to *Time,* were novelist Kurt Vonnegut Jr. and former Nixon energy czar John Love.) *Newsweek* put Loretta Lynn on the cover. *Time* went for an edgier choice: Haggard, aka California inmate number 845200.

Country—and its equally raffish cousin, southern rock—stood at the opposite end of the musical spectrum from another genre that was introduced to the mainstream in the mid-'70s: disco. Where sports fans came down on that little battle in the summer of 1979 was answered in Chicago two and a half weeks before the Coca-Cola 500 at Pocono. The Chicago White Sox staged a promotion that allowed fans to attend the team's doubleheader against the Detroit Tigers for 98 cents provided that they brought a disco record, which would be placed inside a giant crate in center field and blown up between games. The Sox expected 20,000 people to show up. More than 75,000 did—20,000 more than Comiskey Park's capacity and 60,000 more than were at the Sox game the night before. DJ Steve Dahl, wearing an army helmet, circled the field in a jeep, then detonated the records, which tore the outfield grass to shreds and incited the crowd—which, having spent much of the first game drinking beer and smoking pot, was already good and rowdy—to a full-fledged riot. Shirtless fans poured onto the field, setting bonfires, throwing firecrackers, and hitting each other. "I didn't know people could have such little regard for other people's safety," said White Sox pitcher Ross Baumgarten, who clearly had never listened to Donna Summer's *Bad Girls* from start to finish.

A distinctive southern twang was also heard in movies and on TV. *Smokey and the Bandit* was the fourth-highest grossing movie of 1977 and spawned two sequels and scores of imitations, including *Every Which Way but Loose,* which was the fourth-biggest draw of 1978. The *Alice* spinoff *Flo,* set in a roadhouse in Houston, was the seventh-highest-rated show in 1979–1980 and was responsible for otherwise urbane types going around telling each other to kiss their grits. The following year, *Dallas* and *The Dukes of Hazzard* were numbers one and two in the Nielsen ratings.

"You couldn't do a show like that about people from the North,"

Richard Petty said of *Dukes*. "They don't seem to have as much fun as people down South." Maybe, but it wasn't for a lack of trying. Had H. L. Mencken seen how many northerners were embracing redneck chic, he would have swallowed his cigar. The nation's most visible redneck was Jimmy Carter's brother, Billy, a gas station proprietor who was so fond of beer that he promoted his own brand, Billy Beer.* The First Brother was perhaps the republic's staunchest advocate for what he called "Redneck Power," a phrase that was painted on the hood of his pickup and emblazoned on the shirt he wore when he played in softball games with members of the White House staff, Secret Service, and press corps. Instead of being appalled, people followed Billy's lead, snapping up boots and hats and vests. Ralph Lauren created an entire line of cowboy duds that he couldn't keep on the shelves. "Imagine," Lauren said in February of '79, "it took me 12 years to build a $12 million menswear business. It took me two months to sell almost $30 million in Western wear." Less pricey options were available at Billy Martin's Western Wear, the national chain of boutiques started by the New York Yankees manager in 1978. Even the pointy-headed intellectuals were getting in on it. Hendrik Hertzberg, President Carter's New York–bred, Harvard-educated speechwriter, confessed to the *Washington Post* that he had started wearing cowboy boots because they made him "feel close to being a movie star." Another Beltway consultant raved to the *Post* about his boots, saying that he wore them to fancy dress balls.

And if dressing like a cowboy wasn't enough, one could always pretend to be one. In September 1979, *Esquire* ran Aaron Latham's "The Ballad of the Urban Cowboy: America's Search for True Grit," which chronicled the lives of a group of Texas oil workers who killed their time riding mechanical bulls. It spawned the John Travolta movie *Urban Cowboy,* which in turn inspired countless

---

* Carter pitched the beer by saying, "I had this beer brewed just for me. I think it's the best I've ever tasted. And I've tasted a lot. I think you'll like it, too."

American men to risk doing irreparable damage to their reproductive systems.

So as NASCAR started to come of age in 1979, it did so in a society that had begun to admire people who had dirt under their fingernails, guys who wore cowboy boots and belt buckles and weren't afraid to fight now and again. If Middle America was ready to embrace Bo and Luke Duke, then it sure as hell would be willing to embrace a real bootlegger like Junior Johnson or a real brawling hotfoot like Cale Yarborough.

Or, as Yarborough later put it, "All Yankees, secretly, deep inside their hearts, want to be Rebels."

High on Yarborough's list of shortcomings in the first six months of the 1979 season was that he hadn't won a pole. If he didn't rectify that by the end of the season, the 1980 Busch Clash would be run without the Busch-sponsored car. Yarborough thought he had spared his sponsor that indignity at Pocono when he put up a time that looked unbeatable. But late in Saturday's qualifying, Harry Gant, a thirty-nine-year-old rookie driving a car owned by the proprietor of a Hartford school bus company, nipped him. Unlike almost every other driver in the field, all of whom used Goodyear tires, Gant used a set built by McCreary, a small Pennsylvania operation. No one expected the softer tires to hold up during the race—and they didn't—but Gant didn't care. The bonus for winning the pole, combined with the berth in the 1980 Busch Clash, was worth at least $12,000 to him, which was more than all but the top two finishers in the Pocono race would take home.

Waltrip qualified third in Bertha despite missing most of Friday's practice. He had been playing in a celebrity golf tournament in Chicago, and when he showed up at the airport Friday morning to fly to Pennsylvania, his pilot delivered some bad news: he had somehow locked the keys inside the plane. A locksmith was summoned, but busting into a jet proved a little more delicate than jimmying the door on a '55 Oldsmobile. As the locksmith worked on getting into the plane, Bertha sat in the Pocono garage, all dressed up with no one to take her out. Waltrip finally got to the track with only fifteen minutes left in the five-and-a-half-hour session. He had the good fortune to turn a fast qualifying lap, but his luck ran out in Saturday afternoon's final practice. Bertha's engine blew, and Waltrip couldn't keep the car out of the wall. The damage was too serious to fix in a day, and without a backup car—bringing more than one ride to the track was rare—Waltrip had no choice but to buy his way into the race.

Al Rudd Jr. had been the engine builder for his younger brother, Ricky, but when Ricky left the family operation at the start of 1979 to drive for Junie Donleavy, the Rudd family Chevy was without a driver. Al decided to give it a crack at Pocono, one of the trickier tracks on the circuit. Tucked away in the Pocono Mountains of eastern Pennsylvania—an area known for heart-shaped bath tubs and honeymoon suites—Pocono Raceway is a two-and-a-half-mile triangle, and all three turns are radically different. Finding a setup that works through two is a chore; finding one that works through all three is impossible. But Rudd, who had never driven on a big track in his life, still put up the eighteenth-fastest time. Then after Waltrip put Bertha into the wall during Happy Hour, D.W. came calling. Rudd gave Waltrip his car in exchange for some much-needed cash and engine parts. He also got to keep his motor; Waltrip had Robert Yates put a new one in the loaner.

The race was scheduled for 1:00 p.m. Sunday, but rain pushed it back to Monday. The weather was better, but there were still enough clouds in the sky to pose a threat of rain. With a shortened race a possibility, there was going to be hard racing from the start. And that meant there were going to be wrecks.

Dale Earnhardt thought he was dead. He opened his eyes, felt himself flying, saw the clouds approaching, and connected the dots. Then he

234 • MARK BECHTEL

saw a helicopter pilot and figured that unless the dress code for angels had been drastically relaxed, he was probably still alive.

Earnhardt was being airlifted to Pocono Hospital. He had been leading the Coca-Cola 500 as it approached the midway point when his right rear tire blew. His car did a one-eighty and smacked the wall on the driver's side. In the days before head restraints, Earnhardt drove with his head cocked to the left, almost like he was trying to look out his window to see what was happening in front of him. When his tire blew, Waltrip was behind him. After the race he said he was pretty sure that Earnhardt's head hit the wall. He was conscious when he was pulled from the car, and when his crew gave him a ball and told him to squeeze it, he was able to. But after a few minutes at the infield care center, it became clear that Earnhardt was going to need more serious medical attention. He was kept in the intensive care unit at Pocono Hospital, but his injuries weren't as bad as feared. He had broken both his shoulder blades.

As expected, no one had wasted any time rushing to the front. As soon as the green flag flew, Waltrip dropped down low and passed eleven cars by the time he exited the first turn on lap 1, moving from nineteenth to eighth in a matter of seconds. The first serious wreck came a lap later, when Al Holbert's car hit the wall, nearly flipped, and burst into flames. Roger Hamby got caught up in it, staggered out of his totaled car, and lay down on the infield grass before being carted off to the infield medical center.

When it wasn't slowed by caution flags—eight, for forty-six laps—the action was intense, with cars at times stacked five-wide on a track with only one real groove. After Earnhardt fell out, it became a three-car race between Yarborough, Petty, and Waltrip. Yarborough went to the point—the fifty-sixth lead change of the race—after a series of green-flag gas-and-go pit stops with about ten laps left. He was pulling away when the yellow came out on lap 196 for Nelson Oswald's blown engine. Waltrip, who was in second place, decided to duck into the pits for tires. The upside was that the fresh rubber would give him a good chance of running down Yarborough on the restart. The downside was that there might not be a restart.

Waltrip took his spot at the end of the line of lead-lap cars, in seventh place, as the field completed lap 197. The track workers were still cleaning up the mess from Oswald's motor. When the pace car crossed the start/finish line after lap 198, it became official: the race was going to finish under caution.* Waltrip's gamble had cost him $8,250 and 19 points, the difference between a second-place finish and seventh. "Cale might have won anyway, but not starting the race back is what made him win," said Waltrip. Still, it seemed like a reasonable risk to take, as Waltrip still left the track with a 209-point lead.

Yarborough won the race with a fast pit stop and a better race strategy. The win was a reminder of just how good Junior Johnson's operation was. It didn't salvage Yarborough's disappointing season, but it did put an end to the speculation that it would be his last with Johnson. "I'm glad I've got all the press here," Yarborough said after the race. "I don't know who started it, but Junior and I have signed with Busch beer for 1980. I'll be driving whatever Junior wants me to."

Standings After the Coca-Cola 500

1.	Darrell Waltrip	3,061
2.	Richard Petty	2,852
3.	Cale Yarborough	2,850
4.	Bobby Allison	2,845
5.	Dale Earnhardt	2,588

---

* The field had to be given a one-lap heads-up before the green flag came back out. In 2004 NASCAR changed its rules to add extra laps—enough to guarantee two green-flag laps—if a race was going to finish under yellow.

Chapter Eighteen

The Gatorade Kid

Sunday, August 5
Race 20: Talladega 500
Talladega, Alabama

ASTRONAUTS AND race car drivers have much in common: The love of speed. The ability to stare down danger. The big helmets. The inordinate amount of time spent answering questions from strangers about how they go to the bathroom on the job. Unlike their orbiting brethren, racers aren't fitted with special devices to handle the call of nature. Their trips are substantially shorter, and at least before the development of cockpit cooling systems, they tended to sweat so much that dehydration made it a largely moot point. Still, occasionally a driver needs to make a pit stop, one that has nothing to do with tires or fuel. If he does, he has two choices. One is to hold it in. You can figure out the other one.

This was among the many things on Darrell Waltrip's mind leading up to the Talladega 500. He'd been sick with an intestinal virus since the day after the Pocono race. He was off solid food, had dropped ten pounds, and was subsisting, for the most part, on glucose and Gatorade. His fever spiked at 102, and he suffered from aches, chills, and lower gastrointestinal issues of the type one never wants to be afflicted with, especially if one is going to be buckled into a car for three hours. Waltrip wasn't about to miss the race, though. He said he'd rely on a supply of what he indelicately called "cork stoppers."

Waltrip's access to a bottomless bottle of Gatorade was one of the things that put off other drivers. He'd had a sponsorship agreement, one of NASCAR's most valuable and most visible, with the drink company since 1976. Not every driver knew every detail of how the deal had come about, but most at least knew enough of the keywords — "father-in-law," "fraternity brother," "golf course" — to come to the conclusion that it involved rich people scratching each other's backs. That led to the assumption that Waltrip had had it easy, which went a long way toward explaining why Waltrip was so desperate to stick it to the old guard. Talk of silver spoons put Waltrip on the defensive, and his MO when that happened was to strike back. The funny part of it all was that Waltrip hadn't even had a privileged upbringing. Yes, his father-in-law had money, but that didn't mean he was just going to give it to Darrell.

Frank Rader wasn't at all happy with his daughter Stevie's latest boyfriend. Darrell Waltrip was known all over Owensboro, Kentucky, as a reckless hood-in-training, whose reputation preceded him to the point that he was once arrested for "attempted drag racing." (The cops had staked out a strip, and when Waltrip showed up in a Corvette, they popped him.) Waltrip did everything fast: he held the state record in the 440 for almost ten years. And when he wasn't running track, Waltrip's idea of fun was to goad the cops into chasing him by throwing beer bottles at their black-and-whites. It was just like *The Dukes of Hazzard*: the police would chase Waltrip and his pals all over town, up and down alleys, out on country roads. One memorable adventure ended with Waltrip ditching a car in a cornfield after it had been shot up by an officer with Barney Fife–like aim who had been trying to flatten the tires.* As if Waltrip needed to drive home the point that he was not prime son-in-law material, he once flipped a car while being chased on his way to the Rader house to pick up Stevie for a date.

And then there was the pumpkin incident.

Waltrip drove a '55 Oldsmobile that he had painted blue—by hand, with a paintbrush. He called it the Blue Goose. One night he and five buddies piled into the Goose, drove up to Reid's farm, and stole some of the biggest pumpkins they had ever seen. They took them to the drive-in, where everyone was hanging out, and smashed them in the entrance, creating a patch of orange "ice" that, by the end of the night, had sent three cars sliding into the Wax Works record shop next door.

A little while later, at a stoplight, a kid in the car next to Waltrip's tossed a water balloon at the Blue Goose. Waltrip had wisely held back a pumpkin—because you never know when the situation is going to require a giant gourd. Waltrip tossed the pumpkin at the kid's windshield, thinking it would splatter. Instead, it went through the glass and wound up in the driver's lap. Some might call that overreacting. Waltrip, however, wasn't interested in quibbling about what was or wasn't an appropriate retaliation. "I didn't care about that," he said. "I had lost my school ring throwing that pumpkin, and I was too busy looking for it. You couldn't go steady without it, you know."

Stevie clearly didn't mind a ring with a little pulp in it. She'd always thought Darrell was cute. They started dating in 1968 and were married a year later. "When we decided we were going to get married, her family about disowned her," Waltrip wrote in 1979.

Waltrip was, by the time they married, fairly serious about racing. He fell in love with it when he was six. His parents would let

*Waltrip beat the charge because the cops couldn't tell who was driving.

him go to the track with his grandparents only if they asked him, so young Darrell would call his grandmother and gently remind her to call him back with an invitation. When he was twelve, he convinced his dad to buy him a lawn mower and a go-kart. The idea was that he would use the lawn mower to raise enough money to pay his dad back for the go-kart, though no one seems to remember him ever doing that. Past forgiving that debt, there wasn't a whole lot more LeRoy Waltrip could do to help his son's career. His job as a Dr Pepper delivery truck driver didn't provide him with the means to finance a racing operation. The family made the odd sacrifice, but for the most part Darrell was on his own. When he was old enough to drive, he scraped together $500 and bought a '36 Chevy coupe. He didn't have enough of one color paint for the entire car, so he took a page from the Pettys and put everything he had — a little red, some black, and some brown — in one bucket. Richard and Maurice got a beautiful cerulean blue. Darrell got puke brown. "It sort of looked like somebody threw up on it," he said.

He raced at Ellis Speedway outside Owensboro, and when there was nothing left to win there, he and Stevie moved to Franklin, Tennessee, just south of Nashville, where Waltrip dominated at the Fairgrounds Speedway. Frank Rader had finally warmed to Darrell after going to the track with some friends and being pleasantly surprised at how dedicated his son-in-law was. Liking the kid was one thing; bankrolling him was another. Rader set Waltrip up with Terminal Transport, a subsidiary of Texas Gas, but that deal was worth only $25,000. Waltrip owed various creditors three times that much.

He put together a Grand National team, including Jake Elder and Robert Gee, and on occasion he even paid them. But not often. They tried to run a full schedule in 1975, but the debts kept mounting. "I was getting good finishes," he said thirty years later, "but they didn't pay anything. You could finish in the first five or six and you didn't make enough to hardly pay your tire bill. I was in debt over my head, I owed the bank money, I owed Huggins Tire Company money, I owed [parts supplier] Hutch-Pagan money."

Relief came in Daytona. Waltrip passed Donnie Allison on the last lap of the 1975 Firecracker 400, which pushed Bill Gardner over the edge. After the race Gardner summoned Allison to the *Captiva* to give him his pink slip. Gardner and his brother, Jim, decided that if Waltrip could outrun their man in a bad car, he'd be downright dangerous in a good one. Waltrip and Stevie spent a short vacation in Vero Beach after the race, then stopped in at the NASCAR office on their way back to North Carolina to pick up Waltrip's $8,810 check. Someone in the office told Waltrip that Allison had been fired by the Gardners; Waltrip shrugged and got back in the car.

A few hours later the Waltrips made a pit stop. As Darrell was gassing up his car, a familiar face appeared: Jim Gardner. "Funny that I should run into you here," Gardner said. "We've been trying to find you. We want you to drive for our team." Waltrip told him he was committed to his own team, as underfunded as they were. Gardner gave Waltrip his card and told him to think about it. The more Waltrip and Stevie discussed it on the trip home, the more they realized he had to take the Gardners up on their offer. He was just too far in debt. By the time they stopped for dinner, he was pretty well convinced he was going to do it. Then who should appear at the same restaurant but Jim Gardner, whose stalking skills left much to be desired. He tried to pass it off as another coincidental meeting, but Waltrip wasn't fooled. This time he told Gardner he was inclined to accept, and he did, the next day.

While all of this was going on, Bill Stokely was stewing. The head of Stokely–Van Camp, the company that made Gatorade, had just been to the Brickyard for the Indy 500. It hadn't been a pleasant experience. As they had done to Bill France in the 1950s, the stewards had hassled Stokely and his frat brother Dennis Hendrick, a Texas Gas vice president, for not having the proper credentials, despite the fact that Gatorade was paying a lot of money to sponsor Johnny Rutherford's car. Stokely decided if that's how they were going to treat him, he was going home. Not long after that, Hendrick was playing golf with Frank Rader and suggested that Rader should put his son-in-law in touch with Stokely. They talked, and when the meeting was over, Stokely agreed to a $200,000 deal to have Gatorade sponsor Waltrip. "All of my racing career, I've heard people say what a lucky S.O.B. I am," Waltrip said a few years after he signed the deal. *"Everything he's ever had has been handed to him. He was given the Gatorade ride, he was given this or given that.* I wonder if people ever thought how hard I worked and planned to get where I am. I wonder if they thought about some of the turmoil I had to go through."

"If the people who thought we were wealthy could have known how we lived [then]," said Stevie, "they'd have thought we were on welfare." The only way her husband changed after they started to make a little money, she said, was that Darrell didn't "eat as many Rolaids as he used to." He was still eating them, though, and not just at Talladega. His situation — reviled by most fans, disliked by many peers — ate at him. It also motivated him. Probably. It was kind of tough to get a good read on Waltrip. "Darrell is really a complex individual," Stevie said in 1979, after ten years of marriage. "I'm still getting to know him. There are so many different sides."

The field for the Talladega 500 included a couple of moonlighters. David Pearson, who had been tabbed to do commentary for the race alongside Ken Squier on CBS — an interesting call, given Pearson's well-documented skittishness in front of the camera — took Rod Osterlund up on his offer to drive Dale Earnhardt's car while he recuperated from his injuries. And Richard Petty had to find a new front tire carrier after he qualified for the race. Kyle would start a respectable eighteenth, one spot ahead of Bobby Allison.

The two had different expectations. Kyle's was to stay out of trouble and not "mess up anybody." Pearson set the bar higher. His performance at Talladega had been one of the sticking points in his falling-out with Glen Wood, so a strong showing would prove that Pearson still had the necessary nerve and gumption to race at the superspeedways. Driving Earnhardt's car meant that Pearson would be reunited with an old colleague: Jake Elder, his crew chief for two of his championships at Holman Moody. "Jake hasn't changed a bit," Pearson happily reported. "He's still cussing and fuming like he always has."

The forty-one cars rolled off pit road at 1:00 p.m., and Brock Yates of CBS set the scene from the pits: "It's a classic afternoon in the Alabama summertime. Great wads of humidity hanging around us like moist bales of cotton, the horizon covered with marauding thunderheads." Those wads of humidity were bad news for Pearson, whose crew forgot to fill his water jug. Waltrip's support staff was more vigilant. Several of the wives made ice packs and made sure his water jug wasn't dry, while their husbands added more insulation to the car to keep the temperature down inside the cockpit. Waltrip was showing some signs of improvement. After a nearly sleepless night, he had a hamburger the morning of the race and was able to keep it down. But he was still light-headed, so when Donnie Allison fell out of the race with another engine failure, the DiGard crew recruited him to stand by should Waltrip need relief.

The race unfolded without a Big One, but the field was still thinned out by the heat, which put as much strain on the machines as it did on the drivers. Seventeen of the forty-one cars that started, including a slew of favorites, dropped out with motor problems. For the last fifty laps, only Waltrip and Pearson were on the lead lap. But any chance the Silver Fox had of winning was lost when his clutch, which had been replaced that morning, went bad. Without a low gear, Pearson's crew had to push him out of the pits on his last four stops, enabling Waltrip to eventually put him a lap down and cruise to the win.

Richard Petty finished fourth, in a pack of cars two laps down, but he was more interested in his son's finish than his own. He parked next to Kyle's car and asked him, "Hey buddy, how did you do?"

"All right," said Kyle. "But we've got to get more padding in this seat. I wore out my rear end." Kyle finished ninth, seven laps behind Waltrip, but he accomplished what he had set out to do: he stayed out of the way of the faster cars and did some drafting with the slower ones. "The thing that bothered me most about those crashes was the feeling the other drivers would write me off as just another rookie who didn't have what it takes," he said. "I accomplished what I set out to do, and the next time I get into a car for a Grand National, I'll feel a lot better."

On Talladega's spacious infield, two fans hoisted a large banner that read WALTRIP IS NO. 1 E'VILLE, IND., which suggested that his white-hat routine was actually working. (Of course, the fact that the nearest Waltrip fans apparently lived in Indiana said something.) As several bemused fans watched the sign bearers celebrate, Waltrip pulled Maybelline into Victory Lane, took a hit of oxygen, and beckoned Brock Yates to the car so that he could get in a few words before CBS signed off. Spending three hours driving nearly 200 miles per hour was enough to make a healthy man's stomach do backflips, and Waltrip was nowhere near healthy. But he hadn't just survived. He'd won his sixth race and stretched his lead over Petty to 229 points, the biggest it had been at any point in the season. "What Darrell did," said his crew chief, Buddy Parrott, "is another indication of this being our year."

Standings After the Talladega 500

1.	Darrell Waltrip	3,246
2.	Richard Petty	3,017
3.	Cale Yarborough	2,946
4.	Bobby Allison	2,924
5.	Benny Parsons	2,662

Chapter Nineteen
The Beginning of the Trouble

Monday, September 3
Race 23: Southern 500
Darlington, South Carolina
through
Sunday, October 14
Race 28: Holly Farms 400
North Wilkesboro, North Carolina

SEPTEMBER 3 was Labor Day, and in Bristol, Connecticut, there was plenty of laboring going on. Workers had been building a large structure on Middle Street for five months, and judging by the amount of activity on what was supposed to be a day of rest in their honor, they had a deadline approaching and were nowhere near as close to being finished as they should have been. Painters were at work on the outside of the building, but there was only so much they could do, because the masons were still putting up the walls. As soon as a section was finished, the insulation and drywall guys would start their work, almost before the mortar had dried.

The building, which dwarfed everything else on Middle Street, was to serve as the broadcast center for a cable television network called the Entertainment and Sports Programming Network. Cable TV was a novelty at the time—in 1979 only 16 million American homes had it—so the giant building exuded an air of mystery that became even more pronounced in early August, when the thirty-foot satellite dishes were installed out front. They looked ominously anachronistic, like something out of an H. G. Wells novel. One mayoral candidate insisted that they would fry anything that came near them, leaving the good people of Bristol with a pile of dead, irradiated birds on Middle Street.

ESPN's launch was four days away. The network had been conceived in the summer of 1978 by Bill Rasmussen—who, having just been fired as director of communications for the New England Whalers of the World Hockey Association—had plenty of time on his hands. Rasmussen's original plan was to offer some local college events and maybe some Whalers-related programming to viewers in Connecticut. When he looked into purchasing time on Satcom I, which had been sitting in orbit for three years without doing much of anything, he discovered something odd. A five-hour block under the hourly rate would cost $1,250. The daily rate was $1,143, though that wasn't even on the rate card, because nobody in their right mind would consider trying to fill that much time. But 107 bucks was 107 bucks, so Rasmussen expanded his vision from a few hours here and there in Connecticut to an around-the-clock, coast-to-coast network because it was cheaper that way.

Getty came on board with financial backing later in '78, and in early 1979—a few months before he poached NBC Sports president Chet Simmons—Rasmussen signed a deal with the NCAA to show a wide range of college sports. But he still had a problem. There was no way he was going to be able to fill his calendar, even if he showed the same college soccer and football games over and over, which he did.* Rasmussen plugged gaps with programming such as hurling, Irish cycling, and softball. The first competitive event the network aired after its September 7 launch was a slow-pitch game between the Kentucky Bourbons and the Milwaukee Schlitz, which was, at best, the second-most-intense booze-related rivalry of its day, behind the war waged by the "Less Filling" and "Tastes Great" factions in countless Miller Lite commercials.

The broadcast of the 1979 Daytona 500 is rightly hailed as a watershed moment in NASCAR's history. It showed that racing was a viable TV commodity, but in no way did it trigger a mad rush to acquire the rights to races. Promoters were still left to cut their own deals, and the major networks were still skittish about devoting too much time to racing. Humpy Wheeler tried selling the 1980 World 600 on its own merits. When the networks said no, he tried to make it a more attractive show. He threw out all kinds of ideas. Qualifying. *No thanks.* The Sportsman race. *Pass.* Car jumps. *No dice.* Motorcycle jumps. *Not gonna do it.* "I thought, *What the hell am I going to do with these guys? What do people in New York like?*" says Wheeler. "And I thought, *Taxicabs.* So I said, 'What about the Great American Taxicab Race?' They lit up like a 400-watt bulb. And I'm thinking, *Holy crap, what am I going to do? I made all that up on the spot.*" So Wheeler set about finding cabbies from all over the country to drive their cars through an on-track obstacle course: a tollbooth on the backstretch, a hotel in the first turn.†

But there were only so many gimmicks that were going to lure the networks into showing a race. And that's where ESPN came into play. Rasmussen had everything NASCAR wanted: a medium for getting

---

*In the early days ESPN was on the air for twelve hours a day on weekdays and nineteen on weekends.

† When they ran the race on Memorial Day weekend in 1980, a hack from Indianapolis won. "We dropped the flag," says Wheeler. "The first lap they knocked the tollbooth down. Then they knocked the hotel down. It was the funniest thing you ever saw."

the sport into the homes of sports nuts (who, given a chance, might really like it), a little money to splash around, and no reservations about airing something as arcane as stock car racing. No one at the network was in any position to be picky. No one at the network—or at NASCAR—knew it yet, but the two would spend much of the next two decades helping each other grow.

Of course, in September 1979 Rasmussen had no idea if his channel would even make it. When the videotape machines he'd ordered arrived, there was no place in the incomplete broadcast center for them. So Rasmussen had them delivered to his son's condo, where the editing was done up until launch. Everything got done in time—or close enough to done—and the network hit the airwaves on September 7 as planned. There were glitches, to be sure (the first remote aired had no audio), but all in all things went well. And there was no shortage of events to talk about, the Southern 500 included, on the network's nightly highlight show, *Sports Recap,* which three days later would be rechristened *SportsCenter.*

While ESPN was preparing for its first week of broadcasting, the mainstream media were keeping alive a story that brightened up their dreary summer. In late August a White House press secretary let slip to an Associated Press writer that back in April, President Jimmy Carter had come face-to-face with an angry rabbit while vacationing near his home. The next day the AP ran a story that began: "A 'killer rabbit' attacked President Carter on a recent trip to Plains, Ga., penetrating Secret Service security and forcing the chief executive to beat back the beast with a canoe paddle." Writers had a field day, writing pieces that looked at the incident from every conceivable angle: Did Carter hit the rabbit? Could bunnies swim? Was this the same rabbit from *Monty Python and the Holy Grail*?

Bob Dole—who, based on his sponsorship of an unsuccessful bill advocating rabbits' rights, considered himself the Senate's foremost authority on the critters—said that Carter should apologize for "bashing a bunny in the head with a paddle." Dole said, "I'm sure the rabbit intended the president no harm. In fact, the poor thing was simply doing something a little unusual these days: trying to get aboard the president's boat. Everyone else seems to be jumping ship." The *Washington Post* ran an editorial pondering, "What did Mr. Carter ever do to rabbits?" And on September 3 a group called the Defenders of Wildlife unveiled a seven-point program to protect rabbits and advised the president that in the event of a future attack, his best course of action was to sound bells, rattle pots and pans, or "play recordings of feeding calls of hawks and owls," which no casual boater leaves home without. It was the kind of stuff that's hilarious—unless it's directed at you.

While the president was going about his business as the butt of so many *Paws* jokes, Jaws was feeling good about where he stood. Darrell Waltrip's motivation in the points race was simple. "I wanted to beat Richard because I didn't like Richard," he says. "That was just the underlying fact." It was a chance to get back at Petty for making Waltrip feel like an outsider, for not accepting him. And now that he had a 160-point lead* with eight races to go, it was starting to look like his crew chief had been right when he'd declared that it was his year. Waltrip had already clinched the $10,000 Olsonite Driver of the Year Award. The voting was done quarterly, and he had an insurmountable lead after three quarters. That meant ten grand and a banquet at the 21 Club in Manhattan after the season. In Darlington he was the one being asked to ride in parades and judge the Miss Southern 500 beauty pageant. He felt he could safely start crowing. And that was one thing Darrell Waltrip was very good at. He took aim at the aging Petty, suggesting that he should get a "prescription windshield."

---

*Petty had cut into Waltrip's lead, which had been 229 points after Talladega, by winning the Champion Spark Plug 400 in Michigan, where Waltrip had mechanical problems and finished nineteenth.

Before the Southern 500—a race held on a day that was insufferably hot—he'd told ABC, "I'm in good shape. I've run hard everywhere I've been this year. I'm going to run hard today. But I know when this five-hundred miles is over, I'll be a worn-out thirty-two-year-old man. I can't imagine being forty-two and going through the same thing." He didn't have to remind anybody that Richard Petty just happened to be forty-two.

But Darlington was something more than a chance for Waltrip to stick it to Petty. David Pearson, another of the old schoolers who didn't care for Waltrip, was still filling in for Dale Earnhardt. He was back at a track where he'd won eight times, and he was in a very strong car. He seemed to be a real threat to win, and talk of that didn't sit well with Waltrip, who felt that he had established himself as the favorite by driving so well in the Rebel 500 in the spring. "So here I've got Richard on the ropes," Waltrip remembers. "Now we're going to Darlington. Well, Pearson's the king of Darlington. So here's another opportunity for me to knock out another big-time racer. I've beat Richard for the championship; they've got Pearson coming in. That's all I heard going into Darlington: 'Aw, Pearson's going to do this, Pearson's going to do that, and Pearson's the king of Darlington.' And I said—typical redneck—'Yeah, watch this.'

"So sure enough, they drop that green flag, and we took off. We raced all day long, and as the day wore on, my car was just so much better than every other car. I drove Darlington great. I had a great car that day."

Petty didn't, at least not at the outset. After just eighteen laps engine problems forced him behind the wall, where his Chevrolet was descended upon by a dozen guys in matching red pants and blue shirts. They had the hood up for all of three seconds, time enough to switch the ignition box and send him on his way. But the failure of a $125 part put Petty down a lap, which meant that he couldn't drive his usual smooth race. He had to tax himself to get back on the lead lap. And on a sultry South Carolina day, taxing oneself wasn't a good idea. As Waltrip had smugly predicted, the King wilted in the heat. But he was in good company. Bobby Allison got out of his car and was taken to the infield medical center in an ambulance. Ricky Rudd, a whippersnapper of twenty-two, needed a relief driver because, as he confessed to the ABC cameras, he wasn't entirely sure where he was. Donnie Allison, who started on the pole but went out with engine problems, took over for Petty mid-race. Petty got out and collapsed into the arms of a crew member, who laid him on the pavement in the garage. Maurice Petty shooed away onlookers with a broom handle. With his flat cap, his bearish frame, and his thick beard, he looked like Led Zeppelin's notorious manager Peter Grant, keeping groupies off an overworked Robert Plant.

Two drivers were unaffected by the heat: Waltrip and Pearson, whose crew once again forgot to fill his water jug. Waltrip took the lead just past the halfway point and drove away from the pack. He put a lap on every car in the field except one. "Pearson's running second, and I'm determined I'm going to lap him," Waltrip recalls. "I'm slicing through traffic...he's running second, and I'm going to lap him. Buddy [Parrott] and all the guys said, 'Please slow down. Just slow down and ride it out. You've got this thing won.' And I said, 'Shut up and leave me alone. I know what I'm doing.' And sure enough, I lapped him. I mean I just drove by him and left him, and in five laps couldn't even see him."

In the pits Parrott was pleading with him to take it easy. "I was shaking my fist at him," Parrott says. "I was begging him. Please, you got a lap lead on the field. And he'd say, 'Oh, it feels so good. Ohhh, it feels so good.'"

A little too good. "I wanted to lap him again," remembers Waltrip, "because I was that much faster, and it was late in the day, and the longer we ran, the better I got. I was in great shape, and my car handled good, and that's all you needed at Darlington."

Well, that and a brain. And Waltrip's had apparently been under the impression that, this being Labor Day and all, it had the day off.

Waltrip's quest to embarrass Pearson by putting him two laps down ended on lap 298 of 367. "I just kept on going and going and going until I finally drove and turned a little too hard one time and hit the outside wall," says Waltrip. "Bam, bam, bam. I couldn't get it out of the wall; the thing is just eating the wall up. Knocked the right tire off of it. And there I sat, in the infield, wrecked."

Parrott radioed a message: "I said, 'How's it feel now, you...'"

Waltrip made it to the pits, and his crew made a few cursory repairs before rushing him back onto the track. In their haste, they didn't fix the right front suspension, which ten laps later caused the right front tire to go down and put Waltrip into the fence again. This time the crew had to fix the suspension, and by the time Waltrip rejoined the race, he was twelve laps behind Pearson. He finished eleventh. He actually gained 2 points on Petty, who struggled, but had he not thrown away a certain win, he would have picked up 51.

"That," Waltrip said thirty years later, "started our trouble."

After the bad judgment came the bad luck. In the CRC Chemicals 500 in Dover, Delaware, on September 16, both Waltrip and Petty had to deal with flat tires. Waltrip hit the wall and spent an hour in the garage getting repairs. Petty didn't hit anything, and as soon as his tire went down, the yellow flag came out for an unrelated incident, allowing the King to pit without losing a lap. Petty won, Waltrip finished twenty-ninth, and the lead shrank from 187 to 83. Now it was Petty's turn to talk. "I ain't settled into second," he said. "We picked up a hundred points on Darrell. Maybe a couple more licks like that will knock him in the head." Then Petty introduced what would be his main talking point down the stretch — that he had no reason to feel any pressure. "We're going for wins, not the championship," he said. "I've won six championships already, so that deal would mean a lot more to Darrell than it would to me."

The pressure was starting to eat at the entire DiGard outfit. "Darrell was not psychologically prepared to contend for a championship," says Gary Nelson. "Our team was not." As their lead dwindled, they started tinkering with the car more, tried to push the engines harder than they should have. "We were cracking more [cylinder] heads trying to make more power to get back what we had lost," says Nelson. "In those days there were no aluminum heads. They were cast iron, and they would crack if you ported them too much.* But if you ported them, they'd pick up power, so there was a fine line of how much you could port a head and have it last through the race."

They crossed the line in Martinsville the week after the Dover fiasco. The Old Dominion 500 was postponed after Martinsville got hit with five inches of rain.† When they made it up the next day, Waltrip led 184 of the first 275 laps and was out in front when his engine let go. Robert Yates, Nelson, and the rest of the crew reacted heroically, installing a new motor in less than twelve minutes, which most writers claimed was some sort of record. The change happened so fast that one Waltrip fan in the stands went to the bathroom and missed it entirely. When he got back to his seat, another guy told him his driver was now twenty-nine laps down. Thinking he was being messed with — there was no way an engine could be changed that fast — the Waltrip fan called the other guy a liar, which earned him a black eye, a torn shirt, and a cut lip.

While Waltrip was behind the wall getting a new motor, Petty was once again catching a break. He was racing Cale Yarborough for second place when their cars touched. Yarborough broke a ball joint and had to go to the pits for repairs. Petty got stuck on the curb on the inside

---

* Porting a head entails reshaping the intake and/or exhaust ports to make them more efficient — at the risk of damaging them.
† Part of the Wood Brothers shop was washed away. Twenty of their tires were found a mile away.

of the track and had to be pushed free, but his Chevy was unscathed. After the race Yarborough, who came home eighth, blamed the wreck on Petty, who finished second. "I'm sorry I didn't give you just a little more room," Petty told him. "Not much more, just a little bit."

"Where am I supposed to race? I was up on the curb, and I ain't supposed to run on the grass," said Yarborough, who, given his Daytona experience, would know. Some more words were exchanged, and Petty rescinded his apology. "I'm sorry I apologized if that's the way you're going to be about it," he said, and they went their separate ways.

Petty had made up 35 points on Waltrip, who finished eleventh. With five races left, the margin was a very manageable 48 points.

And then came more bad judgment. Waltrip's hubris had done him in at Darlington; at North Wilkesboro on October 14, it was impatience. On lap 310 of 400, Waltrip was racing Bobby Allison for the lead. Waltrip's brand-new Chevy Caprice was the fastest car on the track, but Allison was throwing some good blocks. Frustrated at not being able to get around Allison, Waltrip did what racers do: he used the chrome horn—his front fender. "We nudged ol' Bobby," Parrott recalled thirty years later as he sat in the infield at Daytona. "He'd race you clean, but the one thing you don't do to Bobby Allison, probably even now, is put one little bumper on him. If Bobby Allison was racing today and one of these guys came in and bump drafted him, he would be over there in Lake Lloyd somewhere, swimming."

There was no lake at North Wilkesboro, just a wall. It would have to do. "Bobby, for whatever reason, had gotten upset with me and he didn't like me anymore, and he'd just as soon as wrecked me as look at me," says Waltrip. "I should have been smarter, but I wasn't. So I got to racing him, and he'd bump me and I'd bump him. Bobby was kind of like Dale [Earnhardt]—if you hit me once, I'm going to hit you twice. First thing you know, we come off Turn 4, I start to go by Bobby on the inside, and he clips me."

Allison claimed he didn't do it on purpose, but he hooked Waltrip's car in the right rear. And, says Parrott, "the worst thing you can do in a race car is be hooked in the right rear. And Bobby Allison was a master." Waltrip spun out and hit the fence head-on near the start/finish line. "He stuffed us into the wall and nearly knocked the flag stand down," says Parrott. "The flag guys jumped out of the stand because Darrell was coming up in there." The car bounced off and continued to spin until the passenger side banged the fence. It was a mess. Waltrip got it into the garage, where he remained behind the wheel, a strange combination of pissed and loopy, as his crew tried to get the car fixed. "Why did he do it? Why did he do it? He's been cutting me off all day. I haven't laid a fender on him," he said, his eyes welling with tears.

The nose of the car was knocked in, and the frame needed to be straightened, so Nelson hooked a chain to the front end and attached the other end to the truck the team used to haul its trailer. He told Waltrip to stand on the brake while he floored the truck, which took off in the direction of the fence that kept the fans in the infield out of the garage. Just when it looked like Nelson was going to run over a pack of paying customers, the chain went taut and the truck jerked to a halt, giving the groggy Waltrip another jolt. "Darrell's eyes were kind of rolling around, and all of a sudden that chain got tight and his head hit the headrest," says Nelson. "We told him, 'Uh, Darrell, we got it fixed. Go back out there!'" Bill Gazaway, who was watching from the control tower overlooking the garage, came down to personally raise hell. "You're going to kill somebody!" he bellowed at Nelson.

The repairs took nine minutes, and Waltrip lost twenty-five laps. When he got back on the track, he was looking for revenge. He positioned himself in front of Allison and started running interference. It looked like another wreck was in the offing until NASCAR black-flagged Waltrip. Twice. He finished thirteenth, ten spots behind Petty. The lead was all but gone, a meager 17 points.

As the DiGard team loaded up what was left of the Caprice, someone asked Buddy Parrott if he wanted to take the front bumper, which had been yanked off the car, back to Charlotte. "Hell no," said Parrott. "I want to wrap it around somebody's neck."

Standings After the Holly Farms 400

1. Darrell Waltrip   4,357
2. Richard Petty   4,340
3. Bobby Allison   4,187
4. Cale Yarborough   4,089
5. Benny Parsons   3,813

Chapter Twenty

Pretty Good Americans

Sunday, October 21
Race 29: American 500
Rockingham, North Carolina
and
Sunday, November 4
Race 30: Dixie 500
Hampton, Georgia

RICHARD PETTY left North Wilkesboro enmeshed in the tightest points race in NASCAR history, but before he could consider his strategy for the suddenly relevant final three races of the season, he had to address more pressing concerns. Like figuring out what role he'd play in the selection of the leader of the free world.

Petty had a meeting later in the week with Ronald Reagan, the front-runner for the 1980 Republican presidential nomination. Jimmy Carter had won the 1976 election by holding on to the traditional Democratic power bases: the Northeast and the Solid South. With Carter's approval rating dipping below 30 percent, the GOP sensed he was going to be vulnerable, especially among the hordes of white evangelical southern males who'd helped put him in office. As the Reverend Jerry Falwell explained before the 1980 election, "Carter last time got that vote because he campaigned as a born-again Christian. But this time people will be more concerned about issues than characterizations. Carter has proceeded to undermine the American family." Falwell estimated that there were 3 million to 4 million evangelical voters who could swing either way, many of them southerners. It would be twenty-five years before someone came up with a name for them, but "NASCAR dads" were clearly going to play a role in the 1980 election.

And that's why Dutch was courting Richard and Lynda Petty. They met in a hotel suite and chatted amiably for an hour about their families and their general visions for America. Carter was hip to the importance of the NASCAR set, too. In September 1978 he'd had a slew of them to the White House. Never before had so many cowboy boots trod upon the South Lawn, where the five hundred guests—more than one dressed in a three-piece polyester suit—ate baked southern ham, jalapeño corn bread, and potato salad as Willie Nelson sang "Whiskey River" and "Up Against the Wall, Redneck Mother." During the 1976 campaign, Carter had painted himself as a friend of stock car racing, dropping the green flag at the Atlanta Motor Speedway—where he had been an occasional ticket seller when his peanut crops were poor—and promising to invite the racing community to the White House if elected. On the night he made good on that pledge, though, he was detained by the Middle East peace talks at Camp David. Instead of trying to explain the significance of "tradin' paint" to Menachem Begin and Anwar Sadat and excusing himself from the negotiations, he sent his regrets to the NASCAR dinner. "It would take something of the magnitude of the Camp David summit to keep him away," First Lady Rosalynn Carter told the guests by way of apology.

It was probably just as well, though. Carter could count few support-
ers in the very conservative stock car racing circles.* Big Bill France
told the *Washington Post* that the only reason he showed up at the White
House was that he "got an invitation. I didn't vote for Jimmy Carter in
the last election. Frankly, I've always been a [George] Wallace man. If
he hadn't been shot, I think we would have been here four years earlier." Most of the drivers were similarly underwhelmed by Carter, but
they weren't going to let that keep them from visiting the White House.
Several went inside and had their pictures taken under the portrait of
a president they could admire: the old Scots-Irish man of the people
himself, Andrew Jackson. One of the few allies Carter had in the sport
was his close friend Cale Yarborough, and he became a Democrat only
because his buddy got elected president. Yarborough was a conservative at heart: in 1974 he had become the first Republican commissioner
in Florence County, South Carolina, since Reconstruction.

Petty also dabbled in politics. In 1978 he threw his ten-gallon hat in
the ring for Randolph County commissioner. The timing was peculiar. Petty was in the midst of the worst losing streak of his career, and
here he was spending his spare time driving the other GOP candidates
around the county in a van, going door-to-door, signing autographs,
and discussing pressing issues—taxes, crime, why he'd left Dodge for
Chevy—with the voters. But his motives were sincere. Petty first entertained the idea of running when the Peacock Massage Salon—home,
if the marquee was to be believed, of the "Prettiest Girls in the
South"—opened up on Route 220, not far from the Petty compound.
Eventually, Petty's platform grew into a sort of Appalachian Village

---

* The same couldn't be said for Billy Carter. The NASCAR dinner marked the first
time in well over a year the president's brother had made an appearance at the White
House. He was an extremely popular guest with the drivers—primarily because he,
like them, looked and felt like an outsider. A reporter asked Billy if he was comfortable on the South Lawn. "Yes," he told the writer before turning to a friend and
stage-whispering, "Shit, no!"

Green Preservation Society. In the King's eyes, the sheriff (a Democrat) and the commissioners (four of five of whom were Democrats) were not adequately protecting the small-town values that made Randleman the kind of place where a man would want to raise a family. As Petty put it simply, "It's the kind of a deal where it's time for a change."

So he occasionally turned his pit wall bull sessions into stump speeches. He referred to the leader of the free world as "Peanut" in public. Before one 1978 race he asserted, "Since Carter came in, the country's just gone *bllllumphhh,*" as his finger made the international symbol for a nosedive. "I'd rather have Ford still in there. We were better off when Nixon was in there." Petty endorsed Jesse Helms in his successful reelection campaign for the U.S. Senate, going so far as to film a commercial for him. The message Petty put out resonated. Despite alienating the Dart-driving segment of the electorate, he easily collected the most votes in the race for county commissioner, and the other two GOP candidates rode his coattails into office.

With unemployment and inflation on the rise, the 1978 elections brought good results for all Republicans. They picked up three seats in the U.S. Senate and fifteen in the House, and with the economy still struggling in the fall of 1979, they had their eyes on the White House, which looked ripe for the picking. *Time* explained the political landscape: "For much of the year, Carter appeared so ineffective a leader that his seeming weakness touched off an unprecedentedly early and crowded scramble to succeed him."

Carter's approval rating had dipped below 30 percent during the summer. "In many respects this would appear to be the worst of times," his domestic adviser, Stuart Eizenstat, wrote to him. "I do not need to detail for you the political damage we are suffering." Eizenstat wrote the note in July; after that things got worse. Following the gas riots and the malaise speech came the killer rabbit. Just as that aquatic fiasco was dying down, on September 15 Carter entered a 10K race at Catoctin Mountain Park near Camp David. Wearing a yellow headband and a T-shirt with the number 39, Carter struggled as he climbed a hill early in the race. "I've got to keep trying," gasped the fifty-four-year-old president, who was sweating profusely. "If I can just make the top, I've got it made." And with that he collapsed into the arms of a Secret Service agent. He was rushed back to Camp David, stripped, covered in cold towels, and given a quart of saline solution intravenously.

There were factors that mitigated the president's apparent wimpiness. The hilly course was brutal, and Carter, a devoted runner who jogged between forty and fifty miles a week and was in very good shape, simply pushed himself too hard as he tried to shave four minutes off his personal-best 10K time of fifty minutes. But it was another PR debacle. The *Washington Post* described him as "ashen" and "in distress." One aide mused, "I suppose this will replace the rabbit stories." Another asked a writer, "Are you going to headline it, 'Carter Drops Out of Race'?"

The crack was a reference to the percolating talk that Carter might not even seek reelection in 1980. Senator Ted Kennedy had already launched a viable campaign to challenge him for the Democratic nomination, and beyond Kennedy—if Carter made it that far—lurked a strong field of Republicans, led by Reagan and John Connally. The former Texas governor, like Reagan, realized the value of an endorsement from someone like Richard Petty, so Connally scheduled his own meeting with the King, in New York on Monday, October 22.

But first Petty had a race to run.

Like the first go-round in Rockingham, the air at the American 500 was charged with the electricity that's generated by the distinct possibility of a fight. This time the combatants weren't Cale Yarborough and Donnie Allison. Neither one of them had much to fight for. Cale was languishing in fourth place, while Donnie had, since abandoning his quest to run the entire schedule, skipped eleven of the last eighteen races. No, this time everyone was watching Darrell Waltrip and Bobby Allison.

The day after their run-in in North Wilkesboro, Waltrip ranted to the *Tennessean,* "It's the worst thing that's ever happened to me in racing. The incident cost me the race, probably the national championship and the best friend I had in auto racing." The possibility of innocent drivers once again losing their cars because of someone else's bad blood at the Rock wasn't lost on the rest of the field. "Everybody's concerned about the potential for problems, even more so than we were here in March," said Benny Parsons.

Allison wasn't apologetic about wrecking Waltrip, and he didn't sound like he was losing any sleep over the damaged state of their relationship. "I feel sorry for him," Allison said. "I think the pressure may be getting to him." Waltrip, meanwhile, dropped the defeatist tone once he got to the track and did his best to chill out. In the garage he put his arm around Petty and told the assembled reporters, "I just wish it was me and him racing each other." Then he went on the attack. "[Allison is] someone to talk about pressure," Waltrip said. "He's 42 years old, almost ready to retire as a driver, and he's never won a Grand National driving title. What can he say about pressure? If I don't win this year, at least I have several years left in which to win it. That's something he can't say."

Petty, meanwhile, just stood there and smiled. Whenever he was asked if the fact that he was now in the running for another championship meant there was any pressure on him, he'd just grin, chew on that thin cigar, and insist he'd never felt pressure in his life. "The way I look at it is that it's the kind of deal where a beagle is running a rabbit," he said. "The rabbit is in the lead, but the pressure is all on him. And if people keep talking about it like they apparently are, I don't see how Darrell and his team can help but to start thinking along those lines. That's just human nature."

Whatever role Petty's mind games played in Waltrip's demise, they would have meant nothing had Petty not backed up his talk with one of the most impressive driving stretches of his career. He'd won more races and sat on more poles before, but never against such deep fields.* Throughout 1979 he had been consistent and stayed out of trouble, and the engines built by his brother, Maurice, had made it to the finish of every race. In years past that probably wouldn't have been enough to win a championship, but the infusion of so many new, well-funded teams placed a premium on consistency. Since his wreck in the first Rockingham race, Petty had finished in the top 5 in twenty of twenty-five races, and he'd been worse than eleventh just once.

Petty qualified seventh in Rockingham, four spots behind Waltrip, and both seemed content with the way their cars were running. The day before the race, Waltrip didn't even take his car onto the track, instead moseying around the garage in an autumnal outfit—brown slacks and a matching brown sweater—and consulting with Buddy Parrott before slipping away. Petty left early in the day as well. One of the few drivers who stuck around was Benny Parsons. He was in the garage because that's where the radio was, and he wanted to listen to the Duke-Maryland football game.

No one suffered for missing practice. Both Petty and Waltrip picked up five bonus points for leading early in the race, and Waltrip led the pack at the halfway point of the 492-lap race. He gave the lead up to Petty on lap 267 and was still running second a few minutes later when race officials noticed small puffs of smoke coming from Waltrip's car. A small crack had developed in the oil pan, sending small drops onto the header. All of the oil burned off before it could get onto the track, but Bill Gazaway and the rest of the officials had no way of knowing that. All they knew was that Waltrip's engine was smoking, which meant it was leaking. On lap 294 they black-flagged Waltrip, forcing him into

---

*Petty won ten straight races in 1967, a mark that hasn't been approached since. Not to belittle the accomplishment, but in only four of those ten races was the field bigger than thirty cars, and David Pearson ran in only three of the ten.

the pits to have the crack repaired. He lost eight laps and any chance he had of winning.

The rest of the race offered spectacular wrecks and even more spectacular racing. A few laps after Waltrip was black-flagged, Harry Gant started to feel a vibration in his Chevrolet. Before he had time to get the car into the pits, his front right tire popped off and bounced over the fence, crushing the roof of a car in the parking lot. That was nothing compared to the carnage on lap 426, when Bobby Allison and Ricky Rudd got together, sending both cars hard into the wall backward. The filler neck on Allison's fuel tank broke, causing a fuel leak that ignited before the car stopped moving. "Did I know I was on fire? Damn right!" Allison said later. "I started getting my straps loose long before the car stopped. I wasn't paying much attention to traffic when I bailed out. I just wanted to get away from the car." A groggy Rudd got out of his car and lay down next to it, unaware that it was also leaking fuel. Allison ran to Rudd and pulled him out of the gas puddle.

As Allison was dragging Rudd to safety, Petty was stuck behind leader Benny Parsons, who had lapped the field. Shortly after the restart, Petty and Yarborough got around Parsons, and eight laps later they got the break they needed when Baxter Price spun out in front of them. Petty and Yarborough were both able to swing inside and avoid hitting him, and the yellow flag allowed them to pull up onto Parsons's bumper for the restart. Petty got around Parsons on lap 445, but Parsons returned the favor the next time around, with Yarborough lingering close by in third. Waltrip, eight laps down, could do nothing but watch and root like hell for anyone but Petty. "I was setting back there yelling, 'Hold him, boys! Hold him!'" Waltrip said. But Petty took the lead for the last time on lap 484 and held off Parsons by a car length, with Yarborough glued to Parsons's back bumper in third. Waltrip came home sixth. Petty, who had come to Rockingham trailing by 17 points, had made up 25. Waltrip was no longer the leader. He was livid after the race, convinced that NASCAR was still punishing him for his late-race obstructing of Allison the week before. "There wasn't any [oil] going on the race track," he said. "NASCAR knew that. What it amounts to is that you get into something one week like the deal at Wilkesboro, and the next week you can expect something like this to happen."

While his conspiracy theory was just that, Waltrip did have legitimate cause to feel that he'd been harshly done by. So no one blamed him when he offered NASCAR a piece of unsolicited advice: "They can take their black flag and do you know what with it."

After a week off, the fun resumed at Atlanta. The Friday night before the race saw the long-awaited premiere of "Dukes Meet Cale Yarborough," Yarborough's small-screen debut. In the episode Yarborough was down the Duke boys' way to practice for the Illinois 500 (or as all the Hazzard County locals called it, the "Illinoise" 500), a race that paid its winner the unheard-of sum of $100,000.* As Waylon Jennings explained in his narration, "Well, it seems Mister Cale Yarborough has been doing a little shade-tree mechanic work. They come up with a real, live thingamajig." The thingamajig in question was a turbocharger, which was activated by a giant red switch on the dash, right next to a giant red flashing light. (Apparently, either the race inspectors in Illinoise were a laissez-faire bunch or they were a bit slow on the uptake.) Rumors of the existence of the thingamajig spread through racing circles and piqued the attention of the rival Jethro brothers, who decided to steal it from Yarborough. The episode ended with Yarborough driving a Dodge Charger—the same make as the Duke boys' General Lee—seven-hundred miles to Illinois and winning the race with it. The plot was preposterous but all in good fun, and it won its time slot handily.

---

*Richard Petty got $73,900 for winning Daytona, the biggest purse of the season.

The following night, as the racers slept, a situation that would dominate the national landscape for the next year was developing half a world away, in Tehran. The day after the American 500 in Rockingham, President Carter had allowed the deposed shah of Iran into the United States to receive treatment for his pancreatic cancer, ratcheting up the already fervent anti-American sentiment in Iran. On the morning of November 4, scores of students overran the U.S. embassy there, originally intending to stage a sit-in and then go home. But as more protesters showed up—they were bused in at one point—the event snowballed. Ayatollah Khomeini went on the radio and issued a call for the students to take over the embassy. Sixty-six hostages were seized. Two weeks later thirteen were let go, but the remaining fifty-three were still being held, and their captors showed no signs of releasing them.*

The immediate reaction in the United States was to unite and offer unconditional support. Although Carter made little progress in procuring the release of the hostages, his approval rating immediately soared to 60 percent. That bump—combined with increased scrutiny of the 1969 Chappaquiddick incident in which Ted Kennedy pleaded guilty to leaving the scene of a car accident in which a female passenger was killed—effectively knocked Kennedy out of the presidential race. But as the hostages remained in captivity ABC started airing a nightly update (which would become *Nightline*), the ongoing crisis became another scarlet W, a symbol of the president's perceived weakness.

The Republicans nominated Reagan at their convention in Detroit in July 1980. Richard Petty spoke on the first night as part of the "Together...A New Beginning" entertainment program that also featured Jimmy Stewart, Donny and Marie Osmond, Wayne

*One was released in July 1980, leaving the fifty-two who would remain until the crisis came to its conclusion in January 1981.

Newton, Vicki Lawrence, Michael Landon, Buddy Ebsen, and Lyle Waggoner.* Throughout the fall Reagan hammered Carter on the hostages. Carter's situation wasn't helped by the fact that Election Day was November 4—the one-year anniversary of the start of the crisis. Still, Carter's pollsters had him ahead by three points until the only debate between the two candidates, on October 28. The next day most major news outlets declared Carter the winner of the debate, but voters saw it differently. "There were two things that signaled Carter's demise," says Craig Shirley, a longtime Republican adviser and the author of *Rendezvous with Destiny,* a book about the 1980 campaign. "One, the debate. Two, the hostage crisis. The American people basically said, 'That's it.' The crisis was the final bit of evidence of the impotence of America and the American government." Reagan won in a landslide. Southern white males—the NASCAR dads who had helped put Carter in the White House—abandoned the president en masse. Sixty percent of them voted for Reagan.

As much as NASCAR had benefited from Carter's election in 1976, it may have benefited even more from his defeat. Dutch was more of a NASCAR kind of guy. One of his speechwriters compared him to a former president: Andrew Jackson, the old Scots-Irish man of the people who had been such a popular photo backdrop during NASCAR's White House visit. And the ideals Reagan preached as he ascended to the presidency meshed perfectly with the ideals the sport prided itself on, ensuring that as NASCAR built on the foundation laid in 1979, it would do so in an atmosphere conducive to acceptance and rapid growth.

On the day of the 1979 Daytona 500, the *Washington Post* had run a long story on NASCAR in which David Pearson had talked politics: "What really gets me hot is welfare, taxes and food stamps. Too many people aren't interested in working because they can do better in the welfare line. The

---

*The program was put together by Mike Curb, a Reagan aide and record producer. He later got into NASCAR as a car owner.

cities, counties and states should get them off their butts and put them to work. The American people's taxes are paying them to sit on their butts." It echoed a statement Richard Petty had made earlier: "Democrats are trying to help too many people who don't want to work for a living just because they were born in America." Virtually every driver had slogged his way to the top on his own. A race wasn't five-on-five, nine-on-nine, or eleven-on-eleven. It was one man working by himself. And anything he was going to get, he was going to get himself. More than any other sport, there were no handouts in auto racing. That by-the-bootstraps work ethic embraced by the drivers dovetailed with the new brand of populism Reagan preached, one that stressed the importance of the individual. "In this present crisis, government is not the solution to our problem; government is the problem," he said in his first inaugural address in January 1981. Any man, he was saying, could thrive on his own with a little hard work.

The second pillar of Reagan's message was that there was nothing wrong with the country. Reagan wouldn't be caught giving a speech suggesting that the people of the Republic were in some way responsible for its shortcomings. Throughout the campaign Reagan spoke of America as a beacon of hope, a world leader, "a shining city on a hill." Displays of patriotism—jingoism, his critics would label it—came into vogue, especially as the cold war escalated in the early 1980s.

The NASCAR family has always been quick to rally round the flag. "All I know," Bill France Jr. said of his customers in February of '79, "is that when we play 'The Star-Spangled Banner,' they all stand up and cheer. They're pretty good Americans." Similarly, whenever anyone asked France's father who NASCAR fans were, he'd tell them, "They're the people who win wars for this country."*

---

*In keeping with that theme, Humpy Wheeler's prerace productions in Charlotte often included military exercises. In 1984 he staged a reenactment of Operation Urgent Fury, the United States' 1983 invasion of Grenada. The show lasted fifteen minutes and featured thatched huts being strafed by planes and palm trees splintered by simulated gunfire.

Reagan's ascension transformed the national mood. His message celebrated the rugged, God-fearing, patriotic individual. And NASCAR was offering up forty of them on display every weekend.

Petty and Waltrip staged the same production in the days leading up to the Dixie 500 that they they'd been putting on for weeks: Petty insisting he didn't care about the championship—"If I win it, it'll be a pure money thing"—and Waltrip defending himself from charges that he couldn't handle the p word. "I'm not saying the pressure has gotten to me," Waltrip lectured the media. "You're saying the pressure has gotten to me." Then, as he walked away, he pointed to Petty and said, "The King is here. So let this poor second-class SOB change his clothes."

Atlanta International Raceway is big and fast, the kind of track that suited Buddy Baker's let-it-all-hang-out style. Baker won his seventh pole of the season—clinching the $25,000 bonus for winning the most poles—and then, as he had all year, went out of the race early with mechanical trouble. Neither of the two title contenders had qualified well—Petty was thirteenth, one spot ahead of Waltrip—but by lap 64 of 328, Waltrip had taken the lead, which meant a five-point bonus. Waltrip was again out in front on lap 129 when he ran over some debris in the first turn. As he pulled into the pits to get fresh tires, Dave Marcis pulled out of his pit stall right in front of him. Waltrip slammed on his brakes and went skidding sideways past his box.

Backing up in the pits is against the rules, but, like many NASCAR regulations, there's some wiggle room. Moments earlier Grant Adcox had thrown his car in reverse and backed up a few feet into his stall, and the officials in the pits didn't say a word. Adcox—a middle-of-the-packer making just his sixth start of the year—had little to lose. Waltrip, however, couldn't afford to chance being black-flagged for the third race in a row. Forced to make a split-second decision as his car sat sideways on pit road, he opted to go back onto the track, circle around—on two flat tires—and enter the pits again. When he exited with new tires, he was two laps down.

Petty had problems of his own. He spun out on lap 208 and had to stop for tires, which left him one lap down. Like Waltrip, he had no chance to win the race. The two of them were now worried about one thing: racing each other. As they waged their personal battle back in the field, Neil Bonnett, Dale Earnhardt, and Cale Yarborough were putting on a show up front. Bonnett had used a soft set of tires to qualify. Rules stipulated that a car had to start the race on the same tires it had used for qualifying, so Bonnett and Wood Brothers were gambling that there would be a caution early in the race and they'd be able to stop and get some better tires on the car. But the race stayed green for 175 laps, and Bonnett got lapped. Once he got fresh rubber, he got back around the leader, Yarborough, as the caution flag came out on lap 199, and sixteen laps later he passed Yarborough again to take the lead. Over the next one hundred laps, Bonnett, Earnhardt, and Yarborough exchanged the lead twelve times. With seventeen to go, Bonnett came to a realization: all this battling was killing his tires. He radioed Eddie Wood that he was going to drop back to third place for a while. "I felt if I could make one more run at 'em, I just might win it," Bonnett said later. "And I knew I had to have cooler tires to do that."

While Bonnett was playing possum, the Petty-Waltrip duel turned on an unexpected alliance. Waltrip had gotten one of his laps back, joining Petty as the only two cars one lap down. Petty was ahead of Waltrip by about two hundred yards when Bobby Allison, who was on the lead lap in fourth place but out of touch with the leaders, pulled up on Waltrip. At a mile and a half, Atlanta isn't as wide-open as Daytona, so drafting is less of a factor. But two cars will run a little faster than one, so Allison, who was trying desperately to run down the top three cars, began towing Waltrip, with whom he was no longer on speaking terms. With nine laps to go, the enemies got around Petty.

Five laps later Bonnett and his cool tires made their move. He whipped around Yarborough and then Earnhardt, and he stayed there as the three came out of the fourth turn on the last lap. Unable to get inside Bonnett, Earnhardt tried to rattle him by passing him on the outside. Earnhardt got alongside Bonnett—two of the sport's rising stars, side by side—but he came up half a car length short. A few seconds later, Waltrip crossed the finish line ahead of Petty. Fifth place was worth 5 points more than sixth, and Waltrip had picked up 5 more points for leading a lap. The 10-point swing put Waltrip 2 points ahead going into the final race. And it wouldn't have happened without Allison. "That's the way the sport is," said Buddy Parrott, who had been apoplectic after Waltrip had overshot his pit stall but was now flashing a wide grin. "One week you're cussing a fella, the next week you want to kiss him."

Standings After the Dixie 500

1.	Darrell Waltrip	4,672
2.	Richard Petty	4,670
3.	Bobby Allison	4,458
4.	Cale Yarborough	4,434
5.	Benny Parsons	4,068

Chapter Twenty-one

The Shootout

Sunday, November 18
Race 31: Los Angeles Times 500
Ontario, California

WITH THE exception of the guy who owned the operation, the DiGard crew wasn't exactly filled with Vegas types. They weren't high rollers, they didn't wear pinky rings, and no one was telling Buddy Parrott that he was so money and he didn't even know it. But there they all were on the Strip, just days before the final race of the season, the one that would decide whether they would complete a historic collapse. DiGard owner Bill Gardner had originally planned the field trip as a precursor to an even bigger celebration, the one that would follow the clinching of the Winston Cup championship, but Darrell Waltrip's October demise gave the getaway more of a condemned-man's-last-meal kind of vibe.

Most of the team members had flown in, but Parrott and his wife couldn't get a flight from Charlotte, so they flew into LA and drove a borrowed Lincoln Continental through the desert. The Lincoln lost a tire along the way, so Parrott had to foot the repair bill, leaving him only $15 to play with at the Sands.

It was tough to glean a portent from the team's performance at the casino. Waltrip stuck to the slots. "He won three or four jackpots," says Gardner. "I thought it was an omen. People go their whole lives and don't win one." The boss was less fortunate. "I watched Bill Gardner lose $50,000," remembers Parrott.* "I had never been to Vegas. I thought it was just a show. He had these chips, and I thought, *It's not real money.*"

Parrott's fifteen bucks didn't last long, but he still had a high time. "Gardner took us out, fed us food that I had never seen before," he says. "Them snails." And Gardner planned on bringing everyone back for another celebration after the Ontario race. He booked a gourmet room at the Sands and planned a menu that would blow Parrott's mind.

All they had to do was win the championship.

The math was simple. Waltrip's lead on Richard Petty was 2 points. The difference between any two spots in the race standings ranged from 3 to 5 points, so whoever had the better day in Ontario would be the Winston Cup champ. It was easily the tightest points race ever; the last time the final race of the season had even mattered in the standings was in 1973.

When Waltrip's team got to Ontario, they discovered that they were staying at the same Holiday Inn as Evel Knievel, who just happened to be defying death in that neck of the woods that weekend. And Knievel was up for some fun: "If you liked Crown Royal, you could drink all the Crown Royal you wanted to," says Parrott. Petty was staying at the Holiday Inn, too, and relations were cordial. Parrott had a long talk in

---

* As is usually the case with casino-related endeavors, no one remembers it quite the same. Gardner says that he thought he came out ahead. Waltrip recalls Gardner losing a hundred grand.

the bar with Petty, who employed Parrott's sister. At the track Petty was still telling anyone who would listen that all the pressure was on Waltrip. "I'm already here," Petty said as he leaned against the back of his hauler, pointing to an imaginary ladder rung with the thin cigar in his hand. "I can't go nowhere else. Pressure? I don't know how to spell the word." And then, after everyone left the hauler, he took a swig of his stomach medicine.

But there was some truth in what Petty was saying. Unlike Waltrip, he had a sparkling résumé to stand on. No one was going to judge him on how he handled the '79 points race, so he had no need to play it close to the vest come race day. He'd caught Waltrip with a stretch of aggressive, carefree racing. "He has been bumping and banging and spinning out, doing everything," Waltrip said in Ontario. "And he has been getting away with it."

The novelty of an important season finale drew a larger-than-usual crowd to the press box, as many of the East Coast papers that normally decided against sending a writer across the country for a meaningless race sent someone to Ontario. The track was a knockoff of the Indianapolis Motor Speedway, a two-and-a-half-mile rectangle with four straights and four very sharp turns. The front stretch and backstretch seemed interminable. You just pointed the car down the track and stood on the gas for twenty seconds. If you needed to fix your hair in the mirror—or, if you were David Pearson, you craved a butt—this was the place for it. The pressing question Ontario presented teams with was how big a gear they should use. A bigger ratio meant more speed—and more risk of a blown engine. Most drivers were using a ratio of 3.64:1. Petty went with 3.70.

Without the luxury of six championship trophies to fall back on, Waltrip had a more difficult decision—one that was made trickier by the fact that Petty's campaign to convince the garage that Waltrip was cracking seemed to be working. Waltrip said, "People have come up to me and put their arm around my shoulder and looked at me with real concern in their faces and said, 'You all right?' I'd like to haul off and deck them when they do that. Richard's using good tactics. They all believe everything Richard says because he's the King. They don't bother him about his feeling any 'p-p-p-pressure.'" The Pettys' mind games weren't all played out through the press. "Lee Petty would come by and talk to Darrell—'How's it going?'" says Gary Nelson. "I can remember Lee standing there talking to Darrell and Darrell thinking this guy's his friend." Waltrip heard through the grapevine that the Pettys were using different spindles in Ontario, so he made the DiGard crew change his, too, an extreme tactic. Nelson never found out for sure who started the spindle rumor, but he's always believed someone in the Petty camp planted the story. "I realized why Petty had won so many championships," says Nelson. "They found certain nerves within a team and jumped on them."

The prerace festivities featured a shoot-out motif, with the two title contenders dressed up as Wild West gunslingers. Waltrip was in a frilly vest that looked like someone's leftover Village People Halloween costume. Petty brought his own accessory to his snappy outfit: an STP Winston Cup champion belt buckle. Their crews dressed up as well, all in western gear, except for Maurice Petty, who was decked out in a set of Union army blues. Before the race Ken Squier, who was doing the tape-delay broadcast for CBS, stood between Petty and Waltrip and asked if they had any thoughts on the race.

"No," said Waltrip with a laugh.

"It's just another race," Petty insisted, and if the mood of his crew—especially his crew chief and cousin, Dale Inman—was any indication, he wasn't feigning insouciance. They seemed more interested in what was happening 2,500 miles away, in Washington, than in Ontario. The Redskins were the closest NFL franchise to the Petty compound, so Richard and Dale had grown up as Washington fans. The Los Angeles Times 500 was taking place the same day as the

Redskins-Cowboys game. First place was on the line in what was an especially tasty edition of the rivalry. Dallas had run up the score the year before, and a few days before the rematch Washington's Diron Talbert had fired up his teammates by getting up at a team meeting and saying of the Cowboys, "Just pretend they're Iranians." All day Inman had been pestering the CBS guys about the Redskins' chances. "I can get more excited about a close ball game, a basketball game or a football game, than I do for the race," Inman said. "Because when the race is real close, I know Richard's putting out all the effort and we've done all we can do for him."

Petty started fifth. Waltrip, whose team had decided not to be too risky with their setup, qualified tenth. Cale Yarborough won the pole—his first of the year, which spared his sponsor, Busch, the embarrassment of having to stage the 1980 Busch Clash without its car in the field—and Kyle Petty qualified twenty-sixth. Petty and Waltrip each picked up 5 points early in the race for leading a lap. Petty took his Chevy to the front on lap 6. Waltrip inherited the lead by staying out an extra lap when the caution flag came out following a John Rezek spin-out on lap 9. Waltrip was lingering about half a lap behind the front pack, near the edge of the top 10, when Rezek spun again on lap 41. This time Waltrip was right behind him. The smoke from the spin was heavy, with Rezek lurking in it somewhere, like an iceberg in the fog. Waltrip didn't want to go into the smoke blind, so he spun his car on purpose, looping around Rezek and coming to rest on the grass with the engine still running. The car was clean, but the abrupt stop flat-spotted the tires. Waltrip pulled all the way around and into the pits. "They'll change all four tires on this," the wry Englishman David Hobbs said on the CBS broadcast. "Possibly change the driver's underwear."

It was a hell of a save, but it was followed by another mistake—this one massive—by the DiGard team. Waltrip was about half a lap behind the leaders when he entered the pits. His crew changed the tires and took a long look at the car to make sure they didn't have a repeat of Darlington, when the broken suspension had led to a second flat tire. The only constraint on their time was that they had to get back on the track ahead of the pace car, but that shouldn't have been a problem, since it took the pace car forever to complete a circuit. "That big old racetrack—there ain't no way you lose a lap," says Waltrip. "But we did."

Waltrip was the only car in the lead pack that didn't beat the pace car out of the pits. He pulled in behind it—passing the pace car is a no-no—and was forced to trudge around the track at something near the legal speed limit. The rest of the leaders tore around at racing speed, crossed the start/finish line, and queued up behind him. When the race restarted, Waltrip was the first car in line, but he was actually the last car on the lead lap. It's an oddity in racing, and when it occurs, it confuses everyone, even the drivers. Waltrip, whose radio was down, thought he was leading the race. Only when his communication with Parrott was restored did he find out that he was a lap down. "It was like someone had kicked a ladder out from under me," Waltrip said later.

Hope wasn't lost, though. As Yarborough had shown in Daytona, getting unlapped wasn't impossible. If Waltrip could keep the leader behind him when a yellow flag came out, he'd be back in business. But Benny Parsons blew by him on the restart, and Waltrip didn't have the muscle to pass him back. ("We guessed wrong on the combination," said Parrott.) The only way he was going to regain his lap was if someone gave it to him, and Waltrip wasn't high on anyone's gift list. Every time a caution came out, Parsons raced Waltrip back to the stripe. Parsons said he was doing it because he didn't want to let a car that could possibly win the race back into the mix. Parrott made a couple of trips to Parsons's pit stall to ask for a break, but none was forthcoming. "He didn't want me to win the championship," Waltrip recalled. "I don't think anybody wanted me to win it." Waltrip finally told Parrott, "I don't want to do this, but if that happens again, I'm going to wreck him, because he's doing that on purpose. He knows if I get that lap back, I'll win the championship." But the opportunity never presented itself.

Waltrip's last hope was that Petty would blow up or wreck, which for a while looked entirely possible. Petty had said all along that he was going to race for the win, but that seemed like just another mixed signal meant to screw with Waltrip's head. Apparently he meant it, though. "The champion should be the cat out there running as hard as he can every race he runs," Petty explained later. "I've found out you can get in just as much trouble if you cool it as if you don't. Basically, a cat's better off if he runs hard all day." On lap 75, he brushed the wall hard enough to dent some sheet metal. "The driver just lost it," Petty joked later. He continued to fight for the lead, hard, in the last fifteen laps, giving Inman fits (though he was buoyed by the news that the Redskins were beating the crap out of the Cowboys). In the last laps, when it was apparent he couldn't beat Parsons, Petty finally backed off a little and cruised home in fifth place. Waltrip was eighth, the first car a lap down. Petty won the Winston Cup by 11 points, the narrowest margin in history.

Petty pulled onto pit road, and Inman lowered the window net. Petty braced for an invasion, a hug, a Pepsi bath, something. Instead, Inman screamed, "The Redskins won! The Redskins won!"

"Is that any way to treat a champion, now?" Petty asked.

After the race, the King held court, twirling his little cigar. "Last year was the low ebb of my twenty years in racing, no doubt about it," he said. "From that standpoint, winning the title again is very satisfying." As he considered where he'd come from, he also had to feel pretty good about where Petty Enterprises was going. His front tire changer — Kyle, his heir apparent — came home fourteenth. And they didn't know it yet, but a fourth-generation driver would soon be in the picture. Pattie Petty was pregnant.

Back in the garage, Waltrip — who was expected to attend a joint press conference with Petty — was in no mood to answer questions. He closed the door on his garage stall, emerging after a few minutes only to go directly into the back of the team's hauler to change his clothes.

Only Stevie was granted admittance. They pulled the door of the truck down almost all the way, so the only thing the curious onlookers could see were the green shoes he had put on. A track worker knocked on the truck. "Do you want an escort to the press box?"

"No, thank you," came the reply through the door. "Not today, I think. Please give everybody my regards and regrets."

Waltrip finally emerged, looking like a man who had been stripped of not only his dream but also his fashion sense. His green shoes were complemented by matching pants and a garish purple and white shirt. "I ain't never going to figure it out," he said of the lost lap. "Never. They took it away from me and broke my heart."

He did a few TV interviews, reiterating that he didn't understand what had happened. But he realized that ultimately what had done him in was that he hadn't brought a strong enough car. "I told everybody Richard was coming to race," he said. "Richard always comes to race. We prepared the car more to go five hundred miles than to race."

He sounded ready to do some more finger-pointing, and a writer gave him the perfect opportunity by asking if he was saying that Parrott had made the fateful decision.

Waltrip thought for an instant. "No," he said. "No, it was a unanimous decision."

Another competition was decided in Ontario. Dale Earnhardt finished ninth to sew up the Rookie of the Year title. It had been a foregone conclusion for a couple of weeks that he'd win the award. NASCAR had an elaborate formula that took each rookie's fifteen best results into account, but that was just a guide. The winner was picked by a four-man panel made of the reigning Winston Cup champ, in this case Yarborough, and three NASCAR officials. Not only did Earnhardt have the best results—he finished seventh in the season points race despite missing four races after the wreck at Pocono—but he had clearly shown the most moxie, heart, allure, and every other intangible that would appeal to the voters. Earnhardt had done things no other rookie had done. He'd won races. He'd put a legitimate fear of God into the old pros. He'd inspired fans. He'd started a movement.

Yet as the forces of the racing universe tugged at him, pulling him on the road from simple country boy to icon in a sport America was finally ready to embrace, you wouldn't know it by looking in his garage or his closet. In late October, when it was pretty clear that he was going to win the award, Earnhardt bummed a ride to the shop with Nick Ollila because Earnhardt and his soon-to-be third wife, Teresa, had only one car. "You know, I'm going to win this rookie of the year thing, and they got this banquet in Ontario," Earnhardt said to Ollila. "Have you got a sport coat I could borrow?"*

Now, before he had occasion to wear it, he and the boys were going to do a little less formal celebrating. Earnhardt and Lou LaRosa rode back from the speedway to the hotel in a rental car with Jake Elder. Deeming some sort of trick driving an appropriate way to honor his latest protégé, Elder came flying into the parking lot at about 35 miles per hour and threw the car into reverse. They spun, transmission fluid went everywhere, and the car caught on fire. No one seemed to think it was a big deal. The Rookie of the Year Award meant ten grand to Earnhardt, plus $1,000 for each race he entered in 1980. All told, the thing was worth close to $50,000 — and that was on top of the money from the Winner's Circle program. That was the kind of money that would cover the damages on a rental car. It was almost the kind of money that would buy a man a diamond the size of a horse turd.

They went up on the balcony. LaRosa, the tough Staten Island native, thought about what he and the rugged linthead had accomplished. This was as touchy-feely as it was going to get: "That was great, Dale," LaRosa said, "you being Rookie of the Year."

---

* Ollila obliged. He doesn't remember what it looked like, but, he says, "there was polyester involved in it. Absolutely."

"That don't mean shit to me," Earnhardt said, flashing that Mona Lisa smirk. "I want to be the Winston Cup champion."

Final 1979 Standings After the Los Angeles Times 500

1.	Richard Petty	4,830
2.	Darrell Waltrip	4,819
3.	Bobby Allison	4,633
4.	Cale Yarborough	4,604
5.	Benny Parsons	4,256

Epilogue

DARRELL WALTRIP's refusal to put the blame for his Ontario disaster on his crew might have been a sign that he had turned over a new leaf, become more of a team player.

It might have, but it wasn't.

Shortly after the 1979 season finale, Waltrip convinced Bill Gardner to fire Buddy Parrott as his crew chief. Parrott did not take the news well. "I let everybody know I was going to kick his ass," he says. It didn't take long for word to make its way to Waltrip. He walked into the DiGard shop one fall day, and a worker came up to him and said, "You seen Buddy? He's looking for you. He says he's going to beat the shit out of you."

Waltrip's reaction: "He's a big strong guy. Damn, I hate this."

A few nights later, after dinner and a few beers with a couple of his pals, including Slick Owens, who was also a friend of Parrott's, Waltrip finally decided he'd had enough of looking over his shoulder. "Somebody said something about Buddy, and I said, 'Yeah, I guess I'm going to have to just go over to his house,'" says Waltrip. "They said, 'You can't go over to his house—he'll kill you.' I said, 'Well, riding around worrying about it is about to kill me, so I don't know anything else to do except go over to his house. I got to get this over with.'

"So we did. We drove over to his house and I knocked on the door, and it sort of disarmed him. Because when he saw me, he grabbed me, but he said he had another job offer anyway." *

That offer fell through, though, and when Gardner and Waltrip couldn't decide on a new chief, they hired Parrott back. Waltrip finished fifth in the points in 1980, and it was clear that his time with DiGard was coming to an end. "After we lost that championship in '79, Bill Gardner called me and he said, 'The one thing you'll never have to worry about as long as you drive for me is winning a championship, because I ain't ever going to spend that much money again trying to win a championship. That's the most ridiculous thing I ever did. I'm going to spend money to win races, but I'm not going to get involved in that championship thing anymore.'" After the 1980 season Waltrip paid $300,000 to get out of his contract and sign with Junior Johnson, who was in the market for a new driver because Cale Yarborough had decided that he wanted to drive part-time and signed with M. C. Anderson.

Like much of NASCAR's old guard, Johnson had been on the receiving end of some unwanted Waltrip smack talk in the past, but he had no qualms about kicking in part of the buyout to hire him. "The best driver, that's who you want," Johnson says. "Personality is not a big thing with me because you both have the same desire." The combination of Waltrip's ability and Johnson's know-how proved unbeatable. "All I needed was somebody to tell me what to do," Waltrip says. "When I went to drive for Junior, Junior told me what to do." They won the Winston Cup their first two years together and took it again in 1985.

All the while, Waltrip was gradually gaining acceptance. He still bragged too much and said what was on his mind, no matter how insolent or obnoxious. Sure, he'd egg the crowd on, asking them to

---

* Parrott remembers it slightly differently: Owens called and told him Darrell wanted to get it over with, but in the end Waltrip "was too scared to come over to my house."

boo him in Victory Lane and then telling his sponsor, Mountain Dew, that they had been chanting, "Dew!" But he was winning races and championships, so he didn't need to use his mouth to manufacture any buzz. The press was going to pay attention to him no matter what he said. Waltrip also benefited from having such a popular, likable wife, who had the couple's first daughter in 1987. "Seeing me and Stevie and Jessica in the winner's circle, people saw I had a softer side," he says.*

The defanging of Jaws was completed on May 21, 1989. With $200,000 on the line in the Winston, then the name of the NASCAR all-star race, Rusty Wallace spun Waltrip out with two laps to go and ended up winning. The teams came to blows on pit road after one of Waltrip's crew members kicked Wallace's car as it drove to Victory Lane. Wallace claimed that he'd barely made contact on the track, but Waltrip was suddenly a victim. People actually defended him, advocated for him. It was like Red Sox fans hearing that Bucky Dent's car got totaled and chipping in to buy him a new one.

By that point Waltrip was heading into the downhill side of his career. He won fifty-seven races in the 1980s, just five in the '90s, and none after 1992. He kept driving, though, turning the 2000 season into his own personal victory tour, on which the same fans who had thrown fruit at him fifteen years earlier fattened his wallet by buying everything from hats to Hot Wheels at Kmart, which was his sponsor. Waltrip had become so popular with the masses that when Fox acquired a share of the sport's broadcast rights beginning in 2001, he was the logical choice to become the network's voice of NASCAR.

Under the terms of the television deal that expired after the 2000 season, NASCAR had been paid $100 million a year. The sport had

---

* It also bears mentioning that Waltrip, though certainly obnoxious in his younger days, was always, at heart, a good and decent guy. After Buddy Parrott was fired in 1979 but before he was rehired, he didn't receive a Christmas bonus from the Gardners. Waltrip gave him one. "Biggest one I ever got," says Parrott.

grown gradually as a TV commodity in the 1980s, thanks largely to Bill Rasmussen's creation, ESPN, which had first started showing races in 1981. But the new deal with Fox and NBC was worth more than four times that: $2.47 billion over six years, a staggering sum for a sport that hadn't been deemed viable programming fifteen years earlier. Fox's first race was the 2001 Daytona 500, which provided ample drama: Darrell Waltrip calling the first career win of his little brother, Michael. That should have been the enduring memory of the race, but seconds before Michael crossed the finish line, Dale Earnhardt hit the wall between Turns 3 and 4. It wasn't the kind of spectacular barrel-rolling wreck that leaves observers marveling *I can't believe he survived that* when the driver invariably walks away unscathed. It was a relatively innocuous-looking hit. But it broke Earnhardt's neck, killing him instantly.

If the 1979 season was the start of NASCAR's transformation from a regional curiosity to a major sport, then the beginning of the 2001 TV deal represented the culmination of that evolution. The sport had arrived. Those two events also roughly bookend Earnhardt's career: his rookie season and his last race. The confluence is no accident. Earnhardt, as he told Lou LaRosa he would, won the 1980 Winston Cup title, despite the somewhat predictable departure of Suitcase Jake Elder in the middle of the season. Doug Richert, who was just twenty, took over, and Earnhardt relied on a 148-point lead he'd built up under Elder to hold off Cale Yarborough by 19 points to win the first of his seven championships, which equaled Richard Petty's total.

But it wasn't numbers that made Earnhardt an icon. It was how he did it. The Osterlund team imploded in 1981, and after a few fallow years Earnhardt hooked up with Richard Childress, an independent driver who had just climbed out of the cockpit to focus on being an owner. The two of them built the team that would win Earnhardt's last six titles. It only reinforced the notion that nothing ever came easy to Earnhardt, and it added to the proletarian appeal that had won over all those fans at Charlotte on Memorial Day weekend in 1979. He was one of them, even when he cut his hair and stopped shooting off guns in other people's yards, as he did when he remarried (this time it took) and settled down. He never really settled down on the track, though. As he led the sport to new heights, he picked up the nickname that would stick with him until he died: the Intimidator.

Perhaps the most tragic element of Earnhardt's death was that it came just as he was embarking on a late-career resurgence. Earnhardt's last title came in 1994, and his yearly finishes were getting gradually worse until his youngest son, Dale Jr., made his Winston Cup debut in '99. Having the kid around seemed to spark the old man. He was noticeably peppier, and in Junior's first full season, 2000, Senior finished second in points. He had a legitimate shot at winning his eighth title in 2001, but he never got the chance to topple the King.

Earnhardt's death ignited a fierce debate over safety in the sport. He was the third Winston Cup driver to die in an eight-month period. In July 2000 Kenny Irwin had been killed in practice at the New Hampshire International Speedway, the same track where two months earlier a nineteen-year-old rookie had lost his life in a similar accident. His name was Adam Petty.

When the Petty clan celebrated Richard's 1979 title, Pattie was pregnant with her first child. Eight months later, in the middle of Kyle's second season, she gave birth to Adam. Being pregnant and then a new mother wasn't easy. When Kyle traveled, he usually shared a hotel room with a couple of crew guys, so Pattie couldn't tag along. Kyle drove half of the Grand National schedule in 1980 and a full season in '81. He improved gradually, leading a few races here and there, including the 1984 Firecracker 400 in Daytona.

Just how far stock car racing had come in the first four years of the decade—and just how inextricably linked it was with the patriotic message of President Ronald Reagan—became evident on that Fourth of July afternoon. Reagan, who was running for reelection, chose to spend the most red, white, and blue day of the year at the track, giving the command to start engines from *Air Force One* and then landing on the runway beyond the backstretch shortly after the race began. He was inside the track in time to see Richard Petty's two hundredth—and final—win.

Following the 1984 season Kyle created a stir when he left Petty Enterprises to drive for Wood Brothers. It wasn't unprecedented; the King himself had taken a two-year leave from Petty Enterprises to drive for Mike Curb. But whereas Richard's move had been about hooking up with what he thought would be a more competitive team, Kyle's was about forging his own identity. He'd always viewed the Petty name as a blessing and a curse. No matter what he did, he'd always be "Richard's son." He wanted to see what would happen when his boss wasn't his old man. "When you get out in the real world, it's make-or-break. When you drive for your daddy, he's going to overlook a lot," Kyle said.

The move was also another indication that Kyle was a little bit different. Racing had been his father's life, and his grandfather's, too. But Kyle—the high school basketball and football star, the kid who could pick up a guitar and set a roomful of toes a-tapping without having had so much as one lesson—was destined to develop other interests. It wasn't uncommon; Dale Earnhardt would occasionally have someone fill in for him in practice while he went hunting. What was uncommon was Kyle's preferred diversion: singing.* This wasn't like when his daddy and five of his rivals had caterwauled their way through a bunch of hillbilly standards on a lark. This was real guitar-playin', voice-twangin' Grand Ole Opry stuff. He lost the perm, grew his hair out, got an earring, and started writing songs. It landed him on the

---

*Of course, Kyle's old buddy Marty Robbins did both, but he was always a singer first and a driver second.

pages of *People,* which was just one more reason for the old guard to view him with suspicion. "You're only supposed to want to drive a race car," says Pattie. "You're not supposed to want to do anything else. So it was frowned on by his father; it was frowned on by everyone in racing. *Well, Kyle's not committed. Kyle doesn't take racing serious. He wears an earring and has long hair. He's just a fruitcake that's out singing.* Two things: he was talented, and it paid $5,000 a show to open for Randy Travis or Hank Jr. or the Oak Ridge Boys. And $5,000 is a lot of money. It's more than he made getting in a race car."

Being away from Petty Enterprises made it easier for Kyle to indulge his inner Randy Travis, but he eventually felt the pull of home. In 1997, after winning eight races and $7 million for the Woods and Felix Sabates, Kyle came back to race for his father, who had finally retired in 1992. They set up an offshoot called PE2 that Kyle would oversee, but the idea was that one day he'd take over the running of Petty Enterprises from his dad. The driver would be Adam.

Having grown up as he did, Kyle was acutely aware of the pressure his son would be under to drive, and he was careful not to push Adam into anything. But Adam was one of those kids, like Dale Earnhardt had been, who spent his time in school thinking of nothing but driving cars. And he was good at it. So Richard and Kyle mapped out a plan. Adam entered some ARCA and Grand National races, and he made his debut in NASCAR's top level in April 2000, driving the number 45 car. Six weeks later, on a Friday afternoon during practice for his second race, his throttle stuck, he hit the wall, and he was gone.

The funeral was three days later. Doug Carty, the same man who had married Kyle and Pattie twenty-one years earlier, performed the service in front of a thousand family members and friends at High Point University.

It's human nature to look for silver linings during the darkest days. And it's also almost always a load of bull. But at Adam Petty's funeral, something truly remarkable happened: Bobby Allison got his life back.

Allison finally won that elusive championship in 1983 driving for, of all people, Bill Gardner.* Two years later Allison's son Davey, who had made his dad and uncle so proud before that race in Talladega in 1979, made his first start in the Winston Cup series. In 1988 father and son finished one-two in the Daytona 500, one of the most memorable races ever run—except, ironically, for Bobby.

That June, Allison was racing at Pocono when his left rear tire started to go down during the parade laps. Allison planned to pit on the second lap, but before he could, the tire blew, sending his car into the wall and back down the track, where it was T-boned on the driver's side by another car. It took workers fifteen minutes to get Allison out of the car. He had a broken leg and ribs and internal injuries, including a bruised heart. The wreck ended Allison's career at age fifty-one, but worse, it robbed him of his memory of the '88 Daytona 500. To this day Allison can recall how much he paid for his very first car and where he and Donnie ate after they won their first race in Alabama, but he can't remember what he can only surmise "had to be" the happiest day of his life.

Donnie's career was also cut short by an injury. His relationship with Hoss Ellington continued to crumble during the '79 season. Part of the problem was that Ellington's boys were still spending more time than they should bellied up to various bars. ("Hoss told me one time if his crew quit drinking Budweiser, they'd have to lay off the night shift at Anheuser-Busch," says Donnie.) More significantly, they never got past the fact that Hoss had given Cale Yarborough that ride home from Daytona. "That might have been the deterioration of our relationship," says Donnie. "That was just the way Hoss was. I shouldn't have let that

---

*Donnie Allison had no problem with his brother driving for the man who had fired him. Says Donnie, "The only conversation we had was I told him, 'You better have your ducks in a row, or buddy, you're going to get screwed.' And when everything was said and done and he left DiGard, he got screwed."

get under my skin, but I did." They parted ways in 1980, and the fact that Donnie's first attempt at running a full schedule had been aborted after just ten races did little to help his reputation for being less than serious. He couldn't get a decent ride. He drove a few races for coal magnate Kennie Childers, then found himself in someone else's piece of junk in Charlotte in 1981 and tried to push it too hard. He hit the wall and almost got killed. He drove a few more races but never came close to winning again.

Donnie doesn't hold a grudge against Yarborough (or against Ellington or even Gardner). But he can't help but think about what would have happened if he hadn't wrecked with Yarborough on the last lap in Daytona. "It would have been a lot different," he says. "That would have been the determining factor in my whole career. I wouldn't have gotten upset with Hoss. We wouldn't have parted company. I went and drove for the coal miner a little bit, but then from then on…"

From then on, things only got worse for the Allison family. In August 1992 Bobby's younger son, Clifford, was killed in practice for a Busch Series race. Less than a year later Davey died in a helicopter crash at Talladega. Always headstrong, Bobby coped with the situation by putting his head down and soldiering through. He shut out his wife, Judy, who had been with him since the early days in Hueytown. They separated in 1996 and divorced the following year. Alone and broke—he had no pension or insurance to fall back on, and Bobby Allison Motorsports had just gone belly-up—Allison was forced to leave the house he had moved into on Christmas Eve 1969 with Judy and the kids. He moved across the street to live with his ninety-year-old mother, Kitty.

A priest who is a family friend was asked to compare Allison to Job. He decided that Allison had it worse.

Then, after four years, Bobby and Judy ran into each other just after Adam Petty's death. They decided to put aside their differences and go to the funeral together to support the Petty family. They began to talk, and they came to realize that they'd both done some healing in their time apart.

They remarried two months later.

A number of other figures from that landmark 1979 season can still be found hanging around the track. Jeff Hammond, who spent much of Daytona pulling mud out of the undercarriage of Cale Yarborough's car, went on to become crew chief for Darrell Waltrip and now works with Jaws on Fox broadcasts. Steve Hmiel is the director of competition for Earnhardt Ganassi Racing. His former Petty Enterprises colleague Robin Pemberton is now working for NASCAR as its VP of competition. Michael Waltrip still drives, and Terry Labonte and Geoff Bodine occasionally get back behind the wheel. Ken Squier runs the Thunder Road International SpeedBowl in Vermont and still does some on-camera work. After a successful run as a crew chief and as NASCAR's director of competition and VP of research and development, Gary Nelson runs a motorsports consulting company. And Waddell Wilson — who finally saw the Gray Ghost get to Victory Lane in the Daytona 500 in 1980 — is still building engines.

But most have moved on from a sport that has changed radically over the past three decades. The cars look different (more modern). The drivers look different (better haircuts). The tracks look different (actual seats and luxury boxes). A handful of big teams — Roush Racing, Hendrick Motorsports, Joe Gibbs Racing — that got into the sport as it was beginning to grow, brought with them a bigger-is-better mentality that has changed how things are done. That hasn't made it easy on the mom-and-pop teams that fielded cars for so many years. In 2003 the Wood Brothers were finally forced to move from the hills of southern Virginia to the Charlotte area. The Woods still field a car, the old number 21, but they haven't won a race in eight years.

And in 2008 Richard Petty had to take on an investor to keep Petty Enterprises afloat, which proved to be just a stopgap solution. In early

2009 he merged with Gillett Evernham Motorsports. Under the new deal—which didn't provide a seat for Kyle, who has turned his attention to announcing—the team is called Richard Petty Motorsports. Petty has little say in how the team is run, but it's his name on the truck, so every week the King is at the track, roaming the garage, taking it all in from behind his sunglasses, calling people from all walks of life "cats," and serving as a reminder of a time when stock car racing was a little rougher and a little more colorful and when its brightest days lay just ahead.

Acknowledgments

WRITING A book, as I discovered, can be a laborious, tedious, and grueling process. But it can also be incredibly rewarding, not least because it's something that can't be done alone. A lot of people played a part in this book — some old friends, and some new ones whom I had the pleasure of meeting as this project took shape.

Thanks first to my agent, Scott Waxman, and my editor, Junie Dahn, who were both enthusiastic about the book from the start. Many a brilliant idea of mine has died on the vine (I had that whole teenage vampire idea like twenty years ago. No, really...). But Scott made me keep this one alive, and Junie did a terrific job helping to shape and hone it. (And though he proved tough when he had to be, Junie was refreshingly lax when it came to contractually mandated deadlines. Thanks, man.)

Originally my plan was to focus solely on the 1979 Daytona 500, but the more research I did, the more sprawling the idea became. Zack McMillin was one of the first to encourage me to think big; I'm pretty sure his advice was, "I'd hope to learn more than Cale Yarborough's drafting strategy." For better or worse, that was my mantra for months.

The research process introduced me to several great people. I found a guy on an Internet message board, Jay Coker, who was willing to share his race DVD collection. Thanks for the DVDs and the friendship. Tim

Boyd, a history professor at Vanderbilt, was full of thoughts on how NASCAR fit into American culture in the late 1970s. He suggested working in Disco Demolition Night at Comiskey Park; pretty impressive baseball knowledge for a Brit. Professor Kevin Fontenot at Tulane provided plenty of background on country music, and Bill Malone was helpful as well. Craig Shirley did much to explain how NASCAR and Ronald Reagan were made for each other. And Suzanne Wise at Appalachian State and Frank Barefoot at the Greensboro Library came up huge in providing clips and research materials.

Many drivers, writers, and crewmen shared their memories, and to a man (and woman), they seemed to relish their time in the sport. I hope that enthusiasm comes through in the book. A few of my subjects went above and beyond the call: Junior Johnson (who provided an amazing home-cooked breakfast), Humpy Wheeler, Tighe Scott, James Hylton, Bobby and Donnie Allison, Darrell Waltrip, Neal Pilson, Jim Hunter, and Bill Gardner. Reading old newspaper and magazine stories was almost as much a pleasure as talking to the men who wrote them. Thanks Ed Hinton, Steve Waid, Tom Higgins, Benny Phillips, and Dick Berggren. And special thanks to Ken Squier, who didn't let massive amounts of snow or dental work get in the way of a great talk in Vermont.

One group of interview subjects deserves its own paragraph: the Pettys. Richard, Kyle, and Pattie couldn't have been more helpful or generous with their time. That's the kind of people they are, and it's the kind of person Adam Petty was. After Adam died, his family opened Victory Junction, a camp in Randleman for kids with chronic or serious medical conditions, that had been Adam's dream. And they've broken ground on a second camp in Kansas City. I can't think of a better tribute to Adam. The camp's website is www.victoryjunction.org. It's well worth a look.

Big thanks also to copyeditors Peggy Freudenthal, Marie Salter, and especially Barb Jatkola, whose many catches helped (I hope) prevent me from looking like I failed seventh-grade English.

Writing a book while holding down a full-time job isn't easy. Thanks to my boss at *Sports Illustrated,* Terry McDonell, for letting me moonlight. Of course, it would have been impossible without someone to pick up my slack, which Steve Cannella did more times than I care to mention. Cannella also was an excellent reader and sounding board. I'd repay him the favor if he ever writes a book. Until then, I'd like to think his reward is that his kids—who are, against all odds, avid NASCAR fans—will find it cool that he helped out a friend who once drank moonshine while discussing tractors with Sterling Marlin's best friend.

You can say what you will about the prose on these pages, but I won't hear a bad word said about the pictures, which are uniformly awesome. Dozier Mobley took many of them (and countless other cool ones not seen here), and Bryant McMurray dug through his old film to come up with some great action. Procuring the shots and the rights to them would have been impossible without Maureen Cavanagh, Mark Mobley, Linda Bonenfant, and Frankie Fraley. (Moe gets top billing for calling with picture info literally hours before giving birth to her third kid. That's dedication, if slightly questionable parenting.)

And finally, like a best cinematography Oscar winner facing the flashing red light and the swelling orchestra music, I come to the rushed laundry list of people who offered everything from advice to encouragement to transcription services to interview assistance to boozy lunches to spare hotel beds. In no particular order, and with fingers crossed that I'm not forgetting anyone, they are: Mark Beech, Lars Anderson, Rich O'Brien, Allison Hobson Falkenberry (and Little Cat), Rebecca Shore, Scott Price, Jon Wertheim, Gabe Miller, Rob Goodman, Rosalind Fournier, Tim Layden, Chris Stone, Jeff Pearlman, Jon Edwards, David Hovis, Grace Paeck, and all the Bechtels and Valentines I know. Couldn't have done it without you.

Notes on Sources

Virtually all of the events of this book took place more than thirty years ago. That's a pretty long time—too long to expect someone to remember the particulars of, say, the Northwestern Bank 400, which, for most of the men who drove in it, was one of hundreds of races in a decades-long career. Whenever possible, I relied on the memories of the drivers, their crew members, and others in the NASCAR community. Although it was obviously not possible to reconstruct the 1979 season from firsthand observations, the interviews were essential in putting the events of that year in context.

For the forgotten details, I relied on various contemporaneous race accounts. I am very fortunate that a small band of outstanding writers were on the beat in 1979: Dick Berggren and the rest of the staff at *Stock Car Racing* magazine, Tom Higgins of the *Charlotte Observer*, Ed Hinton down in Atlanta, Benny Phillips of the *High Point Enterprise*, and Steve Waid of *Grand National Scene* wrote stories that were not only essential as source material but also a joy to read. Interviews with those five gentlemen also proved to be invaluable.

Chapter 1: Something Borrowed, Something Blue
Interviews with Richie Barsz, Steve Hmiel, Dale Inman, Robin Pemberton, Kyle Petty, Pattie Petty, Richard Petty, and Ken Squier. Much of the great detail of Kyle's practice runs in Daytona came from stories by Benny Phillips in the *High Point Enterprise*, and *Stock Car Racing* magazine covered the Petty wedding extensively. Richard's recollection of the discussion that he and Kyle had when Kyle decided to become a racer is detailed in his book *King Richard I*.

Chapter 2: Birthplace of Speed
Loads of books have been written about the history of Daytona. Perhaps the most comprehensive is *Racing on the Rim* by Dick Punnett, which notably debunks the oft-repeated story that the "first race" on the beach in Daytona, between Ransom Olds and Alexander Winton in 1902, ended in a flat-footed tie. A nice story, but as Punnett shows, it never happened. Like Punnett, I stuck with newspaper accounts whenever possible. I did rely on

a few books, to gain insight into what Daytona Beach and Ormond Beach were like in the late 1800s and early 1900s. Also, an interview with Bill Tuthill in William Neely's *Daytona U.S.A.* proved to be extremely helpful in understanding Bill France's strategy in the formation of NASCAR, and Brock Yates's profile of France in the June 26, 1978, issue of *Sports Illustrated* was very illuminating.

Chapter 3: The Good Ol' Boys

Interviews with Bobby Allison, Donnie Allison, Junior Johnson, and Cale Yarborough. (I don't think I've ever met a better storyteller than Bobby Allison. As the epilogue mentions, he can't remember finishing just ahead of his son in the Daytona 500, but trust me, he has no problem remembering the exact paint scheme of his first car.) Yarborough's autobiography, *Cale,* written with William Neely, and a profile by Kim Chapin in *Sports Illustrated* (August 5, 1968) were particularly helpful. Sam Moses's *Sports Illustrated* piece (November 6, 1978) shed much light on Yarborough's day-to-day existence at that time.

Chapter 4: The Prince

Interviews with Donnie Allison, Buddy Baker, Hoss Ellington, Phil Finney (who ruined the perfectly good story Kyle told about the seagull breaking Finney's windshield by telling the truth about what really happened), Bill Gardner, Steve Hmiel, Dale Inman, Kyle Petty, Pattie Petty, Richard Petty, Lou LaRosa, and Waddell Wilson. Tom Higgins was among those atop the hauler during the ARCA race. His *Observer* story related what the atmosphere was like as the vets watched Kyle race for the first time.

Chapter 5: The Man in the White Hat

Interviews with Richard Childress, Gary Nelson, Buddy Parrott, Ken Squier, Butch Stevens, and Darrell Waltrip. Ed Hinton still remembers his first encounter with Dale Earnhardt, in the garage after the 125-mile qualifier, a scene he wrote about in his excellent book *Daytona: From the Birth of Speed to the Death of the Man in Black.* In addition to interviews with Waltrip and those who know him, several magazine pieces helped me tell the Waltrip story: Sam Moses's profile in *Sports Illustrated* (October 17, 1977), Steve Waid's pieces in *Grand National Illustrated* (May 1982) and *Grand National Scene* (April 19, 1979), and a piece Waltrip wrote himself for *Stock Car Racing,* titled "How I Made It in Grand National Racing" (December 1979).

Chapter 6: On the Air

Interviews with Bob Fishman, Neal Pilson, Ken Squier, and Bob Stenner. Ed Hinton followed the story of Don Williams from the day the accident happened, remaining in contact with the family until Williams died ten years later; it appears in great detail in his *Daytona.*

Chapter 7: So Fair and Foul a Day
Chapter 8: The Fight

Interviews with Bobby Allison, Donnie Allison, Jack Arute, Buddy Baker, Dick Berggren, Joe Biddle, Geoff Bodine, Richard Childress, Hoss Ellington, Bob Fishman,

Jeff Hammond, Tom Higgins, Ed Hinton, James Hylton, Dale Inman, Junior Johnson, Terry Labonte, Lou LaRosa, Larry McReynolds, Gary Nelson, Buddy Parrott, Kyle Petty, Richard Petty, Benny Phillips, Neal Pilson, Tighe Scott, Ken Squier, Bob Stenner, Steve Waid, Darrell Waltrip, Michael Waltrip, Humpy Wheeler, Waddell Wilson, and Cale Yarborough.

Even now, everyone has a different memory of how far back Cale Yarborough was. Thankfully, the race is now available on DVD. After countless viewings I feel confident that the version of events related here is accurate. In addition to the usual suspects, colorful and comprehensive coverage of Speedweeks was provided by Shav Glick of the *Los Angeles Times* and Godwin Kelly and Joe Biddle of the *Daytona Beach Morning Journal*. Stories of cities coping with the blizzard were all over various local papers. The conversation between Jim Bachoven and Bill France was related in a piece by Rick Houston on NASCAR.com (July 26, 2007). Cale Yarborough's quote, which gave this book its title, is from a 2003 story by Al Pearce in the *Hampton Roads Daily Press*. The details of the Tiny Lund fracases were uncovered in the transcript of an interview he did with *Time* correspondent Anne Constable. And as much as I'd like to, I can't take credit for the theory that the roots of NASCAR boys brawling can be traced to Hadrian's Wall. That one came from Humpy Wheeler, who gave me a copy of James Webb's book *Born Fighting*.

Chapter 9: Round Two

Interviews with Bobby Allison, Donnie Allison, Buddy Baker, Benny Phillips, Jim Riddle, Steve Waid, Darrell Waltrip, and Cale Yarborough. The idea for the digression on foot-wear came from a nice offbeat piece in *Grand National Scene*.

Chapter 10: Round Three

Interviews with Bobby Allison, Donnie Allison, Hoss Ellington, Ed Hinton, and Cale Yarborough.

Chapter 11: Wild and Young, Crazy and Dumb

Interviews with Marshall Brooks, Frankie Fraley, Lou LaRosa, Gary Nelson, David Stern, Darrell Waltrip, and Humpy Wheeler. In 1979 Stern, now the NBA commissioner, was the league's general counsel. The best source for Larry Bird's early life is *Drive*.

Chapter 12: Diamonds As Big As Horse Turds

Interviews with Dave D'Ambrosio, Nick Ollila, Darrell Waltrip, Lou LaRosa, and Humpy Wheeler.

Chapter 13: Pearson's Kerfuffle

Interviews with Hoss Ellington, Darrell Waltrip, Jim Hunter, Gary Nelson, Buddy Parrott, Butch Stevens, Eddie Wood, and Leonard Wood. Hunter is now NASCAR's vice president for corporate communications. In the past he was a race promoter and an author. His book with David Pearson, *21 Forever,* is a great source of information on the Silver Fox. The April 1974 issue of *Stock Car Racing* contains everything a fan could want to know about the Woods.

Chapter 14: Old Chow Mein

Interviews with Jeff Hammond, Jim Hunter, Nick Ollila, Leonard Wood, and Cale Yarborough. Benny Phillips spent a lot of time with Pearson after he was fired by Wood Brothers, and he turned out a lengthy, in-depth series of stories.

Chapter 15: Bring on the Dancing Bears
Chapter 16: Gassed

Interviews with Steve Hmiel, Robin Pemberton, Kyle Petty, Richard Petty, Pattie Petty, and Humpy Wheeler. The great details of Kyle's first race, including the chief steward's wonderful monologue, came from Tom Higgins.

Chapter 17: Rising Again

Interviews with Lou LaRosa and Cale Yarborough. Several books provided background on the South and its development, most notably Numan Bartley's *The New South,* Kirkpatrick Sale's *Power Shift,* and Bruce J. Schulman's *The Seventies. Time* magazine's entire September 27, 1976, issue was dedicated to the region, and *Fortune* followed with a lengthy package in June 1977. Peter La Chapelle's *Proud to Be an Okie* and Bill Malone's *Don't Get Above Your Raisin'* were excellent resources for me on southern pop culture and country music, as were cover stories in *Time* (May 6, 1974) and *Newsweek* (June 18, 1973).

Chapter 18: The Gatorade Kid
Chapter 19: The Beginning of the Trouble

Interviews with Bill Gardner, Gary Nelson, Buddy Parrott, Richard Petty, Butch Stevens, Darrell Waltrip, and Humpy Wheeler. Bill Rasmussen's memoir, *Sports Junkies Rejoice!* was useful in helping me piece together ESPN's early days, as was a story by William Oscar Johnson in the July 23, 1979, issue of *Sports Illustrated.*

Chapter 20: Pretty Good Americans

Interview with Craig Shirley. The details of the 1978 White House visit were gleaned largely from the January 1979 issue of *Stock Car Racing* and a *Washington Post Magazine* story by Bill Morris and Joseph P. Duggan, "The Stock-Car Driver as Politician" (April 22, 1979).

Chapter 21: The Shootout

Interviews with Bill Gardner, Lou LaRosa, Gary Nelson, Nick Ollila, Buddy Parrott, Kyle Petty, Richard Petty, and Darrell Waltrip.

Epilogue

Interviews with Bobby Allison, Donnie Allison, Dave D'Ambrosio, Hoss Ellington, Lou LaRosa, Kyle Petty, Pattie Petty, and Darrell Waltrip. Bobby Allison spoke about getting back together with his wife at Adam Petty's funeral; the story is told in much greater detail in Peter Golenbock's book *Miracle.*

Bibliography

Allison, Donnie, with Jimmy Creed. *As I Recall…* Champaign, IL: Sports Publishing, 2005.

Bartley, Numan. *The New South, 1945–1980.* Baton Rouge: Louisiana State University Press, 1995.

Bird, Larry, with Bob Ryan. *Drive: The Story of My Life.* New York: Doubleday, 1989.

Booth, Fred. "Early Days in Daytona Beach, Florida: How a City Was Founded." *Journal of the Halifax Historical Society* 1, no. 1 (1951).

Bowden, Mark. *Guests of the Ayatollah.* New York: Atlantic Monthly Press, 2006.

Cardwell, Harold D., Sr. *Daytona Beach: 100 Years of Racing.* Charleston, SC: Arcadia, 2002.

Cardwell, Harold D., Sr., and Priscilla D. Cardwell. *Historic Daytona Beach.* Charleston, SC: Arcadia, 2004.

Chapin, Kim. *Fast as White Lightning.* New York: Dial Press, 1981.

Cobb, James C. "From Muskogee to Luckenbach: Country Music and the 'Southernization' of America." *Journal of Popular Culture* (Winter 1982): 81–91.

Drackett, Phil. *Like Father Like Son: The Story of Malcolm and Donald Campbell.* Brighton, Eng.: Clifton Books, 1969.

Egerton, John. *The Americanization of Dixie: The Southernization of America.* New York: Harper's Magazine Press, 1974.

Evey, Stuart. *Creating an Empire: ESPN.* Chicago: Triumph Books, 2004.

Fielden, Greg. *NASCAR Chronicle.* Lincolnwood, IL: Publications International, 2007.

Gillispie, Thomas G. *Angel in Black: Remembering Dale Earnhardt Sr.* New York: Cumberland House, 2008.

Golenbock, Peter. *Last Lap: The Life and Times of NASCAR's Legendary Heroes.* New York: Hungry Minds, 2001.

———. *Miracle: Bobby Allison and the Amazing Saga of the Alabama Gang.* New York: St. Martin's, 2006.

———. *NASCAR Confidential: Stories of the Men and Women Who Made Stock Car Racing Great.* St. Paul: Motorbooks International, 2003.

Graham, Allison. "The South in Popular Culture." In *A Companion to the Literature and Culture of the American South,* edited by Richard Gray and Owen Robinson, 335–52. Malden, MA: Blackwell, 2004.

Hammond, Jeff, and Geoff Norman. *Real Men Work in the Pits: A Life in NASCAR Racing*. New York: Rodale Books, 2004.

Hinton, Ed. *Daytona: From the Birth of Speed to the Death of the Man in Black*. New York: Warner Books, 2001.

Hunter, Jim, with David Pearson. *21 Forever: The Story of Stock Car Driver David Pearson*. Huntsville, AL: Strode Publishers, 1980.

Jensen, Tom. *Cheating: An Inside Look at the Bad Things Good NASCAR Nextel Cup Racers Do in Pursuit of Speed*. Phoenix: David Bull Publishing, 2004.

Kirby, Jack Temple. *Media-Made Dixie: The South in the American Imagination*. Rev. ed. Athens: University of Georgia Press, 1986.

La Chapelle, Peter. *Proud to Be an Okie: Cultural Politics, Country Music, and Migration to Southern California*. Berkeley: University of California Press, 2007.

Levine, Lee Daniel. *Bird: The Making of an American Sports Legend*. New York: McGraw-Hill, 1988.

Malone, Bill C. *Country Music, U.S.A.* 2nd rev. ed. Austin: University of Texas Press, 2002.

———. *Don't Get Above Your Raisin': Country Music and the Southern Working Class*. Urbana: University of Illinois Press, 2002.

Montville, Leigh. *At the Altar of Speed: The Fast Life and Tragic Death of Dale Earnhardt*. New York: Broadway, 2003.

Neely, William. *Daytona U.S.A.: The Official History of Daytona and Ormond Beach Racing from 1902 to Today's NASCAR Super Speedways*. Tucson, AZ: Aztex, 1979.

Noonan, Peggy. *What I Saw at the Revolution: A Political Life in the Reagan Era*. New York: Random House, 1990.

Petty, Richard, with William Neely. *King Richard I*. New York: Macmillan, 1986.

Punnett, Dick. *Racing on the Rim*. Ormond Beach, FL: Tomoka Press, 2004.

Rasmussen, Bill. *Sports Junkies Rejoice! The Birth of ESPN*. Hartsdale, NY: QV Publishing, 1983.

Sale, Kirkpatrick. *Power Shift: The Rise of the Southern Rim and Its Challenge to the Eastern Establishment*. New York: Random House, 1975.

Schulman, Bruce J. *The Seventies: The Great Shift in American Culture, Society, and Politics*. New York: Da Capo Press, 2002.

Spencer, Donald D. *Elegance on the Halifax: The Story of the Ormond Hotel*. New York: Camelot Publishing, 2000.

Teachout, Terry. *Skeptic: A Life of H. L. Mencken*. New York: HarperCollins, 2002.

Tuthill, William R. *Speed on Sand*. Ormond Beach, FL: Ormond Beach Historical Trust, 1978.

Waltrip, Darrell, with Jade Gurss. *DW: A Lifetime Going Around in Circles*. New York: G. P. Putnam's Sons, 2004.

Webb, James. *Born Fighting: How the Scots-Irish Shaped America*. New York: Broadway, 2005.

Wilson, Charles Reagan, William Ferris, and Ann J. Adadie. *Encyclopedia of Southern Culture*. Chapel Hill: University of North Carolina Press, 1989.

Wilson, Waddell, and Steve Smith. *Racing Engine Preparation*. Salt Lake City: Steve Smith Autosports, 1990.

Yarborough, Cale, and William Neely. *Cale: The Hazardous Life and Times of America's Greatest Stock Car Driver*. New York: Times Books, 1986.

Index

Sabates, Felix, 287
Sale, Kirkpatrick, 227
Satcom I, 245
Sauter, Jim, 67
Savannah, Georgia, race (1964), 40
Scots-Irish heritage, 124–26
Scott, Tighe, 83, 111
Scott, Wendell, 166, 166n
Shepard, Morgan, 215, 215n
Shirley, Craig, 266
The Silver Fox. *See* Pearson, David
Simmons, J. K., 160n
Smith, Freddy, 92–93
Southeastern 500, 166–76
Southern 500, 39, 82, 247–51
Southern culture: Jimmy Carter and,
   228–29, 256–60; economic growth and,
   227–28; national popular culture and,
   224–27, 229–32
Southern Pride Car Wash, 64, 68, 204
Speedweeks, 19, 35, 36
Sports Illustrated, 34, 35, 42n, 49, 155, 164
Sportsman 300, 87, 91, 92, 94
Sportsman series, 160
Squier, Ken: Bobby Allison and, 57; on drivers'
   lack of education, 79; first televised Daytona
   500 and, 86–87, 89, 110, 117–18; Los Ange-
   les Times 500 and, 274; Kyle Petty and, 12,
   14; Talladega 500 and, 241; Thunder Road
   International SpeedBowl and, 290
Stacy, Jim, 200–201, 201n
Stewart, Jackie, 179, 188, 190
Stock Car Racing (magazine), 5, 11, 52, 108,
   129, 142
Stokely, Bill, 240–41
STP sponsorship, 9, 10–11, 37, 129, 134, 204
Sunderman, Bob, as alias for Bobby Allison, 46
Sundman, Bob, 46

Talladega, Alabama, racetrack, 195–98
Talladega 500, 90, 196–97, 236–43
Teamsters Union, 196, 209
TelePrompTer, 88
Terminal Transport sponsorship, 239
Texas 400, 73
Texas Gas sponsorship, 239, 240
Thunder Road International SpeedBowl,
   89n, 290
Toronto, Canada, race (1958), 4, 8

The Track Too Tough to Tame, 177–79,
   189–90
Turner, Curtis: as airplane pilot, 78, 78n;
   blocking and, 116; Charlotte parties
   and, 205; driver's union and, 196n;
   Junior Johnson and, 49; Tiny Lund and,
   121–22; Bobby Myers and, 123; Glen
   Wood and, 183
Tuthill, Bill, 33, 208
24 Hours of Daytona, 19
24 Hours of Le Mans, 187n
Twin 125 qualifying races, 59, 82–84, 90

Ulrich, D. K., 147, 198
USAC (United States Auto Club), 41, 207–8

Valvoline sponsorship, 68, 72, 134

Wallace, Rusty, 283
Waltrip, Darrell: Bobby Allison and, 210;
   American 500 and, 260, 262–64; Busch
   Clash and, 73, 75; Carolina 500 and, 143,
   144, 147; Champion Spark Plug 400 and,
   248n; Coca-Cola 500 and, 232, 234–35;
   CRC Chemicals Rebel 500 and, 178,
   187–91, 249, 251; Darlington Raceway
   and, 178; Daytona 500 and, 64, 82–84,
   102–3, 106–7, 111, 115, 117, 118, 129–30;
   debt and, 239–40; as DiGard racing team
   driver, 9, 62, 79, 80, 81, 240, 252, 282; Dixie
   500 and, 268–70; driver and crew dislike
   of, 77–80; early racing experiences of,
   238–39; early wins of, 79; Dale Earnhardt
   and, 162–63; "Suitcase" Jake Elder and,
   80, 172–73, 239; fans' dislike of, 76, 101,
   150, 241, 282–83; Firecracker 400 and,
   221–23, 240; first Grand National team
   of, 239; as Fox broadcaster, 283–84; Bill
   Gardner and, 81–82, 281–82, 283n; ghost
   stories and, 197; Grand National series
   and, 135; Jeff Hammond and, 290; Holly
   Farms 400 and, 253–55, 261, 264; Junior
   Johnson and, 77, 151, 151n, 282; Las Vegas
   and, 272; Los Angeles Times 500 and,
   273–78, 280, 281; NASCAR relations and,
   77, 78; Gary Nelson and, 76–77, 79–80,
   81n, 101, 107, 274; Old Dominion 500
   and, 252–53; Buddy Parrott and, 80–81,
   243, 250–51, 253–55, 281–82, 282n, 283n;